# Ansible for Kubernetes by Example

## Automate Your Kubernetes Cluster with Ansible

**Luca Berton**

Apress®

*Ansible for Kubernetes by Example: Automate Your Kubernetes Cluster with Ansible*

Luca Berton
BOURNEMOUTH, UK

ISBN-13 (pbk): 978-1-4842-9284-6          ISBN-13 (electronic): 978-1-4842-9285-3
https://doi.org/10.1007/978-1-4842-9285-3

Managing Director, Apress Media LLC: Welmoed Spahr
Acquisitions Editor: Divya Modi
Development Editor: James Markham
Coordinating Editor: Divya Modi
Copy Editor: Kezia Endsley

Cover designed by eStudioCalamar

Cover image designed by Freepik (www.freepik.com)

Distributed to the book trade worldwide by Springer Science+Business Media New York, 1 New York Plaza, Suite 4600, New York, NY 10004-1562, USA. Phone 1-800-SPRINGER, fax (201) 348-4505, e-mail orders-ny@ springer-sbm.com, or visit www.springeronline.com. Apress Media, LLC is a California LLC and the sole member (owner) is Springer Science + Business Media Finance Inc (SSBM Finance Inc). SSBM Finance Inc is a **Delaware** corporation.

For information on translations, please e-mail booktranslations@springernature.com; for reprint, paperback, or audio rights, please e-mail bookpermissions@springernature.com.

Apress titles may be purchased in bulk for academic, corporate, or promotional use. eBook versions and licenses are also available for most titles. For more information, reference our Print and eBook Bulk Sales web page at http://www.apress.com/bulk-sales.

Any source code or other supplementary material referenced by the author in this book is available to readers on GitHub (github.com/Apress/Ansible-for-Kubernetes-by-Example-by-Luca-Berton). For more detailed information, please visit http://www.apress.com/source-code.

Printed on acid-free paper

*For my son Filippo, the joy of my life.*

# Table of Contents

About the Author ................................................................................................. xi

About the Technical Reviewer ............................................................................. xiii

Acknowledgments ...............................................................................................xv

Introduction ......................................................................................................xvii

Chapter 1: Modern IT Infrastructure and Hello App ........................................... 1

  Modern IT Infrastructure (DevOps and IaC) .............................................................................. 1

  The Move to Containers ............................................................................................................. 4

  Ansible by Red Hat ..................................................................................................................... 7

  The Cloud Native Computing Foundation ................................................................................... 8

    Kubernetes Support ............................................................................................................... 9

    Kubernetes Distributions: OpenShift, Rancher, EKS, AKS, and GCP ..................................... 9

  Containers and Pods ................................................................................................................ 11

  Creating a Hello App ................................................................................................................ 12

    Linux Base Images .............................................................................................................. 13

    Enterprise Linux-Based Images .......................................................................................... 15

  Container Security ................................................................................................................... 17

    The Hello Dockerfile ........................................................................................................... 18

    The Hello Application .......................................................................................................... 19

  Building the Hello App ............................................................................................................. 22

  Running Hello in Docker........................................................................................................... 22

  Deploying Hello in Kubernetes ................................................................................................ 24

  Deploying Hello in Operator .................................................................................................... 25

  Key Takeaways......................................................................................................................... 25

**Chapter 2: Ansible Language Code** ........................................................ **27**

What Is Ansible? ................................................................................... 27

    Provisioning ...................................................................................... 28

    Configuration Management ................................................................ 29

    Application Deployment ..................................................................... 29

    Ansible Open-Source vs Commercial Options ..................................... 29

Ansible's Architecture .......................................................................... 30

    UNIX Target Node .............................................................................. 31

    Windows Target Node ........................................................................ 32

Ansible Installation .............................................................................. 34

Getting Started with Ansible ................................................................. 36

    Running Your First Ansible Ad Hoc Command ..................................... 36

    Creating a Basic Inventory ................................................................ 37

Ansible Code Language ......................................................................... 37

    Ansible Inventory .............................................................................. 38

    Ansible Playbook ............................................................................... 40

    Ansible Roles .................................................................................... 51

    Ansible Collection ............................................................................. 54

    Ansible Execution Environment ......................................................... 55

Key Takeaways .................................................................................... 61

**Chapter 3: Ansible for Containers** ...................................................... **63**

Ansible for Containers .......................................................................... 63

Install Docker on Linux and Windows ..................................................... 63

    Install Docker in Debian Linux ........................................................... 65

    Install Docker in Red Hat Linux .......................................................... 67

    Install Docker on Windows ................................................................. 70

Flatpak in Linux ................................................................................... 71

Snap in Linux ...................................................................................... 74

Deploy a Web Server in a Container ........................................................ 77

    Apache with Docker for Debian-like Systems ...................................... 78

    Apache with Podman for Red Hat-like Systems ................................... 80

Use Vagrant and Packer .............................................................................. 82

    Vagrant ..................................................................................................... 83

    Packer ...................................................................................................... 84

Key Takeaways ............................................................................................ 85

**Chapter 4: Ansible for K8s Tasks ....................................................... 87**

Kubernetes Objects ..................................................................................... 90

Control Plane vs Data Plane ......................................................................... 91

kubectl ........................................................................................................ 92

    GitOps Continuous Deployment ................................................................ 93

Jenkins ........................................................................................................ 94

VMWare Tanzu Application Platform ............................................................ 95

Set Up Your Laboratory ............................................................................... 95

    Virtual Machines ...................................................................................... 96

    Raspberry Pis .......................................................................................... 97

    Kubespray ................................................................................................ 99

    OpenShift Local ..................................................................................... 100

    hetzner-ocp4 .......................................................................................... 103

Create a Cluster with Minikube .................................................................. 104

    Kubeadm ............................................................................................... 106

    K3s Lightweight Kubernetes ................................................................... 107

    Kubernetes Upgrade .............................................................................. 107

Create a Cluster with kOps ........................................................................ 109

Configure Ansible for Kubernetes .............................................................. 109

Ansible Troubleshooting ............................................................................ 113

    401 unauthorized ................................................................................... 113

Kubernetes ............................................................................................... 114

OpenShift .................................................................................................. 116

    x509 error .............................................................................................. 118

    kubeconfig ............................................................................................. 118

Configure a Python Virtual Environment ..................................................... 120

Configure an Ansible Execution Environment ........................................................ 123

Create a Namespace ............................................................................................. 126

Report Namespaces .............................................................................................. 129

Report Deployments in Namespace ....................................................................... 131

Create a Pod ......................................................................................................... 136

Create a Secret .................................................................................................... 139

Use a Service to Expose Your App ........................................................................ 141

    Kubernetes Networking ................................................................................... 143

Scale Your App ..................................................................................................... 148

Auto-scaling ......................................................................................................... 153

Update Your App ................................................................................................... 154

Assign Resources to Kubernetes K8s Pods ........................................................... 157

    Metrics .......................................................................................................... 158

    CPU Resources .............................................................................................. 158

    Memory Resources ......................................................................................... 161

    Namespace Resources ................................................................................... 162

    GPU Resources .............................................................................................. 163

Configure a Pod to Use a Volume for Storage ....................................................... 163

Apply Multiple YAML Files at Once on Kubernetes ................................................ 166

Key Takeaways ..................................................................................................... 167

**Chapter 5: Ansible for K8s Data Plane ................................................. 169**

Configuring a Java Microservice ........................................................................... 171

    The Demo Java Web Application ...................................................................... 172

Stateless: Deploying PHP Guestbook Application with Redis .................................. 180

Kustomize: Do More with Less .............................................................................. 184

Stateful: Deploying WordPress and MySQL with Persistent Volumes ..................... 186

Security Namespace (Pod Security Admission) ..................................................... 191

Security Pod Resources (AppArmor) ..................................................................... 192

Security Pod Syscalls (seccomp) .......................................................................... 193

Ansible Dynamic Inventory ........................................................................ 194

Key Takeaways........................................................................................ 199

## Chapter 6: Ansible for K8s Management .................................... 201

The Helm Package Manager ..................................................................... 202

Helm Repositories ............................................................................. 204

Helm Packages................................................................................. 207

Helm Plugins .................................................................................... 212

Deploy a Monitoring Tool........................................................................ 216

kube-prometheus ............................................................................. 217

Ansible Collections ........................................................................... 218

Helm Chart....................................................................................... 219

Fetch Logs from Resources ..................................................................... 220

Apply a JSON Patch Operation................................................................. 222

Copy Files and Directories to and from a Pod............................................. 224

Manage Services on Kubernetes .............................................................. 225

Taint Nodes ........................................................................................... 227

Drain, Cordon, or Uncordon Nodes........................................................... 229

Kubernetes Dynamic Inventory................................................................ 232

Roll Back Deployments and DaemonSets................................................... 232

Set a New Size for a Deployment, ReplicaSet, Replication Controller, or Job ......... 233

Security................................................................................................. 233

AAA ................................................................................................ 235

OpenID Identity Provider.................................................................... 236

Calico.............................................................................................. 237

Key Takeaways........................................................................................ 237

## Chapter 7: Ansible for Kubernetes Cloud Providers ................... 239

Cloud Architecture................................................................................. 241

Amazon Web Services (AWS) ................................................................... 244

Google Cloud Platform (GCP)................................................................... 251

Microsoft Azure Cloud Services ......................................................................... 255

Other Vendors .................................................................................................. 259

Key Takeaways.................................................................................................. 260

**Chapter 8: Ansible for Enterprise ...................................................... 261**

The Ansible Automation Platform....................................................................... 261

Event-Driven Ansible......................................................................................... 268

IT Trends........................................................................................................... 272

Ansible Trusted Code........................................................................................ 273

What's Next?..................................................................................................... 275

Thank You.......................................................................................................... 276

**Index................................................................................................ 277**

# About the Author

**Luca Berton** is an Ansible automation expert who works for JPMorgan Chase & Co. and previously worked with the Red Hat Ansible Engineer Team for three years. He is the creator of the Ansible Pilot project. With more than 15 years of experience as a system administrator, he has strong expertise in infrastructure hardening and automation. An enthusiast of open-source, Luca supports the community by sharing his knowledge at different public access events. He is a geek by nature, Linux by choice, and Fedora, of course.

# About the Technical Reviewer

**Nikhil Jain** is an Ansible expert with over 12 years of DevOps experience. He has been using Ansible and contributing to it from its inception. He currently works closely with Ansible engineering.

He is an open-source enthusiast and is part of the Ansible Pune Meetup Organizing team. He has presented multiple Ansible sessions at various global and local events. Apart from sitting in front of his computer automating things using Ansible, he loves watching sports and is a regular part of the local cricket team.

# Acknowledgments

To my son, family, and friends, who make life worth living and whose support and encouragement make this work possible.

To all whom I've worked with over the years and shared any ideas for this book: Thank you for the knowledge you've shared.

# Introduction

This book guides you through the process of automating a Kubernetes cluster using the Ansible open-source technology.

If you are an IT professional who wants a jargon-free explanation of the Ansible technology, this book is for you. This includes Kubernetes, Linux, and Windows systems administrators, DevOps professionals, thought leaders, and infrastructure-as-code enthusiasts, as well as information technology team members providing leadership to their businesses.

Infrastructure and operations (I&O) leaders look at the Ansible platform to implement Infrastructure as Code (IaC), Configuration as a Code (CaC), Policy as a Code (PaC), code pipelines, orchestration (K8s), DevSecOps, self-healing infrastructures, and event-driven automation methodologies.

This book is a powerful resource for computer engineers and leaders who believe that innovation, automation, and acceleration are the drivers of the booming business of tomorrow.

A successful infrastructure is a matter of improvements that are made little by little and good habits that you develop using automation during the journey.

In this book, you learn how to become more productive and effective using the Ansible open-source automation technology to deploy world-scale, cloud-native applications and services. Containers have revolutionized the IT industry, but it takes more than container runtime engines like Docker and Podman to handle these modern, huge workloads. This is where Kubernetes come in to play.

Kubernetes applications are designed as microservices, packaged in containers, and deployed in a hybrid cloud in multiple cloud platforms worldwide to serve your customers.

It's also possible to upgrade applications and services without impacting user performance in many ways: by rolling, canary, and blue/green environments.

The scriptable infrastructure of the cloud providers enables you to elastically meet the demands of traffic with a virtually unlimited compute powerhouse. Engineers have a great deal of power and responsibility for their business's success.

# What Is In This Book?

This book provides in-depth content of the following topics:

- The Ansible code language for beginners and experienced users, with examples

- Ansible installation on the latest releases of Ansible

- Ansible for container management (Docker and Podman)

- Ansible for Kubernetes infrastructure examples

- Troubleshooting common errors

# Development Environment

You do not need a specific IDE to benefit from this book. You simply need a base environment consisting of the following:

- A text editor: Terminal-based (VIM, Emacs, Nano, Pico, and so on) or GUI-based (VS Code, Atom, Geany, and so on)

- A workstation with the `ansible` or `ansible-core` packages installed

- Kubernetes or OpenShift cluster

# Conventions Used in the Book

This is a practical book, with a lot of examples and terminal commands. There are also some Ansible language code samples.

The Ansible language code used in the Ansible Playbook examples mostly uses the YAML and INI formats.

Commands and code samples throughout the book are either inline (for example, `ansible [command]`) or in a code block (with or without line numbers), such as this:

```
---
# YAML file example
```

The Ansible language is written in the YAML format, which is a human-readable, data-serialization language that is extremely popular for configuration files. The code follows the latest YAML 1.2.2 specification. It uses Python-style indentation and a more compact format for lists and dictionary statements. It's very close to JSON and can be used as an XML alternative. The YAML code was validated using the YAMLlint popular validator and tested in the most commonly used Ansible versions in the market.

The INI format used in Ansible inventories examples is a well-known format for configuration files since the MS-DOS operating system and uses key-value pairs for properties.

The terminal commands use the standard POSIX conventions and are ready for use in UNIX-like systems such as Linux, macOS, or BSD. Each command is assumed to be used by a standard user account when the prefix is the $ symbol (dollar) or by the root user when the prefix is the # symbol (number sign).

You are going to find this code in installation, code execution, and troubleshooting examples. The commands were tested in the most modern operating system versions available.

The Ansible code included in this book was tested by the author and the technical reviewer in a wide variety of modern systems and uses the Ansible best practices regarding playbooks, roles, and collections. It was verified using the latest release of the Ansible Linter.

Some code may intentionally break a specific Ansible best practice rule only to demonstrate a troubleshooting session and reproduce a fatal error in a specific use case.

## Chapters at a Glance

This book aims to guide you through your journey of automating the Ansible platform for the Kubernetes (K8s) infrastructure. There are eight chapters, and the book is full of code samples and terminal commands to verify the results.

- Chapter 1 explores how modern IT infrastructure is organized inside an organization and outside to its customers and partners. You are going to learn about the history of Kubernetes, from the initial Google project to CNCF. You also learn about its most famous flavor: Red Hat OpenShift, Amazon EKS, and other public cloud providers. A practical example of the Hello App written in Python language is deployed as a container (Fedora, Ubuntu, Alpine Linux), built in Docker and running in Kubernetes.

- Chapter 2 dives deep into the Ansible language code. It explains the architecture, how to set up a target node, inventories, as well as playbooks, variables, filters, conditionals, handlers, loops, magic variables, vaults, templates, plugins, roles, and collections.

- Chapter 3 is all about containers—how to automate the installation of Docker in your operating systems, how to use the Flatpack and Snap technologies in Linux, and how to deploy the popular web server Apache as a containerized application in Debian/Ubuntu. To do that, you use Docker and Red Hat Enterprise Linux with the Podman runtime engine.

- Chapter 4 goes deep into Kubernetes, explaining the difference between the control plane and the data plane and how to use the kubectl utility. You learn how to set up your laboratory using virtual machines, Raspberry Pis, Minikube, Kubespray, Kubeadm, and OpenShift Local. You configure Ansible to interact with Kubernetes, and troubleshoot and fix the most popular errors. There is a lot of Ansible playbook code to create and report namespaces, deployments, pods, secrets, and persistent volumes. You'll apply multiple YAML files at once to Kubernetes. You also explore how to scale up and down your applications and run rolling updates.

- Chapter 5 explains how to build a web, RESTful Java microservice application using Spring technology and deploy it as a containerized image with the Tomcat web server. This chapter includes more use cases that explain how to automate the deployment of two examples of stateless (a PHP Guestbook application with Redis) and stateful (WordPress and MySQL with persistent volumes) applications in Kubernetes. You learn how to apply security to namespaces, pod resources (AppArmor), and pod syscalls (seccomp). You also learn how to save time using the Kustomize tool to generate Kubernetes YAML resources. Ansible Dynamic Inventory is handy for listing all the cluster resources that interact with Kubernetes API.

- Chapter 6 covers how to manage the control plane, which is a more useful tool for cluster administrator use cases, and discusses how to apply Ansible to the deployment of the DEV, SIT, UAT, and

PROD infrastructures. You learn how to deploy a monitoring tool (Prometheus) via the Helm package manager, fetch logs from resources for troubleshooting, and copy files and directories to and from a pod. The chapter also covers the processes of tainting, draining, cordoning, and uncordoning nodes. It also discusses rolling back deployments and DaemonSets and applying Security Authentication, Authorization, and Accounting (AAA).

- Chapter 7 is dedicated to the public could providers, including how you can take advantage of the hybrid/multi-cloud providers, what the shared responsibility model is, and some specific infrastructure implementations of Amazon Web Services (AWS), Google Cloud Platform (GCP), and Microsoft Azure Cloud Services. It also covers how the Certified Kubernetes Conformance Program by CNCF is helping with portability of applications and services between different clusters.

- Chapter 8 is all about Ansible for enterprise, with the completed container-oriented Shiny Ansible Automation Platform providing the Web-UI RESTful API and Ansible Certified Collections. You learn about the future information technology trends of event-driven Ansible, Ansible Trusted Code, and Ansible Trusted Ansible Collections and Signed Ansible Projects. You also learn how artificial intelligence can propel your automation journey.

The sky is the limit with the OpenContainer standard, Kubernetes orchestration, and Ansible automation; you can deploy the cloud-native applications of tomorrow, taking advantage of unlimited infrastructure capacity and worldwide coverage.

# Source Code

All source code used in this book can be downloaded from `github.com/Apress/Ansible-for-Kubernetes-by-Example-by-Luca-Berton`.

# Disclaimer

Any opinions or personal views I express in this book are my own and not those of Red Hat Inc. or JPMorgan Chase & Co.

# CHAPTER 1

# Modern IT Infrastructure and Hello App

Information technology infrastructure is evolving year after year, faster than ever. Following Moore's Law, servers have become more and more powerful and are able to execute more operations in a fraction of a second. Similarly, network infrastructure is evolving faster than ever.

The IT infrastructure is the backbone of a successful business. Companies efficiently manage their IT real estate with powerful tools that save time. The secret to success is a holistic cooperation between the IT Development and Operations teams. Automate, accelerate, and innovate are the mantras of every corporation in the post-pandemic world.

Kubernetes and Ansible are Infrastructure as Code (IaC) platforms that manage a fleet of services and make crucial decisions promptly.

## Modern IT Infrastructure (DevOps and IaC)

All IT departments worldwide face challenges in efficiently delivering top-level customer IT services. In the same vein, it's important to obtain the most you can from your infrastructure (your return on investment). Just to be clear, the IT infrastructure is the whole data center: the servers, network devices, cabling, storage, and so on. Every good system administrator knows how important every piece in the infrastructure puzzle is. Traditionally, infrastructure teams in large organizations or system administrators in small ones carried the burden of manually managing the IT infrastructure, in order to deliver the best service for their internal and external stakeholders. A large organization typically operates multiple on-premise data centers and cloud providers.

Deploying an application in this traditional infrastructure required a combination of operating systems and underlying system libraries, as shown in Figure 1-1.

1

© Luca Berton 2023
L. Berton, *Ansible for Kubernetes by Example*, https://doi.org/10.1007/978-1-4842-9285-3_1

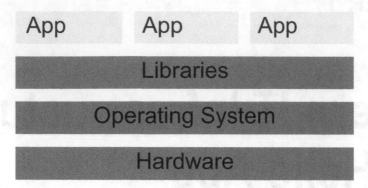

***Figure 1-1.*** *Traditional deployment*

The main drawback of this architecture was that the applications were tightly connected to the underlying operating system and the system libraries. It was sometimes necessary to upgrade the underlying operating system just to update an application, or it was impossible to do so, because another application used a different version of the shared libraries.

The job of the infrastructure team included installing and updating the full lifecycle of the software, changing configurations, and managing services on servers, virtual machines, and nodes. The quality of the service provided could be measured using key indicators.

Some of you are familiar with key indicators, which reveal the uptime of software or hardware. Uptime measures the percentage of time the service is available to receive interactions by users. An uptime of 100 percent means the service is always available. Unfortunately, this was an unrealistic scenario because software and hardware failures negatively affects this in real life. Customers then experience a lower quality of service. You can apply this analysis to any web service, API service, website, web application, hardware, server, network device, or cloud provider. Some businesses also have penalties or insurance associated with poor uptime performance in their contracts.

For all those reasons, it's crucial to boost the performance of your infrastructure to accommodate business needs or to compete better in the marketplace.

Modern processor chips integrate virtualization technology, enabling resource splitting to accommodate increased demand. Static resource partition technology, such as VMware vSphere, allows many organizations to run multiple operating systems in one hardware setup. The ability to run various operating systems using virtualization, resource partition, Linux "cgroup" technologies, and Linux Containers (LXC) delivers virtual machines as base components of resource allocation. See Figure 1-2.

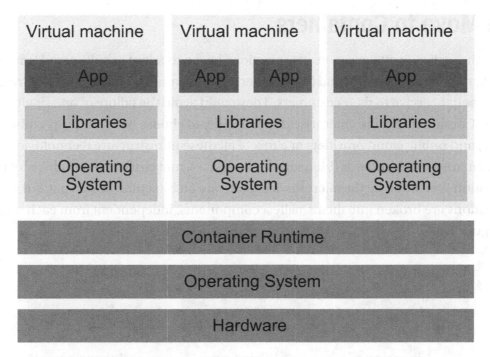

***Figure 1-2.*** *Virtualized deployment*

Business flourished for well-known companies like VMware vSphere, Xen, and so on. Cloud providers such as Amazon Web Services (AWS), Azure Cloud, and Google Cloud Platform (GCP) also benefitted from the rise of virtualization. Their popular products are called Amazon EC2, Azure Virtual machines, and Google Compute Engine.

The most significant disadvantages of virtual machines are as follows:

- Static allocation of resources (CPU and RAM)

- More resources to manage by the IT infrastructure team

- Maintenance and overhead required of multiple operating systems (host and guest)

- Single hardware point of failure (mitigated by cluster premium features and the Veeam backup suite)

# The Move to Containers

Due to those disadvantages, more organizations began to adopt a multi-cloud (multiple cloud vendors) or a hybrid-cloud (data center and one or more cloud vendors) strategy to offer better service to their customers. They could avoid the failure of one single vendor. Containers enable enterprises the flexibility to choose between on-premise, private, and public cloud providers or a mix of all these infrastructure technologies based on universal standards (SLA, quality of services, and cost). The portability of the application is ensured by the microservices software architectural design pattern, where applications are broken into their smallest components, independent from each other. See Figure 1-3.

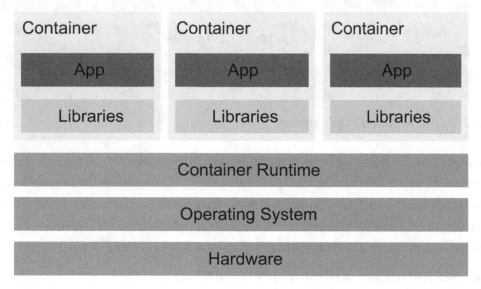

***Figure 1-3.***  *Container deployment*

To deliver the best value in the least amount of time, IT engineers needed more powerful tools than bare metal or virtual machines. Deploying an application in a container is entirely independent of the underlying operating systems, as shown in Figure 1-3.

The Docker company was founded in 2011 by Kamel Founadi, Solomon Hykes, and Sebastien Pah, after the Y Combinator in the summer of 2010. Docker debuted to the public in Santa Clara at PyCon in 2013. Docker specifies how a container image is built and how the image is loaded and runs. Docker created a set of platform-as-a-service (PaaS) products that use OS-level virtualization to deliver containers, for example, the command-line Docker utility.

Podman is an open-source alternative to Docker (its full name is the POD MANager). Its main advantage is that you don't need a service to be running like Docker on your machine; Podman is "daemonless." The command syntax is very similar to Docker's. If you are concerned about security in your applications or planning to use Kubernetes, Podman is a better alternative. This book uses Docker because it's more well-known and widespread in the IT industry. But for most of the commands with the Docker prefix, you can substitute docker with podman and obtain the same result.

The template code of the container is called a *Dockerfile*, which allows you to build a binary version of the container, called an *image*. A more technology-agnostic alternative to Dockerfile is a *Containerfile,* by the Open Container Initiative (OCI), part of The Linux Foundation. Both are configuration files that automate the steps of creating a container image. The OCI promotes open industry standards around container formats and runtimes. The OCI releases three specifications: the Runtime Specification (runtime-spec), the Image Specification (image-spec), and the Distribution Specification (distribution-spec). Dockerfiles and Containerfiles use a combination of system tools, system libraries, code, runtimes, and settings to specify how an application runs. A single image can be run as many times as you want in a local Docker or Kubernetes cluster.

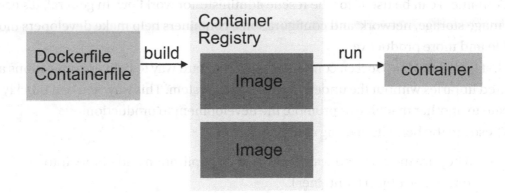

**Figure 1-4.** *Container lifecycle*

Once built, the container image is stored in a Container Registry (see Figure 1-4). The first Container Registry is Docker Hub, but many Container Registries are available in the marketplace nowadays. The first alternative that comes to my mind is Quay from Red Hat. Container Images are stored inside with metadata. That makes it easy for Kubernetes clusters to search within them and find them.

You can maintain multiple versions of your container in a Container Registry. You can also organize images in tags and branches that match the DEV (Development), SIT (System Integration Test), UAT (User Acceptance Test), and PROD (Production) DevOps principles.

Tags simply add a marker to a specific version of the image and make it easy for the users to find it.

If you need more than one container, you must move to a Docker Compose tool, which defines and runs multi-container Docker applications.

Modern business applications require one or more of the following features:

- High availability

- Multi-cloud compatibility

- Multi-tier storage

- Elastic/auto-scaling

- Self-healing

- Security by design (DevSecOps)

Containers can be useful for the rescue administrator workflow. In general, it's easier to manage storage, network, and configurations; containers help make developers more flexible and more productive.

First introduced by Docker, containers are a standard way to deliver applications and required libraries without the underlying operating system. This way, you can quickly relocate to another machine or promote the development to production.

These are the benefits of using containers:

- They are the standard way to package an application and library into one single object (container).

- They are much faster to spin up rather than using a virtual machine.

- They are easy to scale.

- They are portable because you can host anywhere.

- They enable microservices.

Running a container in a virtual machine is possible, but requires extra work to maintain the operating system of the running host and the guest container manually in a virtual machine. It is possible, but a sub-optimal solution.

Orchestration tools such as Kubernetes allow you to easily manage containers at scale.

Global trends of the DevOps and DevSecOps developer-centric methodologies deliver application-as-service, microservices, and serverless applications. They are ramping up faster and faster. In this scenario, containers created by the Continuous Integration and Continuous Delivery (CI/CD) toolset are tested for quality assurance and promoted to production faster than ever. Apache Mesos and Docker Swarm technologies are also often involved.

# Ansible by Red Hat

Ansible is the leading open-source infrastructure automation technology. Infrastructure teams and system administrators worldwide realized that they needed a better way to scale their systems' management scripts to keep up with business demands. The hosted web applications increase the complexity, email flow, and new releases of the operating system. Manual work becomes unsustainable when the number of target devices grows. API-driven server management and configuration management tools like Ansible helped make things manageable.

The main Ansible use case is as follows:

- Provision

- Config management

- Application deployment

Red Hat Inc. (part of IBM since 2019) is leading the development of the Ansible project worldwide, guaranteeing the open-source quality of code.

The Ansible platform is available for a huge variety of modern operating systems and requires only an OpenSSH connection and a Python interpreter on the Linux target node. It supports a wide range of operating systems via different connection technologies. For example, you can use WinRM for Windows target nodes and Network API for network devices.

The learning curve is very rapid. You see this for yourself in Chapter 2, where you learn all about the Ansible programming language.

Red Hat also organizes the yearly AnsibleFest worldwide, usually at the end of October, to educate people about Ansible and share new features and success stories.

# The Cloud Native Computing Foundation

In the early stage of application containerization, runtime systems such as Docker and Podman were extremely useful for manually deploying and testing applications.

However, when the workload became higher and managing failover was crucial, the world needed a more automated way of doing this.

Kubernetes (also called K8s) is the best way to orchestrate and manage a container workload. Kubernetes take care of deploying, scaling, and managing container applications. It is open-source and completely automatic.

Kubernetes has many releases per year; at the moment, there are three releases a year.

While Docker is focused on how a single container image is created, loaded, and run, Kubernetes is a way to schedule and manage a large number of containers.

You can deploy your container in Kubernetes to produce applications at a scale. You can seamlessly move containers and applications at scale. Similarly to Docker and Podman, you can run your container in Kubernetes. Kubernetes run anywhere—on-premise, in a private data center, in a public cloud, and even in embedded hardware such as the latest tiny Raspberry Pi devices. Kubernetes supports multiple processor architectures and modern operating systems.

Updating, upgrading, and managing in Kubernetes is relatively easy and guarantees security for your organization.

The Cloud Native Computing Foundation (CNCF) leads the development of the Kubernetes project, offering a vendor-neutral vision. CNCF is part of the Linux Foundation. CNCF also organizes community events, including KubeCon and CloudNativeCon, where you can meet experts and share stories.

The most inspiring customer stories are from innovation leaders such as BlackRock, Netflix, Zalando, Uber, *The New York Times,* ING, Squarespace, BlaBlaCar, Huawei, Amadeus, PNC Bank, Seagate, Verizon Media, and much more.

In Kubernetes, a *cluster* is made up of at least one Kubernetes master; many Kubernetes worker machines are called *nodes*. A cluster is fundamental for Kubernetes: all containerized workloads and services run within a cluster.

# Kubernetes Support

Kubernetes relies on a vibrant community, external experts, and consultant services. Kubernetes is officially a self-support model, but more private organizations offer support and customization services.

Canonical, the organization leading the Ubuntu project, offers support for Kubeadm, MicroK8s, and Charmed Kubernetes on VMWare, OpenStack, bare metal, AWS, Azure, Google, Oracle Cloud, IBM Cloud, and Rackspace.

# Kubernetes Distributions: OpenShift, Rancher, EKS, AKS, and GCP

There are currently several Kubernetes distribution options. They all integrate the core Kubernetes features, but they differ by the included modules and managing software. Kubernetes is the main framework for developing commercial products and cloud services.

---

**Note**    This book focuses on the generally available Kubernetes, while most of the code also works in some cloud-native Kubernetes services.

---

## OpenShift by Red Hat

OpenShift Container Platform (OCP) is a key product of the Red Hat multi-cloud strategy. It is getting traction in the market because it's easy to set up and maintain. Red Hat packages the core Kubernetes experience with a selection of valuable utilities to simplify the new user onboarding process. OpenShift Container Platform requires having a OpenShift subscription to use it, which includes Red Hat support. For this reason, it supports only Red Hat operating systems underneath, which is Red Hat Enterprise Linux (RHEL) and Red Hat CoreOS (discontinued).

Red Hat has a strong cloud-provider partnership for fully managed OpenShift services with products like Red Hat OpenShift Service on AWS (ROSA), Azure Red Hat OpenShift, and Red Hat OpenShift on Google Cloud Marketplace.

The main differences between OpenShift and Kubernetes are that OpenShift:

- Requires a paid subscription

- Has limited operating system support (Red Hat Enterprise Linux (RHEL) and Red Hat CoreOS

- Uses the `oc` command-line tool instead of `kubectl`.

- Has stricter security policies than default Kubernetes

- Forbids running a container as `root`

- Uses Role Based Access Control (RBAC) security

- Routes object instead of Ingress of Kubernetes based on HAproxy

- Uses ImageStreams for managing container images

- Uses OpenShift projects vs Kubernetes namespaces

OpenShift uses Helm as a software package manager, which simplifies the packaging and deployment of applications and services to OpenShift Container Platform clusters. OpenShift mainly uses Kubernetes operators; however, Helm is very popular in many Kubernetes applications. For Kubernetes-native applications, consider using Kubernetes Operator instead, because Operator continuously checks the application's status and determines if the application is running according to the configuration defined by the software developer.

Red Hat OpenShift Local (formerly Red Hat CodeReady Containers) is the fastest way to spin up an OpenShift cluster on your desktop/laptop for development purposes. This happens in minutes. It supports Linux (x86), Windows (x86), and macOS, even Intel and Apple Silicon (M1 and M2 processors). It is a simplified version relying on a virtual machine (~20GB) to set up, run, test, and emulate the cloud development environment locally. It uses the `crc` command-line utility to spin up a complete lab with an API and web interface. The requirements of the latest 2.10 release are four physical CPU cores, 9 GB of free memory, and 35 GB of storage space.

Red Hat also releases an open-source version of OpenShift called OKD. It's free to use and includes most of the features of its commercial product without support.

## Kubernetes in the Public Cloud

Many cloud provider vendors build their Container Orchestration and Management products. The most popular cloud-native services are as follows:

- Amazon Elastic Container Service (Amazon ECS) by Amazon Web Services (AWS)

- Google Container Engine (GKE) by Google Cloud Platform (GCP)

- Azure Container Service by Microsoft Azure

- IBM Bluemix Cloud Kubernetes Container Service by IBM Cloud

- Oracle Container Cloud Service (OCCS) by Oracle Cloud

- Alibaba Cloud Container Registry

More services are available in the IT industry, but I consider these the major actors in the marketplace nowadays. See Chapter 7 for more details.

## Amazon EKS

Amazon Elastic Kubernetes Service (Amazon EKS) is a service of Amazon Web Services (AWS). It adds the `eksctl` command-line tool for working with EKS clusters and uses the `kubectl` command underneath.

Amazon also provides Amazon Elastic Container Registry (Amazon ECR), an AWS-managed container image registry service that's cross-region and completely integrated within the AWS ecosystem. Specified users or Amazon EC2 instances defined in the IAM policies can access the ECR container repositories and images. Amazon ECR manages private image repositories consisting of Docker and Open Container Initiative (OCI) images and artifacts. Amazon Linux container images are already available in ECR, built with the same software components included in the Amazon Linux AMI for applications in Amazon EC2. See Chapter 7 for more details.

# Containers and Pods

A *container* is a single unit for delivering software. But the real world is more complex; sometimes you need more than one container to provide the complete solution.

A *pod* contains

- One group of one or more containers with shared storage and network resources

- One specification for how to run the containers

The name comes from the fact that a group of whales is called a *pod*. Pods enable microservice deployment. The advantage is that they are loosely coupled, and their execution is autonomous and independent.

Pods are the smallest deployable objects in Kubernetes. The pod's contents are colocated, coscheduled, and run in a shared context. The best practice is to insert only containers that are tightly coupled in a pod for an application-specific task or feature.

As well as a container, a pod might contain an `init` container that runs during the pod's startup.

---

**Note**    For debugging purposes, you can inject ephemeral `contains` if your cluster has enabled this feature.

---

# Creating a Hello App

The "Hello" app is a simple implementation in a container of the "Hello world" message that prints the text message `"Hello world"` onscreen and terminates its execution.

First of all, you need to define a Dockerfile. You can rename the Dockerfile as Containerfile to be fully OCI-compliant. This simple task requires you to execute the UNIX command `echo` into a Dockerfile. Before being able to execute the command, you need to add some lines of code to instruct Docker (or Podman) about the system requirements, some metadata, and finally, the command to execute.

The simple example in Listing 1-1 shows the full Dockerfile to print the Hello World text on the screen using the shell `echo` command.

***Listing 1-1.*** A simple Dockerfile

```
#A simple Docker container image.
FROM busybox
LABEL org.opencontainers.image.title="Hello World image"
```

```
LABEL maintainer="Luca Berton"
#Run a command
CMD echo "Hello World"
```

Every line prefixed with a # (number/pound symbol/hashtag) is considered a comment, so it's ignored by the program. It is useful for documentation or sharing developer information.

The FROM instruction tells Docker that you want to begin a new image using, in this case, another image as your starting point. It is starting from the image called busybox.

BusyBox is a very popular tool in many embedded Linux systems. In a ~5 MB of on-disk storage space, BusyBox delivers a tiny version of many common UNIX utilities into a single small executable. It provides the base functionality for the UNIX most commonly used utilities. The modern Linux distributions use the GNU full-feature alternative tools packaged in GNU fileutils, shellutils, and so on. The utilities in BusyBox generally have fewer options than their full-featured GNU alternatives. Despite the limited size, the included options provide the expected functionality and behave very much like their GNU counterparts. This is why BusyBox is so well known and used outside the embedded domain.

The LABEL instruction adds metadata to the image. The metadata enables the Container Registry to search and organize the images. The label instructions might be multiple and follow a key=value format, where the key is the parameter's name and the value is the associated value.

The CMD instruction tells Docker that what follows is a shell command and is the process to run upon the container start.

This is a very minimal Dockerfile; there are more instructions available but these are the most basic.

# Linux Base Images

There are a huge amount of base images available in the Container Registries for your application development that you can use in the FROM instruction. Deriving an image from another is actually the best way to reuse code and obtain security updates from the original image maintainer. You don't need to reinvent the wheel!

# Fedora Linux

Imagine you want to use the Fedora or Ubuntu images as base images.

For the Fedora Linux distribution, you could specify the following:

```
FROM fedora:latest
```

In this way, you select the latest release of the Fedora Linux distribution. As I'm writing this book, the latest release is Fedora 37. The latest release is typically updated every six months, based on the current release cycle. This acts like a rolling-release pointer.

```
FROM fedora:37
```

You select a specific Fedora version release, 37 in this case.

```
FROM fedora:rawhide
```

In this way, you have selected the rawhide release channel, which is suitable for developers, is sometimes unstable, and updates very often. This should be selected only by users who know what they are doing.

# Ubuntu Linux

Many popular Linux distributions are available as containers. The Ubuntu Linux distribution is also available in a container image.

The Ubuntu Linux distribution is available in Docker Registry:

```
FROM ubuntu:latest
```

In this way, you select the latest LTS release of the Ubuntu Linux distribution. When I was writing this book, the latest release was Ubuntu 22.04.1 LTS Jammy Jellyfish, released on August 10, 2022. It is an LTS release with long-term support, which means five years of free security and maintenance updates, guaranteed until April 2027. Note that the latest release always points to the latest release, so it's updated every six months considering the current release cycle. This acts like a rolling-release pointer.

```
FROM ubuntu:22.04 or FROM ubuntu:jammy
```

You can specify one Ubuntu-specific version using the release numbers or name. In the specific, the version number is 22.04 and the name is `jammy`, which refers to the Jammy Jellyfish release name.

```
FROM ubuntu:rolling
```

You can specify the "rolling release," which is the latest release available, using the `rolling` keyword. Currently, I'm writing this book referring to the 22.10 release, Kinetic Kudu name, with a release date of October 21, 2022. Note the rolling release is supported only for nine months until July 2023.

## Alpine Linux

Another Linux distribution popular as a base for container images is Alpine Linux. Alpine Linux is a security-oriented, lightweight Linux distribution based on a different version of the system `libc` called `musl` against the usual GNU `libc` and BusyBox. It is famous because of its very small footprint and reduced attack surface. The image is ~5 MB in size and has access to the Alpine package repository via the Alpine Package Keeper (apk) package manager.

# Enterprise Linux-Based Images

Enterprise releases of Linux are available as containers as well. They are very powerful, especially for partners and system integrators that develop their solutions on top of them.

Red Hat was the first company to introduce the Red Hat Universal Base Image (UBI) in May 2019 for Red Hat Enterprise Linux (RHEL) versions 7 and 8. RHEL 9, released on May 2022, is also available as a Universal Base Image (UBI). UBIs are a lighter-weight versions of the Linux operating system's userland stripped down to the bare essentials and distributed by the official release channels.

UBIs are designed to be a foundation of cloud and web application use cases. Images are available via Red Hat Container Registry at https://catalog.redhat.com/.

UBIs are tested for Open Container Initiative (OCI) compliance, performance, and security. UBIs are also freely redistributable and deployable on non-Red Hat platforms. Many Red Hat partners distribute solutions on top of UBIs and distribute them as new images.

Red Hat Universal Base Images are available for each released operating system version in four sizes: Standard, Minimal, Micro, and Multi-service for AMD64 and Intel 64 (amd64), ARM (arm64), Power ppcle64, and IBM zSeries s390x processor architectures.

- The standard `ubi` UBI images (compressed ~76 MB) are general purpose and designed for every application that runs on RHEL, including the standard YUM or DNF Package Manager, OpenSSL crypto stack, and basic OS tools (tar, gzip, vi, and so on).

- The multi-service `ubi-init` UBI images (compressed ~80 MB) are on top of the standard (`ubi`) UBI and contain the `systemd` initialization system services, useful for building images to deploy services on top of it. For example, a web application or a file server.

- The minimal `ubi-minimal` UBI images (compressed ~38 MB) are very minimalistic images with a very small footprint; they use the `microdnf` Package Manger (a basic package manager to install, update, and remove packages extensible via modules).

- The micro `ubi-micro` UBI image (compressed ~11 MB) is the smallest possible UBI image, without a package manager and all of its dependencies, reducing the attack surface of container images for highly regulated and security environments. UBI micro was introduced in June, 2021.

Other useful Red Hat Universal Base Images include the following:

- Language runtime images (`nodejs`, `ruby`, `python`, `php`, `perl`, and so on)

- A repository full of packages for the most common applications

There are other Enterprise Linux distributions available as container images.

Since August 2022, the SUSE Linux Enterprise Server Base Container Images (BCI) via the SUSE Container Registry (`https://registry.suse.com`) images for AMD64 and Intel 64 (x86_64), ARM (aarch64), Power (ppcle64), and IBM zSeries (s390x) processor architectures.

At the moment, the following five SUSE Enterprise Linux BCIs are available:

- Base `bci-base` (compressed ~47 MB): SUSE Linux Enterprise general-purpose image with zypper and a minimal set of packages

- Init `bci-init` (compressed ~58MB): Similar to `bci-base` with a `systemd` service manager for managing services

- Minimal `bci-minimal` (compressed ~15 MB): For deployment container RPM-only with manual package dependencies resolution

- Micro `bci-micro` (compressed ~10 MB): For static-binary deployment without a package manager

- BusyBox `bci-busybox` (compressed ~5 MB): The UNIX coreutils tools provided by the BusyBox project instead of GNU coreutils for size reduction

Other Enterprise Linux distribution images include these:

- Rocky Linux image `rockylinux` tags 8, 8-minimal, 9, 9-slim

- Oracle Linux image `oraclelinux` tags 7, 7-slim, 8, 8-slim, 9, 9-slim

# Container Security

Container images are created by software that might be affected by security flaws that could harm your organization. The advantage of using maintained images is that the creator constantly monitors the security of the images through the static analysis of vulnerabilities and releases a new version when necessary. Some examples of impactful security threats that pop up are Log4Shell (CVE-2021-44228), Heartbleed (CVE-2014-0160), and Shellshock (CVE-2014-6271).

Once you create your container image, you can use a vulnerability analysis engine to inspect the image layer-by-layer for known security flaws. Most Container Registries integrate some container image static analysis tools.

- Docker Hub Vulnerability Scanning has been powered natively by Docker, instead of a third party, since February 27, 2023.

- Red Hat Quay uses the open-source Clair security framework.

These tools scan each container image layer and notify you of vulnerabilities that might be a threat. They use the popular Internet thread databases to search for security patterns: NIST Common Vulnerabilities and Exposures database (CVE), Red Hat Security Bulletins (RHSB), Ubuntu Security Notices (USN), and Debian Security Advisories (DSA).

In the market, there are many open-source and commercially available products for this task nowadays. Popular tools include Anchore, Datadog Cloud SIEM, Sophos Cloud Native Security, Bitdefender GravityZone, Sysdig Secure, Red Hat Advanced Cluster Security for Kubernetes, and Aqua Security. Integrating one or more of these products into your DevSecOps process is a good way to address and mitigate security risks.

## The Hello Dockerfile

Now that you know more about the Dockerfile format, you can move forward with your Hello App.

The Hello App is a Python 3 base on the Flask Restful framework. Flask is a popular web application framework for Python, implemented on Werkzeug and Jinja2. Flask-RESTful is a popular Flask extension for quickly building REST APIs. It's a fast way to integrate a web server into a few lines of code.

The two Hello App source files are shown in Listing 1-2.

***Listing 1-2.*** Hello Dockerfile

– Dockerfile

```
FROM python:3
LABEL org.opencontainers.image.title="Hello World image"
LABEL maintainer="Luca Berton"
ADD helloworld.py /
RUN pip install flask
RUN pip install flask_restful
EXPOSE 8080
CMD [ "python", "./helloworld.py"]
```

The FROM instruction informs Docker that you want to derive from the python:3 image. At the moment of writing the book, tag 3 of the python image points to the latest release of the Python image. The same result could be obtained using the tags 3.11.0, 3.11, 3, and latest. The Python image is the official distribution of the Python computer programming language in a slim release. Docker Hub Container Registry is available on top of the latest Debian 11.5 "bullseye" Linux distribution, released on September 10, 2022.

The ADD instruction adds files to the image from the current directory. You need to specify the source filename and the destination.

The LABEL instruction adds metadata to the image—specifically an image title and the maintainer's name.

Line number 4 uses the LABEL instruction:

```
ADD helloworld.py /
```

This line copies the helloworld.py file into the destination directory / (root), which is the base directory of every UNIX file system.

The RUN instruction executes some commands inside the image. Specifically, line number 5 and line number 6 execute the pip command.

```
RUN pip install flask
RUN pip install flask_restful
```

The pip command is the Python Package manager that is used to install additional content inside the container. The advantage of this approach, rather than using the system packages, is that it fetches the latest release of the package and compiles it for your system. The pip command also takes care of the dependencies and ensures that the software is up-to-date on your system. In this example, it added the flask and flask_ restful programs.

The EXPOSE instruction specifies the network port of the service of your container. In this case, port 8080 is required by the web application.

The CMD instruction tells Docker to execute the shell command and is the process to run upon the container start. It runs the concatenation of the two strings of the list. So the python system command and the ./helloworld.py application.

# The Hello Application

The Hello application is a simple Python program that you will execute inside a container. Listing 1-3 details the contents of this helloworld.py application.

**Listing 1-3.** helloworld.py

    - helloworld.py

```
#!/usr/bin/env python3
from flask import Flask, request
from flask_restful import Resource, Api
app = Flask(__name__)
api = Api(app)
class Hello (Resource):
    def get(self):
        return 'Hello World'
api.add_resource(Hello, '/') # Route_1
if __name__ == '__main__':
    app.run('0.0.0.0','8080')
```

A few lines of this code run a web server on port 8080 and serve the default address /
with the Hello World message.

You can test this code in a browser with the target address of localhost and the
local port 8080 by just typing localhost:8080 in your favorite browser. When the
helloworld.py application runs, it returns the Hello World text on the screen, as shown
in Figure 1-5.

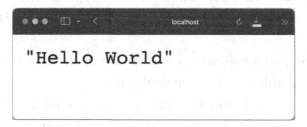

**Figure 1-5.** *The hello app in a browser*

In order to run the helloworld.py file, you must manually install all the necessary
dependencies. In this case, the installation of the packages flask and flask_restful.
This process is boring, repetitive, and error-prone; you need to automate it with a
container image. The best way to test the code is to create a Python virtual environment
using the Python venv module and then use the pip command to install the required
packages.

To install the required dependencies (all the commands listed in the Python import), use:

```
pip install flask flask_restful
```

If you want to share the virtual environment with a friend, you could generate a requirements.txt file with the full dependency tree that's usable on every machine with Python installed. Listing 1-4 shows the requirements file generated on my machine at the moment of writing this book (versions of the dependencies might vary on your system).

***Listing 1-4.*** requirements.txt

```
- requirements.txt
```

```
aniso8601==9.0.1
click==8.1.3
Flask==2.2.2
Flask-RESTful==0.3.9
itsdangerous==2.1.2
Jinja2==3.1.2
MarkupSafe==2.1.1
pytz==2022.6
six==1.16.0
Werkzeug==2.2.2
```

You could easily install all the required dependencies and run helloworld.py typing these commands:

```
pip install -r requirements.txt
python helloworld.py
```

The first command installs all the necessary software dependencies and the second runs your application. The expected output for successfully listening for a new connection is the following:

```
* Serving Flask app 'helloworld'
* Running on http://127.0.0.1:8080
```

# Building the Hello App

Before being able to execute your container, you need to build the binary image, as illustrated in Figure 1-6. The process requires some time but is completely automated. Once you practice, it will become straightforward.

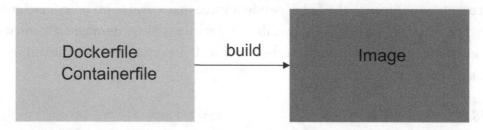

***Figure 1-6.***  *The container build process*

Using the build parameter of the docker command in the terminal, you request the building of your container, specifying the image name using the -t parameter and the name hello-world-python:

```
$ docker build -t hello-world-python .
```

Under the hood, Docker downloads the base image name Python and selects tag 3. After that, Docker adds the helloworld.py file to the file system of the new container and downloads the required Python dependencies.

The result is a container named hello-world-python in your workstation. In case you're wondering, it's ~1GB on my workstation.

# Running Hello in Docker

Once the container image is successfully built, you can execute it as many times as you want or upload it to a Container Registry (Docker Hub, Quay.io, Google's Container Registry, and so on). Figure 1-7 illustrates the container run process.

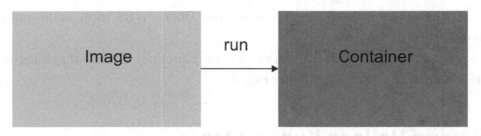

***Figure 1-7.*** *Container run process*

You can run your containers by specifying the port mapping using the 8080 port of the localhost mapped to the port 8080 on the container.

```
$ docker run -p 8080:8080 hello-world-python
```

You can check the status of the Docker execution using the ps parameter of the docker command:

```
$ docker ps
CONTAINER ID          IMAGE
2c66d0efcbd4 hello-world-python
```

The computer-generated string 2c66d0efcbd4 represents the container ID of the running container in your workstation.

You can verify the execution using the command-line browser cURL:

```
$ curl http://localhost:8080
```

If you prefer to use your favorite browser software, just type localhost:8080 in the title bar; Figure 1-8 shows the result.

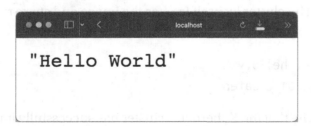

***Figure 1-8.*** *The hello app in a browser*

As you can see, the result of the execution using Docker is the same as the manual Python execution of the Hello App.

The main advantage is that you can execute the container as many times as you want or share it with others via the Container Registry.

# Deploying Hello in Kubernetes

In order to deploy your image to Kubernetes, you need to create a manifest file called `hello.yml`. Manifest files are written in YAML programming code and are very easy for humans to understand. See Listing 1-5.

***Listing 1-5.*** The hello.yml Manifest File

```
- hello.yml
apiVersion: v1
kind: Pod
metadata:
   name: redis-pod
spec:
   containers:
      - name: hello-container01
        image: hello-world-python:latest
        ports:
           - containerPort: 8080
```

Once you create the `hello.yml` manifest file, you can deploy the Hello App to your Kubernetes cluster. The cluster by itself fetches the image and starts running, waiting for new connections:

```
$ kubectl create -f hello.yml
pod/hello-container01 created
```

You can then verify that the Kubernetes cluster has successfully initialized all the Hello App resources using the following command:

```
$ kubectl get pods
NAME                    READY    STATUS     RESTARTS    AGE
hello-world-python      1/1      Running    1           11h
```

# Deploying Hello in Operator

Operator enables you to verify and deploy new applications in your Kubernetes cluster automatically. You need some coding skills, because the code is going to rely on the Kubernetes Operator SDK, which is a Minikube environment for running Kubernetes locally, as well as the Go language (Golang). At the moment, the app is so tiny that it seems overdoing it to create an operator to display a text message, but it's good practice.

The seven steps needed to generate a Kubernetes Operator are as follows:

1.  Generate the boilerplate code using the Kubernetes Operator SDK and Minikube:

    ```
    $ minikube start init
    $ operator-sdk init
    ```

2.  Create the APIs and a custom resource:

    ```
    $ operator-sdk create api --version=v1alpha1 --kind=Traveller
    ```

3.  Download any dependencies.

4.  Create a deployment.

5.  Create a service.

6.  Add a reference in the controller for the deployment and service.

7.  Deploy the service, install the CRD, and deploy a CRD instance.

Operators extend Kubernetes APIs and create custom objects to customize the cluster according to your needs.

# Key Takeaways

IT infrastructure is more critical than ever. It serves the business mission and delivers the best possible service to stakeholders both inside your organization and outside, to customers and partners.

The Kubernetes platform orchestrates your container fleet precisely and efficiently. K8s, combined with Ansible, enables incredible powerful horsepower that allows you to use DevSecOps, Infrastructure as Code, and self-healing infrastructures.

# CHAPTER 2

# Ansible Language Code

Ansible is an IT automation tool that enables Infrastructure as Code (IaC). Michael DeHaan started the Ansible project. The first release of Ansible was made public on the February 20, 2012. Michael took inspiration from several tools he had written, along with some hands-on experience with the state of configuration management at the time. Some of Ansible's unique attributes, such as its module-based architecture and agentless approach, quickly attracted attention in the open-source world. The logo is reminiscent of the Start Trek Communicator device of instantaneous communications between galaxies.

## What Is Ansible?

Ansible is classified as an infrastructure automation tool; it allows you to quickly automate your system administrator tasks. Infrastructure as Code manages and provides computer data centers through machine-readable definition files rather than physical hardware configuration or interactive configuration tools. With Ansible, you can deploy your Infrastructure as Code on-premises and on well-known public cloud providers.

Ansible is used to apply the DevOps principles in worldwide organizations. DevOps is a set of practices that combines software development (Dev) and IT operations (Ops). As DevOps is a cross-functional mode of working, those who practice the methodology use different tools, referred to as "toolchains," rather than a single tool. These toolchains fit into one or more categories, reflective of key aspects of the development and delivery process.

These are the six benefits to using Ansible and counting:

- **Simple**: The code is in the YAML language, a human-readable data serialization language. It is well-known and easy to learn; it is commonly used for configuration files and in applications where data is being stored or transmitted.

27

© Luca Berton 2023
L. Berton, *Ansible for Kubernetes by Example*, https://doi.org/10.1007/978-1-4842-9285-3_2

- **Powerful**: Ansible is robust and battle-tested in configuration management, workflow orchestration, and application deployment.

- **Cross-platform**: Ansible is agentless, which means that it supports all major operating systems, as well as physical, virtual, cloud, and network providers. Agentless support for all primary OS, physical, virtual, cloud, and networks.

- **Works with existing tools**: Ansible can work with existing tools, making it easy to homogenize the current environment.

- **Batteries included:** Ansible is bundled with many modules to automate the most common tasks.

- **Community-powered**: Every month, Ansible has more than 250,000 downloads, an average of 3,500 contributors, and more than 1,200 users on IRC.

Ansible can be easily extended by using additional resources and plugins. The most common way to distribute these is via an Ansible collection that comes with a standardized format. The more than 750 modules include cloud modules for clustering, executing commands, crypto, database, managing files and directories, identity management, inventory, messaging, monitoring, net tools, network, notification, packaging, remote management, source control and versioning, storage, system, utilities, web infrastructures, and interacting with Windows operating systems.

Ansible's three prominent use cases are provisioning, configuration management, and application deployment. After using this technology, you may just invent more ways to use it!

# Provisioning

*Provisioning* is the process of setting up the IT infrastructure: all system administrators know how important it is to manage a uniform fleet of machines. Some people still rely on software to create workstation images. But there is a drawback to that; with imaging technology, you're only taking a snapshot of the machine at a certain time. You have to reinstall software every time because of modern critical activation systems or to update the latest security patches. Ansible is very powerful in automating this process.

# Configuration Management

*Configuration management* is the process of maintaining systems and software in a desired and consistent state. It maintains an up-to-date and consistent fleet, including coordinating rolling updates and scheduling downtime. With Ansible, you can verify the status of your managed hosts and take action in a small group of them. A wide variety of modules is available for the most common use cases, not to mention the typical use case of checking for the compliance of your fleet to international standards and apply resolution plans.

# Application Deployment

*Application deployment* is the process of publishing software between testing, staging, and production environment. For example, Ansible can automate your web application's continuous integration/delivery workflow pipeline. Your DevOps team will be delighted!

# Ansible Open-Source vs Commercial Options

Ansible is a community-driven project with fast-moving innovations. It's open-source with only command-line tools.

Ansible Inc., originally AnsibleWorks Inc., was the company set up to support and sponsor the project commercially by Michael DeHaan, the founder of the Ansible project. In October of 2015, Red Hat acquired Ansible Inc. and evaluated Ansible as a "powerful IT automation solution" designed to help enterprises move toward frictionless IT. Since 2016, *AnsibleFest* has been an annual conference of the Ansible community of users and contributors; previous editions were hosted in Europe and the United States. Since 2023, the event has been part of the Red Hat Summit main event planned in May each year.

Red Hat Ansible Automation Platform is the commercial framework designed by Red Hat. You can interact using a web user interface, an API, command-line interfaces, and Ansible collections. It provides configuration management (CM), CM tools, a GUI, Role-Based Access Control (RBAC), and third-party authentications and integrations to manage your infrastructure. Red Hat Ansible Automation Controller was formerly known as Ansible Tower. Red Hat Ansible Automation Platform has loads of products, including Ansible Automation Controller, Automation Hub, Automation Analytics, and more.

Enterprise needs more services and some stable releases. For example, they need an SLA for support. Red Hat offers this service to companies under the Ansible Tower umbrella, now rebranded as Ansible Automation Controller.

Ansible Tower is a REST API, web service, and web-based console designed to make Ansible more usable for IT teams with members of different technical proficiencies and skill sets. It is a hub for automation tasks. The Tower is a commercial product supported by Red Hat Inc. but derived from the AWX upstream project, which has been open-source since September 2017.

Red Hat maintains Ansible Core (formerly Ansible Engine) with the explicit intent of being used in the open-source community and as an enterprise IT platform. With Ansible Core, organizations can access the tools and innovations available from the underlying Ansible technology in a hardened, enterprise-grade manner.

# Ansible's Architecture

Ansible typically requires two or more hosts—one that executes the automation, called the *Ansible Control Node*, and one (or more) that receives the action, called the *Target Node*. Figure 2-1 illustrates the architecture.

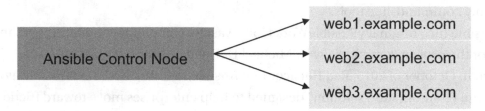

***Figure 2-1.*** *Ansible Architecture*

The Ansible Control Node directs the automation and effectively requires Ansible to be fully installed inside. The Ansible Target Node requires only a valid login to connect.

The Ansible Control Node usually uses Ansible Playbook and Inventories (see Figure 2-2) for the execution. The Ansible Playbook is the automation blueprint and has a step-by-step list of tasks to execute against the target hosts.

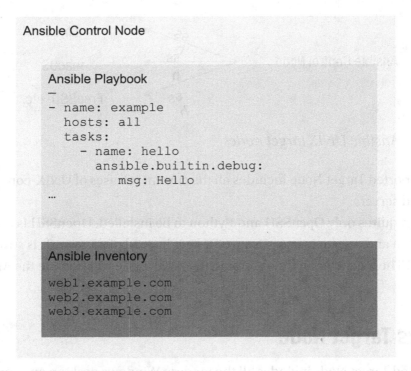

Ansible Control Node

Ansible Playbook
—
- name: example
  hosts: all
  tasks:
    - name: hello
      ansible.builtin.debug:
        msg: Hello
…

Ansible Inventory

web1.example.com
web2.example.com
web3.example.com

***Figure 2-2.*** *Ansible Playbook and Inventory*

Ansible Playbook is coded in the YAML language, so easy to write and human-readable.

The Ansible Inventory is the list of target hosts in INI, YAML, or JSON format. For simplicity, you can group the hosts using a common name. In this way, you can easily specify the group name for the execution.

The next section reviews how to install and configure a control node for Ansible for the most common operating systems.

# UNIX Target Node

You can configure Ansible in the following UNIX target node: Linux distributions, macOS, and UNIX (FreeBSD, OpenBSD, etc.), as shown in Figure 2-3.

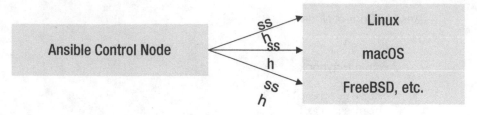

***Figure 2-3.*** *Ansible UNIX target nodes*

The supported Target Node includes all the current releases of UNIX-compliant desktops and servers.

Ansible requires only OpenSSH and Python to be installed. OpenSSH is used for connection and one login user. Using SSH keys instead of passwords is strongly encouraged. The local Python interpreter in the target node will execute the Ansible commands.

## Windows Target Node

The supported Target Node includes all the modern Windows desktop and server releases. The list includes Windows 7, 8.1, 10, and 11 and Windows Server 2008, 2008 R2, 2012, 2012 R2, 2016, 2019, and 2022 at the moment of writing this book, but Windows support is future-proof. See Figure 2-4.

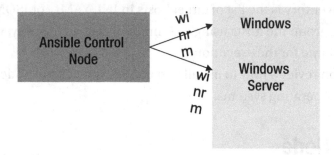

***Figure 2-4.*** *Ansible Windows target nodes*

The Windows host requires PowerShell 3.0 or newer and at least .NET 4.0. You only need to upgrade old Windows 7 and Windows Server 2008 nodes.

The WinRM listener receives and executes the commands between Ansible Controller and the target node. Ansible 2.8 added an experimental SSH connection for Windows-managed nodes for Windows 10+ clients and Windows Server 2019+.

The easier, more straightforward configuration is using the WinRM connection method with the basic authentication.

You can specify more advanced authentication methods: Basic, Certificate, NTLM, Kerberos, and CredSSP. You can do this for local user accounts, Active Directory accounts, credential delegations, and HTTP encryption, as shown in Table 2-1.

***Table 2-1.*** *WinRM Authentication Methods*

| Option | Local Accounts | Active Directory Accounts | Credential Delegation | HTTP Encryption |
|---|---|---|---|---|
| Basic | Yes | No | No | No |
| Certificate | Yes | No | No | No |
| Kerberos | No | Yes | Yes | Yes |
| NTLM | Yes | Yes | No | Yes |
| CredSSP | Yes | Yes | Yes | Yes |

Basic authentication is the simplest authentication option but also the most insecure because it transmits the password encrypted with base64 encoding.

The following example shows the WinRM host variables configured for basic authentication in the Ansible Inventory:

```
ansible_connection: winrm
ansible_winrm_transport: basic
ansible_user: LocalUsername
ansible_password: Password
```

WinRM Certificate authentication uses certificates as public/private key pairs in PEM format. The following example shows how to configure WinRM host variables for certificate authentication in the Ansible Inventory:

```
ansible_connection: winrm
ansible_winrm_transport: certificate
ansible_winrm_cert_pem: /path/to/certificate/public/key.pem
ansible_winrm_cert_key_pem: /path/to/certificate/private/key.pem
```

For all the other installation scenarios and comprehensive configuration details, refer to the documentation on the official Ansible website: `https://docs.ansible.com/`.

# Ansible Installation

The Ansible package must be installed only on the Ansible Control Node (see Figure 2-5). Ansible is available for a large variety of modern operating systems. You can configure the Ansible Control Node in a large variety of UNIX operating systems: Linux distributions, macOS, UNIX (FreeBSD, OpenBSD, and so on).

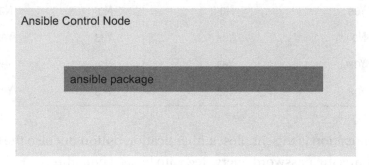

**Figure 2-5.**  *Ansible Control Node*

The supported control node includes the current UNIX-compliant desktop and server releases.

Ansible Engineering Team distributes a minimalist language and runtime called `ansible-core` (it was called `ansible-base` in version 2.10), and the Ansible Community Team has a community package called `ansible`.

Choose the Ansible style and version that matches your particular needs or is available in your operating system.

Ansible Core (`ansible-core` package) focuses primarily on developers and users who want to install only the basic Ansible language and runtime and add any additional Ansible Collections. It contains only the `ansible.builtin` modules and plugins, allowing other Ansible Collections to be installed. The Ansible Core is similar to Ansible 2.9 without any content; it has since moved into external Collections, resulting in a smaller package on disk. The current release cycle at the moment of writing this book of Ansible Core is two major releases per year.

The `ansible` Community package includes the Ansible Core plus 85+ community-curated Collections that contain thousands of modules and plugins. It re-creates and expands on the functionality included in Ansible 2.9 in a bigger package on disk. The current release cycle of the Ansible Community package at the moment of writing this book is two major versions per year, on a flexible release cycle that trails the release of the `ansible-core` package.

The easiest way to install Ansible is to install the `ansible` or `ansible-core` in your package manager or use the `pip` tool for Python.

Use the following command on Red Hat Enterprise Linux, Fedora, CentOS, Rocky Linux, Alma Linux, Oracle Linux, or Amazon Linux systems with root privileges to install Ansible:

```
yum install ansible
```

On Debian and Ubuntu Linux systems, use this command (root privileges required, often `sudo` is used):

```
apt-get install ansible
```

The PyPI is the largest archive of Python modules, and you can interact with it using the popular `pip` command-line utility. Using the `pip` command-line utility, you can download and install the latest release available from the PyPI website on your system. System administrators often configure a Python virtual environment in order to separate the Ansible installation and the library that might be necessary for additional components, such as roles and collection from the system libraries.

Using the Python `pip` tool, you can install Ansible using the following command (root privileges may or may not be required, depending on your environment):

```
pip install ansible
```

The `pip` utility is available in many operating systems inside the `python-pip` or `python3-pip` system package. Some variants are available for Python 3: pip3 or specific versions of Python, for example, Python 3.10: pip3.10.

After successfully installing Ansible on your system, you can use the `ansible --version` command to check the current version of Ansible on your system and, of course, also check if the installation was successful.

The first line of the output of the `ansible --version` command shows the full version of Ansible installed:

```
ansible [core 2.13.4]
```

In Ansible jargon, the full version reads 2.13.4 with 2 as a major, 13 as a minor, and 4 as the revision.

# Getting Started with Ansible

In this section, you learn how to execute a simple Ansible ad hoc command against a list of hosts.

## Running Your First Ansible Ad Hoc Command

Every command is executed by the `ansible` command-line utility (installed with Ansible on your system). Try running the Ansible `ping` command. A command is called a *module* in Ansible jargon. The purpose is to test the connection between the controller and the target node.

The expected result is printing the screen's message `"ping: pong."` If you see this message, the connection was successful, and the execution of the Ansible code went fine. When the connection is unsuccessful, an error message is displayed onscreen.

The expected output after running the `ping` command is shown here:

```
$ ansible localhost -m ping
localhost | SUCCESS => {
    "changed": false,
    "ping": "pong"
}
```

Sometimes, you'll need to execute the command as a root or administrative user. Ansible integrates a proper privilege escalation mechanism.

Adding additional parameters to the command line allows you to specify the connection user `devops` and indicate that you need `root` privileges using the `sudo` mechanism (default).

```
ansible localhost -m ping -u devops --become
```

This command executes under the root user's permission, supplying the sudo password. You must verify the configuration and the policies of your system in order to be able to execute the sudo command via the current user. This is the result of the execution. Some modules have different results for the normal user and the root user. The ping module has the same result, but modules that install packages or perform system-wide configurations have a different result.

## Creating a Basic Inventory

Every execution needs a list of target hosts. Ansible needs to know which nodes to target the execution against. You can specify the list of target hosts in the command line to an inventory file. The inventory is a simple list of target hosts in the default Ansible inventory file. If no Ansible inventory is specified in the command line, Ansible relies on the default /etc/ansible/hosts file. It's simply a text file with a list of host names or IP addresses. It follows the INI format.

The inventory file stores the list of target nodes. For example, you can specify only one host named localhost and the content will look like the following:

```
localhost anisble_connection=local
web1.example.com ansible_connection=ssh ansible_user=devops ansible_ssh_
private_key_file=~/.ssh/id_rsa
```

There are two hosts in this inventory. The first is localhost, so you can execute the automation against the control node and another host web1.example.com using the username devops connecting via SSH using the key file ~/.ssh/id_rsa.

## Ansible Code Language

Ansible is a declarative language, which means that it is focused on the result of the execution rather than the steps to achieve the results, like in traditional programming languages. The code is organized into Ansible Playbook when you want to execute more than one command, like in Ansible Ad Hoc.

Ansible is not a complete computer programming language but relies on multiple common computer programming statements for each code segment. Every task is executed in sequence when a condition is verified and in iteration and uses a module construct. Think about a module like a Lego blueprint for your automation; they could combine together as needed to achieve great results. One important property of some modules is *idempotency,* which means the ability to perform some action on the target host only if needed and to skip the execution whenever it is not necessary.

Ansible relies on Python language underneath, so it has a vast plethora of libraries and tools. The Ansible language, called *Playbook*, is coded in YAML and uses many of the Jinja2 functions and filters.

Ansible can be extended using plugins that extend and propel the integration to many cloud providers and more functions, modules, and so on. Code reuse greatly emphasizes Ansible, and the standard way to distribute and consume the Ansible code is with Ansible Roles and Ansible Collections.

# Ansible Inventory

An Ansible Inventory is the list of managed hosts that target your Ansible automation. You can also organize your inventory in groups or patterns to select the hosts or groups.

The `ansible-inventory` command-line tool is included in every Ansible installation, and its purpose is to show the current Ansible inventory information. It's advantageous to verify the current status of your Ansible Inventory. It accepts Ansible Vault and Ansible Inventory in INI, YAML, and JSON formats. You can get the complete lists of parameters using `--help`. A handy feature is to display the hosts in a list using the `--list` parameter or in a tree view using the `--graph` parameter.

The INI inventory is the simplest inventory type. You can insert all your target hosts or IP addresses. The default location of the inventory is `/etc/ansible/hosts`, but most command-line tools accept a customized path with the `-i` parameter.

Moreover, it's possible to define multiple groups inside, specifying the group name between brackets in INI format `[group]`, or under the `children` node in YAML format. Obviously, hosts might be present in multiple groups inside an inventory.

The particular keyword `all` includes all the hosts of the inventory. The only exception is `localhost`, which you need to specify. The `all` keyword is important and targets all your Ansible example inventory.

One particular host is `localhost`. You might sometimes want to execute your Ansible code with the local machine as a target. You can achieve this result by specifying the `ansible_connection` "`local`" property. By default, Ansible assumes it should use the SSH connection for any target nodes; in this way, you force it to use the local connection instead.

# INI Inventory

The most straightforward Ansible inventory format is INI. The INI format has been around for years and is very popular for Windows and Linux configuration files. The INI inventory file can have some name=value fields inside. Obviously, name is the name of the property, and value is the property's value. The example in Listing 2-1 shows one ungrouped host called bastion.example.com and two hosts inside the [web] group containing web1.example.com and web2.example.com.

***Listing 2-1.*** The example.ini File

```
bastion.example.com ansible_user=ansible
[web]
web[1:2].example.com
[web:vars]
ansible_user=devops
```

You can use your target host directly with the hostname or the additional [web] group. Note that this example specifies some hostnames in a range between brackets, specifying the first and last elements with an alternation of numbers and letters.

You can also specify some variables for each host. This example scenario is common because it defines different connections with different hosts. For example, use the local link for the localhost and ssh, the default, for all the other hosts. For each host, you can customize the login user. This example uses the ansible user for bastion.example.com and the devops user for web1.example.com and web2.example.com. You might like to move the host variable to the host_vars/bastion.example.com file, which contains the variables for the host bastion.example.com. In a similar way, you can store the group variables in the group_vars/web file containing the variables for the web group.

# YAML Inventory

The YAML format is a simple human-readable format that is often used for Ansible inventories instead of the INI format. In this format, the indentation of every single line is essential. The list of hosts or IP addresses descends from the root all node. Each host must be under the hosts field. You can specify the groups under the children keywords.

The same `example-ini` inventory could be expressed, as shown in Listing 2-2.

***Listing 2-2.*** The example.yaml File

```
---
all:
  hosts:
    bastion.example.com:
  vars:
    ansible_user: ansible
  children:
    web:
      hosts:
        web1.example.com
        web2.example.com
      vars:
        ansible_user: devops
```

The YAML inventory is entirely equivalent to the INI format. As you can see, you can specify a group name, some hosts underneath, and some host and group variables.

## Ansible Playbook

An Ansible Playbook is a set of plays to be executed against an inventory. The code is written in the YAML text syntax format, making the files easy to write and human-readable. Each YAML file begins with three dashes (`---`) and ends with three dots (`...`). The three dots (`...`) are often omitted. Be very careful about the indentation; most of the time, improper indentation is the cause of malfunction. You can use the sharp/hashtag symbol (#) for comments, as you can in many languages.

Ansible uses a lot of string variables; you can specify the value directly or with a single or double quote. We recommend using a double quote as a general rule. Using the pipe (|), you can define multi-line strings that keep newlines and a major (>) that doesn't.

The first Ansible Playbook in this book displays a simple "Hi" message on the screen. Listing 2-3 shows the complete Ansible code.

***Listing 2-3.*** The hi.yml File

```
---
- name: Hi example
  hosts: all
  tasks:
    - name: Hi message
      ansible.builtin.debug:
        msg: "Hi!"
...
```

Here is a line-by-line explanation of the hi.yml Ansible Playbook:

1. Start of the YAML file (---)

2. Name of the play ("Hi example")

3. Target hosts of execution (all of the inventory)

4. Beginning of tasks

5. The first task is named Hi message

6. The ansible.builtin.debug module displays messages onscreen

7. The msg argument of the debug module is the message that you want to display

8. End of file (...)

You can execute this code using the ansible-playbook command-line utility included in every Ansible installation. The full command requires specifying the playbook name after it, as shown in Figure 2-6.

```
$ ansible-playbook hi.yml
```

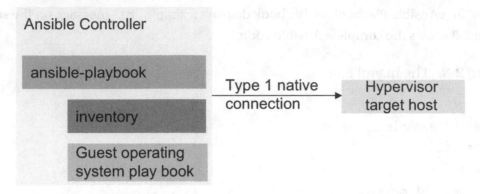

*Figure 2-6.*  *The ansible-playbook process*

The execution produces the "Hi" message on the screen and an OK status for the execution. The Ansible playbook could contain multiple plays targeting different hosts, for example, and executing different tasks.

A good security practice is to execute as much code as possible as standard user permission. However, some operations are only possible at the root/administrative permision level. Ansible has embedded the ability to switch between two users (usually the normal and administrative users) and supports many of the most popular systems for privilege escalation.

You can enable privilege escalation in Ansible Playbook using the following Ansible statements:

- become specifies that privilege escalation is necessary

- become_method selects the escalation method

- become_user specifies the destination user (default root)

The Ansible playbook shown in Listing 2-4 installs the popular fail2ban program, accessing the target host as a normal user then switching to root.

*Listing 2-4.*  The fail2ban.yml File

```
---
- name: install fail2ban
  hosts: all
  become: true
  become_method: sudo
  become_user: root
```

```
tasks:
  - name: install fail2ban
    ansible.builtin.apt:
      name: fail2ban
      status: present
      update_cache: true
```

The --check parameter of the ansible-playbook command allows you to perform a read-only operation on the target node, often used as a dry run for this playbook.

Ansible doesn't have a proper debug system, but you can combine the Ansible debug module with the verbosity parameter (1-4). The debug module allows you to print text on the screen during the execution, and you can specify the verbosity parameter of each message. The verbosity parameter of the ansible-playbook command is expressed by the number -v for level one, -vv for level two, -vvv for level three, and -vvvv for level four.

## Ansible Variables

Like in every language, variables allow you to make your code reusable in the future. These are the variables available in the Ansible language:

- User-defined variables

- Extra variables

- Host and group variables (see the previous Ansible Inventory section)

- Registered variables

The user-defined variables are declared with the vars statement followed by the list of each variable and value. Variable types are the same as in Python: string, number, Boolean, list, dictionary, and so on. You can retrieve the variable value in any part of your Ansible playbook by specifying the name between double brackets, like this: {{ name }}.

The extra variable is a way to pass value from the command line. It's advantageous when you're trying to integrate Ansible into your current toolchain or simply want to parameterize your playbook from the command line. It overrides any value in your Ansible Playbook specific to the -e parameter of the ansible-playbook command.

Array variables are instrumental when you want to specify some properties that apply to multiple objects. For example, Listing 2-5 contains some cars and properties.

***Listing 2-5.*** An Array of Variable Snippets

```
cars:
  bmw:
    model: M1
    fuel: petrol
  tesla:
    model: Model S
    fuel: electric
```

You can access each property using dot (.) or bracket notation [], like in Python. For example, `cars.bmw.fuel` and `cars[bmw][fuel]` both refer to the value `petrol`.

The registered variables save the output of any commands inside registered variables. It is very useful when you want to combine the output of a module with another module.

## Ansible Filters

You can perform some alterations of Ansible variables using the Ansible filters. These are native functions from the Jinja2 filters. They extend the functionality of the Ansible language. Ansible filters manipulate data at a variable level. The most common filters are as follows:

- Assign default mandatory values: `{{ variable_name | default(5) }}`

- Make variables optional: `{{ variable_name | default(omit) }}`

- Assign ternary value: `{{ status | ternary('restart', 'continue') }}`

- Manage data types: `{{ variable_name | items2dict }}`

- Format data to JSON and YAML: `{{ variable_name | to_json }}` or `{{ variable_name | to_nice_yaml }}`

- Work with regex: `{{ "ansible" | regex_replace('^.', 'A') }}`

# Conditionals

Like in every programming language, conditional statements give developers the ability to check a condition and change the behavior of the program accordingly. The Ansible form is the when statement.

The when statement defines when a task will be executed or not based on the Boolean result of the following:

- Complex expression using parentheses ()

- Comparison operators ==, >=, <=, !=

- Ansible facts (ansible_facts['os_family'] == "Debian")

The example in Listing 2-6 reloads the ssh service when the variable reload_ssh is true.

***Listing 2-6.*** The reload_ssh.yml File

```
---
- name: ssh reload
  hosts: all
  vars:
    reload_ssh: false
  tasks:
    - name: reload ssh
      ansible.builtin.service:
        name: nginx
        state: reloaded
      when: reload_ssh
```

Running the code produces one skipped status for the task where the statement is false during the execution. When you switch the variable reload_ssh to true, the task status is going to be executed.

# Handler

The Ansible handler is a special conditional statement that runs operations only when the first task reports a change in status. Handlers execute only when the previous task reports a changed status. If the previous task report has an ok status, the handler is not executed.

In Listing 2-7, the handler code is executed only if a change is detected. Note that the notify statement mentions the handler's name to run. This playbook checks the latest version of the HTTPD web server on all hosts; if an update is available, the yum module executes the upgrade and displays the message on the screen. If an upgrade is not necessary, the handler code is not executed.

*Listing 2-7.* The httpd.yml File

```
---
- name: handler demo
  hosts: all
  become: true
  tasks:
    - name: latest package
      ansible.builtin.yum:
        name: httpd
        state: latest
      notify: httpd update
  handlers:
    - name: httpd update
      ansible.builtin.debug:
        msg: "Webserver updated!"
```

# Loop

Computers are great for repetitive tasks. Loop statements automate repetitive tasks in Ansible Playbooks. The loop variable item is available during the iteration to express the current value in each iteration.

These are the most popular Ansible loop statements:

- `loop`: The `loop` statement is added to the task and takes as a value the list of items over which the task should be iterated.

- `with_items` statement: Like `loop` for simple lists, lists of strings, or a list of hashes/dictionaries. Flatter to list if lists of lists are provided.

- `with_file` statement: This keyword requires a list of control node filenames. The loop variable item holds the contents of the file.

- `with_sequence` statement: This keyword requires parameters to generate a list of values based on a numeric sequence.

- `with_fileglob` statement: This statement lists files matching a pattern. For example, you can specify the *.txt parameter to list all the files with txt extensions on the target node, as shown in Listing 2-8.

***Listing 2-8.*** The checkservices.yml File

```
---
- name: Check services
  hosts: all
  tasks:
  - name: services running
    ansible.builtin.service:
      name: "{{ item }}"
      state: started
    loop:
      - apache2
      - sshd
```

This example shows you how to iterate through a list of elements and pass as a single item to the service module to process one at the time using the `loop` Ansible statement.

## Ansible Facts

Variables related to remote systems are called *facts*. They are powerful because you can obtain a comprehensive vision of the current host, the operating system, the distribution used, the IP address, the networking configuration, the storage configuration, and so on. With Ansible facts, you can use the behavior or state of one system as a configuration on other systems.

Note that this requires `gather_facts` be enabled in the Play section (see Listing 2-9). The `gather_facts` variable is enabled by default and adds an extra "Fact Gathering" task at the beginning of every Ansible playbook execution. You can disable using the `gather_facts: false` statement when you don't want to acquire any Ansible facts from target machines and use them inside Ansible Playbook. It's a good habit that explicitly declares the `gather_facts` variable in your Ansible Playbooks.

***Listing 2-9.*** The facts.yml File

```
---
- name: print facts
  hosts: all
  gather_facts: true
  tasks:
  - name: print facts
    ansible.builtin.debug:
      var: ansible_facts
```

The `facts.yml` playbook prints all the Ansible facts of the target system. The `ansible_date_time` fact, as an example, shows the current date and time on the screen.

## Ansible Magic Variables

Magic variables are Ansible's internal variables that come in handy at times. These are the five most common magic variables:

- `hostvars`: Accesses variables defined for any host

- `groups`: Lists all the groups in the inventory

- `group_names`: Lists which groups are the current host

- inventory_hostname: Hostname configured in the inventory

- ansible_version: Ansible version information

Refer to the Ansible manual for the full list and uses.

## Ansible Vault

Ansible Vault allows you to store encrypted variables and files and then use them, specifying a password in Playbooks or Roles. The AES 256 cipher protects files with strong encryption in the latest versions of Ansible. You can manage the Ansible vault using the ansible-vault command in the terminal, which is included in all the Ansible installations.

Creating a new Ansible Vault is very straightforward:

```
$ ansible-vault create secret.yml
```

You can use Ansible Vault in any Ansible Playbook by specifying the --vault-id @prompt parameter in the command line.

## Ansible Templates

The Ansible templates are helpful for applying variable values to configuration files. Ansible templates work by taking advantage of the Jinja2 programming language, the Ansible built-in template module.

The example shown in Listing 2-10 populates the hi.txt.j2 template with the value of the example variable and saves it in the /tmp/hi.txt file.

***Listing 2-10.*** The templates/hi.txt.j2 File

```
---
- name: template demo
  hosts: all
  vars:
    example: Hi
  tasks:
    - name: apply template
      ansible.builtin.template:
        src: templates/hi.txt.j2
        dest: /tmp/hi.txt
```

**Listing 2-11.** The template.yml File

```
{{ example }}
```

The result is a file with the following contents:

```
Hi
```

# Ansible Plugins

Plugins extend Ansible's functionality to more services and application domains. Every Ansible plugin executes on the Ansible Control Node. The full list of Ansible plugin types include the following:

- `action`: Executes in the background before the module executes

- `become`: Extends privilege escalation systems

- `cache`: Buffers gathered facts or inventory source data

- `callback`: Extends behaviors when responding to events

- `connection`: Extends connection possibilities to the target hosts

- `docs`: Fragments to document common parameters of multiple plugins or modules

- `filter`: data manipulation—extracts a value, transforms data types and formats, performs mathematical calculus, splits and concatenates strings, inserts dates and times, and so on

- `httpapi`: Interacts with a remote device's HTTP-based API

- `inventory`: Data sources for Ansible target hosts

- `lookup`: Extension to the Jinja2 templating language

- `module`: The most common, basic Ansible plugin

- `module_utils`: Helper to write Ansible modules

- `shell`: Expands how Ansible executes tasks

- `strategy`: Controls the flow of play execution

- test: Evaluates expressions and return true or false

- vars: Adds variable data to Ansible

Some plugin types are specific for the Ansible for Network use case:

- cliconf: CLI interface for network devices

- netconf: Interface to network devices

- terminal: Initializes a network device's SSH shell

Refer to the official "Ansible Working with Plugins" guide for more details. The most commonly used are the lookup plugins that enable you to extend Jinja2 to access data from outside sources within your playbooks.

Famous Ansible lookup plugins use cases are as follows:

- Reading from Windows INI style files (ini)

- Reading from CSV files (csvfile)

- Listening for files matching shell expressions (fileglob)

- Reading lines from stdout (lines)

- Generating a random password (password )

- Reading from a UNIX pipe (pipe)

- Returning content from an URL via HTTP or HTTPS (url)

# Ansible Roles

The Ansible Role enables code reuse to Ansible, creating a standard format to distribute playbook code. The standard structure splits the Ansible Playbook statements of Ansible into folders in the local file system.

You can manage Ansible's roles using the ansible-galaxy command-line utility that's included in every Ansible installation.

First of all, create the role-example Ansible role using the ansible-galaxy command and the following parameters:

- role, because you want to interact with an Ansible role

- init, because you want to initialize a new role

- role-example, the name of the new role

Here's the full command to create `role-example`:

```
$ ansible-galaxy role init role-example
```

The following directories were created:

- `defaults`, the `main.yml` file in this directory, contains the default values of role variables that can be overwritten by the user when the role is used. These variables have low precedence and are intended to be changed and customized in plays.

- `files`. This directory contains static files that are referenced by role tasks.

- `handlers`. The `main.yml` file in this directory contains the role's handler definitions.

- `meta`. The `main.yml` file in this directory contains information about the role, including author, license, platforms, and optional role dependencies.

- `tasks`. The `main.yml` file in this directory contains the role's task definitions.

- `templates`. This directory contains Jinja2 templates that are referenced by role tasks.

- `tests`. This directory can contain an inventory and `test.yml` playbook that can be used to test the role.

- `vars`. The `main.yml` file in this directory defines the role's variable values. Often these variables are used for internal purposes within the role. These variables have high precedence and are not intended to be changed when used in a playbook.

Not every role will have all of these directories. The most important file is `main.yml` in the `tasks` directory. The contents of this file is the contents of the tasks of one of the Ansible playbooks.

In the most straightforward Ansible role, you can print text on the screen. You can write the following code inside the `main.yml` file under the `tasks` directory in the `role-example` role, as shown in Listing 2-12.

***Listing 2-12.*** The role.yml File

```
---
name: role-example demo
ansible.builtin.debug:
  msg: "role-example"
```

You can include your roles in an Ansible Playbook using the `roles` statement, as shown in Listing 2-12.

***Listing 2-13.*** The Contents of the tasks/main.yml File

```
---
- name: role example
  hosts: all
  roles:
    - role-example
```

As you can see in Listing 2-12, you can take advantage of Ansible code reuse without knowing the implementation details of the Ansible role.

This concept of sharing code with other developers is the stepstone behind the Ansible Galaxy. It is a public directory where you can find available Ansible resources. There is a search engine that quickly finds the proper Ansible role or collection. Every resource shows the author, the download count, the supported operating systems, and much more information about usage and internal variables.

You can easily download and use Ansible roles from Ansible Galaxy in two ways:

1. By installing roles manually.

   The following command downloads and installs the latest version of the `geerlingguy.redis` Ansible role from the Ansible Galaxy website:

   ```
   $ ansible-galaxy role install geerlingguy.redis
   ```

2. By installing roles via `requirements.yml`.

   You can create a `requirements.yml` file when you want to install more than one role or execute all the operations automatically. See Listing 2-14.

***Listing 2-14.*** The requirements.yml File

```
---
roles:
  - src: geerlingguy.redis
```

You can execute your `requirements.yml` role file using this `ansible-galaxy` command:

```
$ ansible-galaxy role install -r roles/requirements.yml
```

With the following parameters:

- `role install` parameter, which installs a role

- `-r` specifies the usage of the `requirements.yml` file under the `roles` directory

Ansible roles are a good way to distribute Ansible code but the Ansible Collections are more powerful. Each Ansible role might have a different license and support by the author or organization that create it.

# Ansible Collection

An *Ansible collection* is the most modern and complete way to distribute Ansible code between multiple platforms in a standard way: roles, modules, and plugins. An Ansible collection can be stored in a private repository or a public archive such as the Ansible Galaxy website.

The most comprehensive Ansible collection is `community.general`. It has a lot of valuable Ansible resources. It is distributed on the Ansible Galaxy website, under the Community license. At the time of writing this book, there are 500+ modules and 100+ plugins in the latest version 6.0.1.

You can easily download and use the Ansible collection using the `ansible-galaxy` command in two ways:

1. By installing one collection manually.

   The following command downloads and installs the latest version of the `community.general` Ansible collection from the Ansible Galaxy website:

   ```
   $ ansible-galaxy collection install community.general
   ```

2. By installing a collection via `requirements.yml`.

   You can create a `requirements.yml` file when you want to install more than one role or execute all the operations automatically (see Listing 2-15).

***Listing 2-15.*** The requirements.yml File

```
---
collections:
  - name: community.general
    source: https://galaxy.ansible.com
```

You can execute the `requirements.yml` collection file using the `ansible-galaxy` command:

```
$ ansible-galaxy collection install -r collections/requirements.yml
```

Include the following parameters:

- `collection install` parameter installs the collection

- `-r` specify the use of the `requirements.yml` file in the `collections` directory

# Ansible Execution Environment

The latest approach is to create a container for your Ansible code is called Ansible Execution Environment. This is a solution to a growing problem. The more an organization adopts Ansible, the more the dependency tree grows, and the more dependency every piece of code has. Maintaining each piece of code becomes complex. Moreover, the developer environment might be misaligned with the production environment and lead to unexpected results.

The main advantage of the Ansible Execution Environment is that developers can use the same container used locally in production with the same version and library dependencies.

The `ansible-builder` and `ansible-runner` command-line tools help in the creation and execution of the Ansible Execution Environments (EE).

The `ansible-builder` command-line tool was added in 2022 to simplify the creation of Ansible Execution Environments (EE). It is available in the Ansible toolchain package with the Red Hat Ansible Automation Subscription:

```
$ dnf install ansible-builder
```

The `ansible-builder` command-line tool is also available in the PyPI repository (via the `pip` tool):

```
$ pip install ansible-builder
```

Imagine that you want to create a custom `my_ee` Ansible Execution Environment with all the tools to use Ansible for Amazon Web Services (AWS).

The following code creates an Ansible Execution Environment to run Amazon Web Services (AWS) collections and dependencies. A *collection* is a group of Ansible resources that connect to Amazon Web Services. The Ansible collection to interact with Amazon Web Services is `community.aws` and it requires the `boto3` and `botocore` Python libraries to be installed in the system.

The main file is the `execution-environment.yml` file and it provides the description of the steps to build an Ansible Execution Environment using the `ansible-builder` command-line tool, as shown in Figure 2-7 and Listing 2-16.

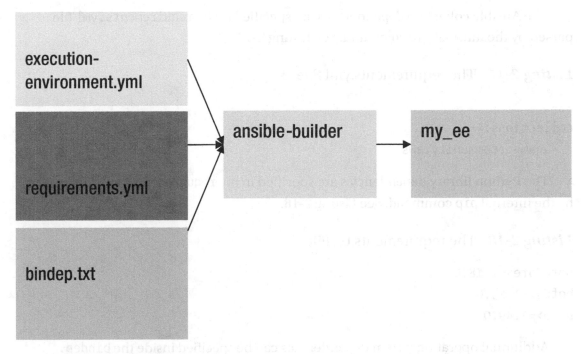

***Figure 2-7.*** *The ansible-builder process*

***Listing 2-16.*** The execution-environment.yml File

```
---
version: 1
dependencies:
  galaxy: requirements.yml
  python: requirements.txt
  system: bindep.txt
additional_build_steps:
  prepend: |
    RUN pip3 install --upgrade pip setuptools
  append:
    - RUN ls -al /
```

The Ansible collection dependencies are specified in the `requirements.yml` file, parsed by the internal `pip` command. See Listing 2-17.

***Listing 2-17.*** The requirements.yml File

```
---
collections:
  - name: community.aws
```

The Python library dependencies are specified in the `requirements.txt` file, parsed by the internal `pip` command. See Listing 2-18.

***Listing 2-18.*** The requirements.txt File

```
botocore>=1.18.0
boto3>=1.15.0
boto>=2.49.0
```

Additional operating system dependencies can be specified inside the `bindep.txt` file. Note that you can specify different package names for the RPM (Red Hat-like systems) or DPKG (Debian-like systems). See Listing 2-19.

***Listing 2-19.*** The bindep.txt File

```
git [platform:rpm]
git [platform:dpkg]
```

The Ansible Execution Environment is created only when the `ansible-builder` command is executed:

```
$ ansible-builder build -t my_ee -v 3
```

With these variables:

- `build,` to specify the build operation
- `-t my_ee,` to specify the desired Execution Environment name, my_ee in this case
- `-v 3`, to specify the verbosity level of the build, in this case, level 3 so pretty verbose

This tool might require access to the Red Hat Container Registry when you use an RHEL UBI8 base image with a Red Hat Ansible Automation subscription (username and password for the Red Hat Portal).

```
$ podman login registry.redhat.io
```

Running the `ansible-builder` command confirms successful execution with the name of the container:

```
Successfully tagged localhost/my_ee:latest
```

If a problem arises, the result shows the specific error.

Under the hood, the `ansible-builder` tool performs the following steps:

1. Generates a Containerfile (the generalized standard version of the Dockerfile that works with different Container engines) inside the `context` directory.

2. Runs the `docker build` or `podman build` in the context to build the `ansible-builder` Container and build the final image.

3. Fetches the base image from `registry.redhat.io` (usually ee-minimal-rhel8:latest).

4. Downloads the Ansible collection(s) and dependencies specified in the `requirements.yml` file using the `ansible-galaxy` tool.

5. Installs the package(s) and the dependencies specified in the `bindep.txt` file using the `microdnf` package manager in Red Hat Enterprise Linux.

6. Installs the Python package(s) and the dependencies specified in the `requirements.txt` file using the Python Package Manager (PIP).

7. Builds the final image with only the necessary files.

After executing the `ansible-builder` tool, you obtain the `context` directory with all the building instructions and the my_ee container to execute your Ansible code.

Once the container has been built, you can execute your Ansible Playbook inside the Ansible Execution Environment using the `ansible-runner` command (see Figure 2-8).

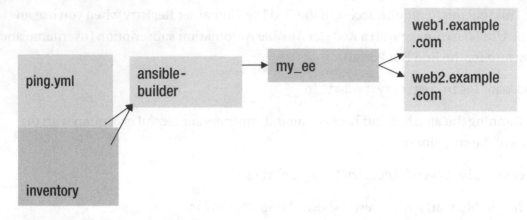

**Figure 2-8.** *The ansible-runner process*

The `ansible-runner` command-line tool was added in 2022 to simplify the creation of Ansible Execution Environments (EE). It is available in the Ansible toolchain package with the Red Hat Ansible Automation Subscription:

```
$ dnf install ansible-runner
```

The `ansible-builder` command-line tool is also available in the PyPI repository (via the `pip` tool):

```
$ pip install ansible-runner
```

The Ansible Runner enables you to run the Ansible Execution Environment as a container in the current machine. Use the following command:

```
$ ansible-runner run -p ping.yml --inventory inventory --container-
image=my_ee .
```

With these variables:

- `run,` to specify the run operation

- `-p ping.yml,` to specify the Ansible Playbook to execute

- `--inventory inventory,` to specify the inventory name, in this case, the inventory file

- — `--container-image=my_ee,` to specify the name of the Ansible Execution Environment

- — `.` (`dot`), to specify the directory of the base path, in this example, the current directory

The `ansible-runner` tool mimics the behavior of the `ansible-playbook` command and returns the Ansible output onscreen.

Under the hood, `ansible-runner` runs your Ansible Playbook inside the Ansible Execution Environment in your favorite Container Engine (Docker or Podman).

The main advantage of using the Ansible Execution Environment is that you can deploy to a Kubernetes Control Plane and scale the resources as needed.

# Key Takeaways

Ansible is a potent computer language for Infrastructure as Code (IaC). This chapter started with a quick overview of the architecture and configuration for all the operating systems (macOS, Windows, and Linux in bare metal), as well as virtual machines, private and public cloud computing, and containers. Ansible includes the expected typed variables, conditionals, and loops statements, plus some extra features for DevOps use cases, such as the handlers, facts, host and group, and magic variables. In this chapter, you about learned the foundation of the language; in the next chapter, you'll apply your knowledge to the Container and Kubernetes environments.

# CHAPTER 3

# Ansible for Containers

Managing containers in your organization might be a pretty daunting task. Especially when you perform manually and deal with repetitive tasks. Sometimes you need to run a container in your workstation or in your server fleet.

Ansible can simplify this workflow and automate the boring and daunting tasks. You can also create some new ways to distribute your application in platform-independent formats. Moreover, a common use case for security is to run your web server as a container, so the content is secured from any tampering.

## Ansible for Containers

Ansible is a great ally to simplify your journey of running containers. In the following pages, you are going to discover how to simplify the installation of the Docker Container Engine and how to automate the flatpak and snap in your workstations.

As a Container Engine, Podman is the preferred way on Linux because it has several advantages compared to Docker, especially because it can run rootless. However, Podman on Mac requires an additional machine to run your code, and Windows requires the virtualized Windows System for Linux (WSL).

## Install Docker on Linux and Windows

Docker is the preferred Container Engine for many platforms. You can start your Ansible journey by automating the installation of Docker. This is very useful when you spin up a new virtual machine. In the following sections of this book, I focus on the Docker Engine, which is part of running a container.

For your reference, there is also a product called Docker Desktop that has a nice GUI that runs on most operating systems. Table 3-1 lists the Docker Desktop-supported platforms.

© Luca Berton 2023
L. Berton, *Ansible for Kubernetes by Example*, https://doi.org/10.1007/978-1-4842-9285-3_3

**Table 3-1.** *Docker Desktop Supported Platforms*

| Platform | x86_64 / amd64 | arm64 / aarch64 |
|---|---|---|
| Debian | Yes | |
| Fedora | Yes | |
| Ubuntu | Yes | |
| Binaries | Yes | |
| Windows | Yes | |
| MacOS | Yes | Yes |

This chapter focuses on the Container Engine, the Docker Engine, only the Docker runtime, called docker-engine, and supported according to Table 3-2.

**Table 3-2.** *Docker Engine Supported Platforms*

| Platform | x86_64 / amd64 | arm64 / aarch64 | arm32 | s390x |
|---|---|---|---|---|
| CentOS | Yes | Yes | | |
| Debian | Yes | Yes | Yes | |
| Fedora | Yes | Yes | | |
| Raspbian | | | Yes | |
| RHEL (1) | | | | Yes |
| SLES (2) | | | | Yes |
| Ubuntu | Yes | Yes | Yes | Yes |
| Binaries | Yes | Yes | Yes | |

*(1) RHEL: Red Hat Enterprise Linux*
*(2) SLES: SUSE Linux Enterprise Linux*

Most Linux distributions, especially the Enterprise Linux distributions (for example Red Hat Enterprise Linux or SUSE Linux Enterprise Linux) prefer Podman as the Container Engine. It usually is included in the system repository or out-of-the-box.

---

**Tip**    The `community.docker.docker` connection Ansible connection plugin turns a Docker container into an Ansible target. Just use the container name as the entry in the Ansible inventory. The Docker container must be running on the Ansible controller, but connecting remotely to a Docker engine on another host is possible. It requires the `community.docker` Ansible collection and the Docker Python library be installed.

---

# Install Docker in Debian Linux

The following steps work in all the Debian and Ubuntu derived Linux distributions. You are trying to automate the following three steps using Ansible:

– Add a Docker GPG key

– Add a Docker repository

– Update `apt cache` and install Docker

The first step is to download the GPG signature key for the repository. Use the `ansible.builtin.apt_key` Ansible module.

This encrypted key verifies the authenticity of the packages and the repository and guarantees that the software is the same as the Docker releases. For the `ansible.builtin.apt_key` Ansible module, you use two parameters: `url` and `state`. The `url` parameter specifies the URL of the repository GPG signature key, and the `state` parameter verifies that it is present in your system after the execution.

The second step is to add the Docker repository to the distribution. It's an extra website where `apt`, your distribution package manager, looks for software. You are going to use the `ansible.builtin.apt_repository` Ansible module. For this Ansible module, you use two parameters: `repo` and `state`. The `repo` parameter specifies the repository parameters, and the `state` parameter verifies that it is present in your system after the execution.

The third step is to update the `apt cache` for the available packages and install Docker (`docker-ce`) using the `ansible.builtin.apt` Ansible module. For this Ansible module, you use three parameters: `name`, `state`, and `update_cache`. The `name` parameter specifies the package name (Docker in this use case), and the `state` parameter verifies that it is present in your system after the execution. Before installing the package, the update_cache parameter performs an update of the apt-cache to ensure that the latest version of the package is downloaded.

---

**Tip**    You can use the Ansible Magic Variable ansible_distribution, which automatically contains the most current operating system. Possible values are Alpine, Altlinux, Amazon, Archlinux, ClearLinux, Coreos, Debian, Gentoo, Mandriva, NA, OpenWrt, OracleLinux, Red Hat, Slackware, SMGL, SUSE, and VMwareESX.

---

Listing 3-1 shows the full Ansible Playbook code.

***Listing 3-1.*** install_docker_deb.yml

```
---
- name: install Docker
  hosts: all
  become: true
  tasks:
    - name: Install apt-transport-https
      ansible.builtin.apt:
        name:
          - apt-transport-https
          - ca-certificates
          - lsb-release
          - gnupg
        state: latest
        update_cache: true
    - name: Add signing key
      ansible.builtin.apt_key:
        url: "https://download.docker.com/linux/{{ ansible_distribution |
        lower }}/gpg"
        state: present
```

```
- name: Add repository into sources list
  ansible.builtin.apt_repository:
    repo: "deb [arch={{ ansible_architecture }}] https://download.
    docker.com/linux/{{ ansible_distribution | lower }} {{ ansible_
    distribution_release }} stable"
    state: present
    filename: docker

- name: Install Docker
  ansible.builtin.apt:
    name:
      - docker-ce
      - docker-ce-cli
      - containerd.io
      - docker-compose-plugin
    state: latest
    update_cache: true
```

As usual, you can execute the code using the `ansible-playbook` command-line utility included in every Ansible installation.

A common way to verify successful installation of Docker is by executing the following command on the target host:

```
$ docker run hello-world
```

When the installation of Docker is successful, it downloads the `hello-world` image from the library, downloads the latest tag of it, validates the sha256 digest file, and prints the onscreen message: `Hello from Docker!`

# Install Docker in Red Hat Linux

The following steps work in all the Fedora or Red Hat derived Linux distributions.

The automation steps are very similar to Debian, but you use different Ansible modules to handle `rpm` packages:

- Add a Docker GPG key

- Add a Docker repository

- Update yum cache and install Docker

The first step is to download the GPG signature key for the repository. You are going to use the `ansible.builtin.rpm_key` Ansible module. For this Ansible module, you use two parameters: key and `state`. The key parameter specifies the URL or the key ID of the repository GPG signature key, and the `state` parameter verifies that it is present in your system after execution. This encrypted key guarantees that the code was not altered and that it is the same as the Docker releases.

The second step is to add the Docker repository to the distribution. It's an extra website where YUM or DNF, your distribution package manager, looks for software. You are going to use the `ansible.builtin.yum_repository` Ansible module. For this Ansible module, you use four parameters: name, baseurl, gpgcheck, and gpgkey. The name parameter specifies the repository parameters and the `baseurl` parameter is the URL of it. The gpgcheck parameter enables the GPG verification with the URL specified in the gpgkey parameter.

The third step is to update the yum cache for the available packages and install Docker using the `ansible.builtin.yum` Ansible module.

For this Ansible module, you use three parameters: name, `state`, and `update_cache`. The name parameter specifies the package name (Docker in this use case), and the `state` parameter verifies that it is present in your system after the Ansible execution. Before installing the package, the `update_cache` updates the yum cache to ensure that the latest version of the package will be downloaded.

The full Ansible Playbook is shown in Listing 3-2.

***Listing 3-2.*** install_docker_rpm.yml

```
---
- name: install Docker
  hosts: all
  become: true
  tasks:
    - name: set mydistribution
      ansible.builtin.set_fact:
        mydistribution: "{{ 'rhel' if (ansible_distribution == 'Red Hat
        Enterprise Linux') else (ansible_distribution | lower) }}"

    - name: Add signing key
      ansible.builtin.rpm_key:
        key: "https://download.docker.com/linux/{{ mydistribution }}/gpg"
        state: present
```

```
  - name: Add repository into repo.d list
    ansible.builtin.yum_repository:
      name: docker
      description: docker repository
      baseurl: "https://download.docker.com/linux/{{ mydistribution
      }}/$releasever/$basearch/stable"
      enabled: true
      gpgcheck: true
      gpgkey: "https://download.docker.com/linux/{{
      mydistribution }}/gpg"
  - name: Install Docker
    ansible.builtin.yum:
      name:
        - docker-ce
        - docker-ce-cli
        - containerd.io
      state: latest
      update_cache: true

  - name: Start Docker
    ansible.builtin.service:
      name: "docker"
      enabled: true
      state: started
```

In the same way as the previous code, you can execute the Ansible Playbook using the ansible-playbook command-line utility included in every Ansible installation.

Run the command-line Docker on the target host:

```
$ docker run hello-world
```

This command is expected, as in the previous Debian code, to return the same onscreen message: Hello from Docker!

# Install Docker on Windows

You can also automate the installation of the Docker Desktop in your Windows 10 and 11 systems with the Ansible Playbook and the Chocolatey Package Manager. Chocolatey is the largest archive of packages for Windows; at the time of writing this book, it includes 9583 community maintained packages.

It also provides a package manager utility that uses the NuGet packaging infrastructure and Windows PowerShell to simplify the process of downloading and installing software.

This section focuses on the Ansible module called `win_chocolatey` to automate the software installation process. Its full name is `chocolatey.chocolatey.win_chocolatey`, which means that it is part of the collection distributed directly by `chocolatey`. The best part is that if the target system doesn't have `chocolatey` installed, it installs the package manager and then performs the installation.

The parameter list of the `win_chocolatey` Ansible module is pretty comprehensive, but these are the most important options for this use case:

- In the `name` parameter, you specify the package's name or a list of packages.

- If you want to install a specific version, you can specify it in the `version` parameter.

- The state specifies the action that you want to perform. In this case, installing is `present` or to have the latest version and upgrade eventually with `latest`.

Listing 3-3 automates the installation of Docker in Windows-like systems with Ansible Playbook.

***Listing 3-3.*** install_docker_win.yml

```
---
- name: install Docker
  hosts: all
  become: false
  gather_facts: false
  tasks:
    - name: Install Docker
```

```
chocolatey.chocolatey.win_chocolatey:
  name: "docker-desktop"
  state: present
```

A successful Windows installation is shown in Figure 3-1.

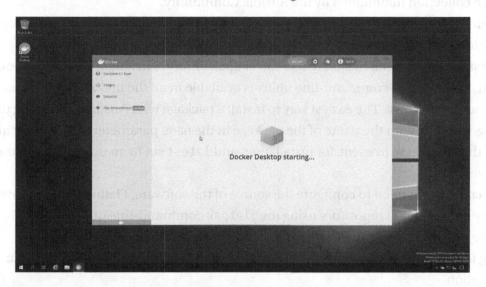

***Figure 3-1.*** *Docker Desktop on Windows installed via Ansible*

You can now execute any Docker container in your Windows target host.

# Flatpak in Linux

The purpose of container technology is to simplify the development and maintenance of applications in Linux, making it simple to deliver the application to every Linux user and distribution. Traditionally, the different libraries between distributions make it difficult to deliver applications to users, to control the update and the bug report process. Flathub is the archive where you can find hundreds of applications available for any Linux operating system.

Flatpak was developed in 2015 by Red Hat, Endless Computers, and Collabora. At the moment of writing this book, Flatpak runs on 36 distributions, and there are 1889 applications available. The main target of the application is desktop-oriented applications. Note that some flatpaks are available only for some architecture.

Here, you'll set up the Podman Desktop Flatpak. The Flatpak installation in a target system is effortless using the `flatpak` Ansible module, which manages Flatpaks in the target system.

The full name is `community.general.flatpak`; it's part of the `community.general` Ansible collection maintained by the Ansible Community.

Before jumping to the `flatpak` Ansible module, you need to prepare your system for managing Flatpak containers.

First of all, you need to ensure that the Flatpak binary is installed correctly in your system. The `flatpak` command-line utility is available in all the major distributions in the system repository. The easiest way to install a package with Ansible is by using the package module with the name of the package in the `name` parameter (`flatpak` in this case), the state set to `present` for installation, and `latest` set to an upgrade to get the latest version.

Secondly, you need to configure the source of the software, Flathub. This archive is seen by an additional repository using the `flatpak` command-line utility.

The Ansible module `community.general.flatpak_remote` takes care of this boring task, verifying that the `flathub` repository is successfully configured for your workstation.

Thirdly, you can use `community.general.flatpak` to install your application.

The only required parameter is `name`, where you specify the Flatpak name. In the example, `io.podman_desktop.PodmanDesktop` was obtained from the Flathub website.

The `state` parameter specifies the action to perform: whether you want to perform the installation action (the `present` option) or the remove an action (the `absent` option).

The `method` parameter specifies whether you want to install Flatpak system-wide (`system` value) or only for the current user (`user` value).

More advanced parameters are available:

- `remote`, which specifies the name of the source of the software; the default is `flathub`

- `no_dependencies`, which ignores the dependency installation (needs to be solved manually)

- `executable`, the flatpak executable path, which is by default the Flatpak program

The full Ansible Playbook is shown in Listing 3-4 and Figure 3-2.

**Listing 3-4.** flatpak.yml

```
---
- name: flatpak module demo
  hosts: all
  become: true
  tasks:
    - name: flatpak present
      ansible.builtin.package:
        name: flatpak
        state: present
    - name: flathub repo
      community.general.flatpak_remote:
        name: flathub
        state: present
        flatpakrepo_url: https://flathub.org/repo/flathub.flatpakrepo
        method: system
    - name: install Podman Desktop via flatpak
      community.general.flatpak:
        name: io.podman_desktop.PodmanDesktop
        state: present
        method: system
```

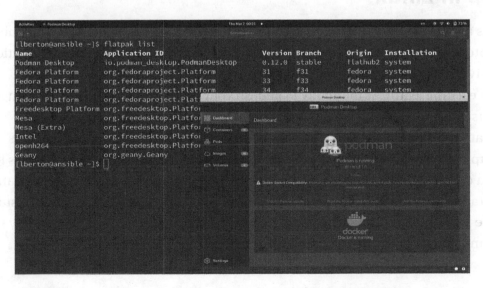

**Figure 3-2.** *Podman Desktop Flatpak on the latest Fedora Desktop*

Once a Flatpak is successfully installed in your system, you are going to continue using the same version. Flatpak doesn't have an auto-update mechanism.

You can automate the update process of all your Flatpaks in the system using the Ansible `command` module. The Ansible `command` module is used when there is no native module available; it literally executes your command to the target host. As you might understand, this is possibly dangerous because you are exiting somehow from the Ansible sandbox mechanism. Actually, the `shell` module also executes the command via a full shell. The difference is that the `shell` Ansible module supports the full variables like $HOME and operations like <, >, |, ; and &, whereas the `command` Ansible module does not. The Ansible Playbook to update your Flatpak is shown in Listing 3-5.

***Listing 3-5.*** flatpak_update.yml

```
---
- name: flatpak update demo
  hosts: all
  become: true
  tasks:
    - name: update flatpak(s)
      ansible.builtin.command: "flatpak update --noninteractive"
```

# Snap in Linux

Snap is another Linux distribution format that distributes applications in a container promoted by Canonical, the company behind Ubuntu. The amount of documentation is pervasive, so it's fairly easy to on board your application in a snap.

An exciting feature is the ability to publish your application for Internet of Things (IoT) use cases. In fact, it supports any class of Linux application, such as desktop applications, server tools, IoT apps, system services, and printer drivers. The snaps auto-update automatically. Under the hood, the `snapd` daemon checks for updates four times a day using a so-called over-the-air (OTA) `refresh` mechanism. The significant advantage is that the old snap is not replaced until the new snap is successfully installed. The file is distributed using the SquashFS compressed file system, so it has a pretty small footprint. Snapcraft is a tool for developers to package their applications.

Snap is supported by 41 Linux distributions. One of the biggest benefits is the adoption of an application sandbox, so applications run isolated, minimizing security risks.

Applications are available in a global Snap Store, and the application archive is hosted and managed by Canonical, but it's free to download. At the moment of writing this book, there are 7885 snaps currently in the Snap Store, but around 800 appear to be test or hello-world snaps.

Snap confinement allows setting the degree of isolation from the system. There are three options—Strict, Classic, and Devmode. Strict is the most restrictive and runs in complete isolation. Classic is the middle way and allows accessing the system resources like your operating system. Devmode is intended only for developers.

The `community.general.snap` Ansible module enables smooth installation of any Snap application. For example, you can install `microk8s`, a small, fast, secure, certified Kubernetes distribution for workstations and appliances.

In Listing 3-6, the Ansible Playbook installs a snap in the Ubuntu distribution.

***Listing 3-6.*** snap_ubuntu.yml

```
---
- name: snap module demo
  hosts: all
  become: true
  tasks:
    - name: snapd present
      ansible.builtin.apt:
        name: snapd
        state: present
    - name: install microk8s via snap
      community.general.snap:
        name: microk8s
        state: present
        classic: true
```

You can execute the Ansible Playbook using the `ansible-playbook` command included in every Ansible installation.

Installing snap in the Fedora-like Linux operating system requires a bit more effort because you need to take care of the SquashFS dependency and create the symlink for the /snap directory. The other part of the code is exactly like in the Ubuntu Ansible Playbook shown in Listing 3-7.

*Listing 3-7.* snap_fedora.yml

```
---
- name: snap module demo
  hosts: all
  become: true
  tasks:
    - name: snapd present
      ansible.builtin.yum:
        name:
          - snapd
          - fuse
          - squashfs-tools
          - squashfuse
          - kernel-modules
        state: present
    - name: symlink /snap
      ansible.builtin.file:
        src: "/var/lib/snapd/snap"
        dest: "/snap"
        state: link
    - name: load squashfs module
      community.general.modprobe:
        name: "squashfs"
        state: present
    - name: install microk8s via snap
      community.general.snap:
        name: microk8s
        state: present
```

The result of the execution is a full microk8s ready to be used in your Fedora machine (see Figure 3-3).

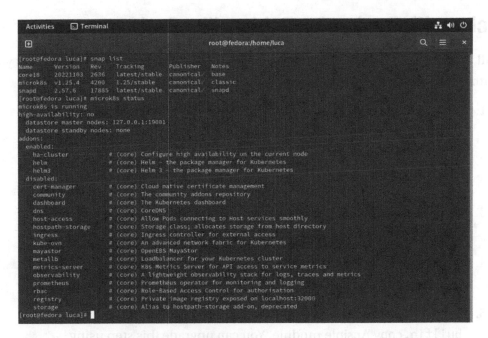

*Figure 3-3. microk8s in Fedora Desktop*

As mentioned, the snap has the auto-update feature so the snapd daemon takes care of the update and the install mechanism behind the scenes.

# Deploy a Web Server in a Container

One of the best characteristics of containers is their ability to separate the application from the data. Let's apply this isolation principle to your services. Running, for example, your webserver in a container lowers the attack surface and enables the service to be updated smoothly, keeping the data in the file system.

The good news is that Apache is available as a container named `httpd` in the most famous Container Registry. It supports all the architectures: `amd64`, `arm32v5`, `arm32v6`, `arm32v7`, `arm64v8`, `i386`, `mips64le`, `ppc64le`, and `s390x`. At the moment of writing this book, the standard image is based on Debian Linux 11 "bullseye" (`latest` or `bullseye` tags) or alpine Linux (`alpine` tag).

If your team prefers to use the web server, Nginx, you can simply switch to the `nginx` container image.

Let's suppose you want to serve files from the `/webroot` directory.

# Apache with Docker for Debian-like Systems

The full process of running the Apache webserver container requires six steps that you can automate with different Ansible modules:

1. First, you need to install some Python packages and dependencies using the `ansible.builtin.apt` Ansible module.

2. Then you need to install the Docker module for Python using the `ansible.builtin.pip` Ansible module.

3. Then you need to pull the image for the Docker hub registry using the `community.docker.docker_image` Ansible module.

4. Now create the document root with the right permission using the `ansible.builtin.file` module.

5. Then create the custom `index.html` file using the `ansible.builtin.copy` Ansible module. You can upgrade this step using the `template` module.

6. Finally, you can run the `webserver` container, setting the right port and volume settings with the `community.docker.docker_container` Ansible module.

This Ansible module requires the `community.docker` Ansible Collection to be installed on the system. If it's not present, you can install it using this command:

```
$ ansible-galaxy collection install community.docker
```

The full Ansible Playbook is shown in Listing 3-8.

***Listing 3-8.*** httpd_debian.yml

```
---
- name: deploy httpd on container
  hosts: all
  become: true
  vars:
    webroot: "/webroot/"
  tasks:
    - name: system packages present
```

```
    ansible.builtin.apt:
      name:
        - python3-pip
        - virtualenv
        - python3-setuptools
      state: latest
      update_cache: true
  - name: Docker Module for Python
    ansible.builtin.pip:
      name: docker
  - name: pull image
    community.docker.docker_image:
      name: httpd
      source: pull
      tag: latest
  - name: webroot present
    ansible.builtin.file:
      path: "{{ webroot }}"
      state: directory
  - name: custom index.html
    ansible.builtin.copy:
      dest: "{{ webroot }}index.html"
      content: |
        Custom Web Page
  - name: run httpd container
    community.docker.docker_container:
      name: webserver
      image: httpd
      state: started
      detach: true
      exposed_ports:
        - 80
      ports:
        - 8080:80
      volumes: "{{ webroot }}:/usr/local/apache2/htdocs/"
```

# Apache with Podman for Red Hat-like Systems

You can obtain the same result as the previous scenario using the Podman Container Engine in Red Hat systems. The full process requires four steps that you can automate with different Ansible modules:

1. First, you need to verify that `podman` and its dependencies are successfully installed on the target system using the `ansible.builtin.yum` Ansible module.

2. Second, you need to create the custom `index.html` file with the `ansible.builtin.copy` Ansible module. You can upgrade this step using the `template` module. Note that modern Red Hat systems come with SELinux enabled, so you need to set the `container_share_t` SELinux Context; otherwise, the files aren't shared between the host and the guest.

3. Thirdly, you need to pull the image for the container hub registry using the `containers.podman.podman_image` Ansible module.

4. Finally, you can run the `webserver` container, setting the right port and settings using the `containers.podman.podman_container` Ansible module.

This module requires additional `containers.podman` Ansible Collections that you can install using this command:

```
$ ansible-galaxy collection install containers.podman
```

The full Ansible Playbook is shown in Listing 3-9.

***Listing 3-9.*** httpd_redhat.yml

```
---
- name: deploy httpd container
  hosts: all
  become: true
  gather_facts: false
  vars:
    webroot: "/webroot"
```

```yaml
tasks:
  - name: podman installed
    ansible.builtin.yum:
      name: podman
      state: latest

  - name: pull image
    containers.podman.podman_image:
      name: docker.io/library/httpd
      pull: true
      tag: latest

  - name: webroot present
    ansible.builtin.file:
      path: "{{ webroot }}"
      state: directory
      owner: "root"
      group: "root"
      mode: '0777'
      setype: "container_share_t"

  - name: custom index.html
    ansible.builtin.copy:
      dest: "{{ webroot }}/index.html"
      content: |
        Custom Web Page
      setype: "container_share_t"

  - name: run httpd container
    containers.podman.podman_container:
      name: webserver
      image: httpd
      state: started
      detach: true
      expose:
        - 80
```

```
      ports:
        - 8080:80
      volume:
        - "{{ webroot }}:/usr/local/apache2/htdocs/:exec"
```

You can execute your Ansible Playbook using the `ansible-playbook` command line included in every Ansible installation. See Figure 3-4.

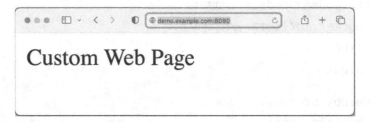

***Figure 3-4.*** *Webserver in a container in Fedora Linux*

---

**Tip**   The `containers.podman.podman` Ansible connection plugin turns a Podman container into an Ansible target. Just use the container name as the entry in the Ansible inventory. The Podman container must be running on the Ansible Controller. It requires the `containers.podman` Ansible collection be installed.

---

# Use Vagrant and Packer

Vagrant and Packer are two tools developed by HashiCorp and distributed open-source. They are designed to simplify your journey with virtual machine images when creating a complex environment for the development of integration tests. HashiCorp also developed the container management software called Nomad, which is open-source in the Cloud Native Computing Foundation (CNCF). The Nomad project is very simple to install and it's portable because it has a lightweight server-client design.

# Vagrant

Vagrant is a tool for creating environments for quick use, reuse, and cleanup. It interacts with a hypervisor (VirtualBox, KVM, Hyper-V, libvirt, Docker containers, VMware, Parallels, and AWS) to quickly create temporary virtual machines from an image. Vagrant uses a "box" template image to spin up your virtual machine. You can search for common boxes on the public Vagrant Cloud website. The Vagrant box usually starts with the minimal software installed. You can define a *Vagrantfile* to tell Vagrant what box to use, including CPU, memory, networks, forwarded ports, and shared directories. Vagrant supports defining multiple machines in the same Vagrantfile, coded in the Ruby programming language. In a Vagrantfile, you can also execute Ansible as a provisioner to execute an automation script automatically at the first boot. Vagrant generates Ansible inventory automatically for all of the defined machines. You can also define Ansible groups. This allows you to create a realistic integration test environment on your workstation machine. The Vagrantfile shown in Listing 3-10 creates two virtual machines (host01 in the group database and host02 in the group web) using the VirtualBox hypervisor with different CPU and memory resources and provisions them using the playbook.yaml Ansible Playbook.

*Listing 3-10.* Vagrantfile

```ruby
# -*- mode: ruby -*-
# vi: set ft=ruby :
cluster = {
  "host01" => { :ip => "192.168.0.10", :cpus => 2, :mem => 2048 },
  "host02" => { :ip => "192.168.0.11", :cpus => 4, :mem => 1024 }
}
groups = {
  "database" => ["host01"],
  "web" => ["host02"],
}
Vagrant.configure("2") do |config|
  config.vm.box = "ubuntu/jammy64"
  cluster.each do |name, data|
    config.vm.define name do |host|
      host.vm.hostname = name
      host.vm.network "private_network", ip: "#{data[:ip]}"
```

```
      host.vm.provider :virtualbox do |vb, override|
        vb.cpus = data[:cpus]
        vb.memory = data[:mem]
      end
      host.vm.provision :ansible do |ansible|
        ansible.playbook = "playbook.yaml"
        ansible.groups = groups
      end
    end
  end
end
```

You can execute the Vagrantfile using the `vagrand up` command, which interacts with VirtualBox to create the virtual machine and provision with the Ansible Playbook.

# Packer

Packer is a tool for building your virtual machine "box" image from physical or virtual machines. Packer uses a configuration language called HCL to connect to a provider via SSH, run a provisioned Ansible, and capture the virtual machine's state in an Amazon Machine Image (AMI) or in the Vagrant box image format. It's useful to build an image as part of the continuous integration process and deploy your application to a test environment.

Packer has a Docker builder that can manage Docker Containers and create container images. It creates a container, runs provisioners, and saves the result as a new image. You can use Ansible as a provisioner to build a Docker image, as illustrated in Listing 3-11.

***Listing 3-11.*** example.pkr.hcl

```
variable "ansible_connection" {
  default = "docker"
}
source "docker" "example" {
  image = "ubuntu:latest"
  commit = true
}
```

```
build {
  sources = ["source.docker.example"]
  provisioner "ansible" {
    playbook_file = "playbook.yaml"
  }
}
```

After you create the Packer HCL configuration file, you need to use the `initialize` parameter to read the file and the `build` parameter to create and push your Docker image to the registry. The full commands are similar to these:

```
$ packer init .
$ packer build .
```

## Key Takeaways

Ansible is a great tool for automating any container workload. You can apply automation to the container and distribute your application in a more secure way. In this chapter, you saw how to apply automation to a web server using the popular distribution-independent formats Flatpak and Snap. In the following chapter, you're going to dive deep into the Kubernetes world and learn how to automate it with Ansible.

# CHAPTER 4

# Ansible for K8s Tasks

Kubernetes (also known as "K8s") is an orchestration platform that automates container management. Deploying, scaling, and rolling service and application updates is easy. There is a vibrant community around Kubernetes because it's an open-source project. Kubernetes was originally developed by Google and is now maintained by the Cloud Native Computing Foundation (CNCF). The platform enables an ecosystem for microservices deployment and cloud-native applications and services, a system design methodology that embraces rapid change, large scale, and resilience. Containers, microservices, immutable infrastructure, and declarative APIs exemplify this methodology.

Kubernetes provides a way to deploy and manage containerized applications at scale across a cluster of servers. It does this by providing a set of APIs and tools that enable users to define the desired state of their applications (for example, how many replicas of a container should be running) and then automatically deploy and manage the containers to meet that desired state.

Kubernetes is designed to be highly available and to provide self-healing capabilities, meaning that it can automatically recover from failures and ensure that applications are running as intended. It also provides load balancing, auto-scaling, and rolling updates, enabling users to easily manage and scale their applications and services.

Kubernetes is commonly used in cloud-native environments and is supported by a wide range of cloud providers. The major players are Amazon Web Services (AWS), Microsoft Azure, and Google Cloud Platform (GCP). Kubernetes is also widely used in on-premises environments and hybrid cloud deployments, as shown in Figure 4-1.

2014: Google → 2015: CNCF → 2016: Mainstream → 2017: Enterprise → 2018: KubeCon

*Figure 4-1.* *Timeline of the Kubernetes project*

© Luca Berton 2023
L. Berton, *Ansible for Kubernetes by Example*, https://doi.org/10.1007/978-1-4842-9285-3_4

Kubernetes was started by Google in 2014. The predecessor was called Borg, a distributed cluster manager created by Google to manage its fleet automatically. With the advent of cloud computing, managing the workload manually became nearly impossible, and applying normal paradigms was also nearly impossible. Docker Corporation came up with a solution that allowed it to scale up and down very easily with immediate benefits. The main advantage of Docker is to create a bundle that can be executed locally, in a remote machine, or in the cloud in the same manner.

Docker has successfully bridged the gap between developers and operators. Docker solved the problem of packaging the software and making it accessible on different platforms. Containers can support any programming language: Ruby, Python, Java, C, C++, and so on.

A lot more was required to manage the workloads, and that was why Kubernetes was created. It was a disruptive approach at the time that Google innovated the whole industry. The official project was announced publicly on June 10th, 2014, and it had a great following and was released on the same day as DockerCon, the biggest event about containers worldwide. The 1.0 version was for web app-style stateless low-scale systems. The initial Google development team was pretty small: Tim Hockin, Kelsey Hightower, Craig McLuckie, Joe Breda, Brian Grant, Xiaohui Chen, and the original manager, Chen Goldberg.

Mesos had a better scheduling feature, so, at the time, companies like Netflix, Airbnb, and Apple were looking for a more mature solution with scaling capabilities up to 10,000 instances. A lot changed from that release and the project grew up to where it is today. In retrospect, the correlation between Docker and Kubernetes looks inevitable, but it wasn't so clear at the time.

The best thing was that Google created the Kubernetes container orchestration platform and published it as open-source. More companies contributed to the project than ever before. They created the open-source community behind and established a de facto standard. The core part is written in the GO programming language.

Kubernetes was built in a way called *Promise Theory* that ensures that you can run the container and don't need to worry about the underlying complexity. Still, it is completely abstract by the hardware and any possible failure that might happen during the lifecycle. This means that when a Kubernetes cluster is alive, it can be broken at any time, but Kubernetes' job is to make sure that the application is always running and serving your traffic. Another important technology is the declarative layer on top of Docker.

OpenShift was started in 2010 as a platform-as-a-service (PaaS) to run containers. Google and Red Hat worked together on the open-source project. Clayton Coleman was the first contributor at the time from Red Hat. The key advantage of Kubernetes compared to other orchestration technologies (Dockeswarm and Mesos) was that it came out with a new project built from scratch, with the vision of a platform built for enterprise users and with plenty of extension possibilities. This vision quickly excited the engineers, who immediately recognized their workflows' value.

The most appreciated feature of Kubernetes is a clean API that manages container workload and works across multiple computers. Once you introduce the network, partial failure modes and different scheduling constraints are available across the capacity.

The killer application for Kubernetes was Pokémon Go, the popular augmented reality game developed by Niantic and running on the Google Kubernetes Engine (GKE). Once they launched in July 2016, they experienced 50 times the amount of load that they expected. Kubernetes was able to meet the demand even if it was challenging at the time, pushing the limits of the infrastructure.

At DockerCon 2017, Docker announced the official support of Kubernetes, which was the beginning of a successful partnership between the two products. After this announcement, many competitors embraced Kubernetes: Mesos, Docker, and Pivotal. By the end of 2017, Amazon Web Server launched a Kubernetes product.

That was the official signal that Kubernetes was here to stay in the market. The major force was probably the vibrant community supporting Kubernetes. The developer experience of using containers and Docker being very easy attracted new people. It was a product that went above and beyond the expectations of the user cases.

Increasing velocity, efficiency, portability, scaling, and reducing latency are some of the great success stories of adopting Kubernetes in your organization. Benefits include a decline in an increase in production load, increase in traffic without issues, SLA achievements, MTTR improvements, cost savings, reduction of load times, better hardware utilization, integration of local data centers and hybrid cloud environments, huge active customers, a high number of transactions per second, smooth production releases per day, more COVID-19 tests scheduled, redesign and standardize CI/CD pipeline, and decreased software development time.

# Kubernetes Objects

The atomic unit to deploy any Kubernetes object is the *pod*. The pod contains one or more containers. It is easy to scale pods to scale your application. The pod is executed in a *worker* node of Kubernetes. The complete number of worker nodes is called a *data plane* because they run your applications.

A Service is a logical way to expose your application and connect a pod without worrying about the internal IP addresses of pods.

To deploy a pod, you use `PodSpec` in Kubernetes, a simple YAML text document (also called YAML manifest) that is a blueprint for Kubernetes to deploy your pod. The most important instruction is the image specified in the `spec` area, which defines the image to use. DockerHub is often the default Container Registry, so you can just specify `ubuntu:22:10`. To specify another Container Registry, you need to specify the full URI and the image name.

The pod is ephemeral, meaning you lose data when the pod is terminated or destroyed.

Volumes persistently store the data of the pod. Volumes are available to be connected for any other pod. You specify the volume in the `spec` area of the PodSpec.

You can mount all the many network storage protocols, for example, NFS, SMB, CephFS, Lustre, GlusterFS, JuiceFS, and OpenEBS. This is supported by the Container Storage Interface (CSI) driver for Kubernetes. CSI drivers are available for popular storage devices (NetApp, Synology, HP, Cisco HyperFlex, Datatom-Infinity, Datera, Dell EMC (PowerMax, PowerScale, PowerStore, Unity, and VxFlexOS), HPE, HPE Ezmeral, Huawei Storage, IBM Block Storage, IBM Spectrum Scale, IBM Cloud Block Storage VPC, Intel PMEM-CSI, HP TrueNAS, and many cloud storage services (AWS Elastic Block Storage, AWS Elastic File System, AWS FSx for Lustre, Azure Blob, Azure Disk, Azure File, cloudscale.ch, GCE Persistent Disk, Google Cloud Filestore, Google Cloud Storage, Hetzner Cloud Volumes, HyperV, oVirt, Tencent Cloud Block Storage, Tencent Cloud File Storage, Tencent Cloud Object Storage, vSphere, and so on).

The `ConfigMap` file keeps the configuration in a key-value database.

A `Secret` is a way to store sensitive information such as usernames, passwords, SSH keys, and keypairs. Note that `Secrets` are base64 encoded but not encrypted.

`Namespaces` within a cluster allow for logical groups of the common resources of an application and set user role permissions for access resources and set limits. If they're not specified, your resources are created under the `default` namespace.

Deployment is commonly used to deploy pods without dealing with pods. Inside a Deployment, you can add a ReplicaSets to specify the expected pod count and ensure that the amount of pods matches the desired count for deploying your application or service. You can also set a label for pods to make them easily recognizable. If a pod terminates for whatever reason, the Deployment spins up another pod replica to maintain the desired pod count of the ReplicaSets.

ResourceQuota sets the hard requests and limits for CPU or memory resources per namespace. Each pod resource request and limit is validated against these hard limits.

You can set some special settings using taints, which are settings of the worker node. Tolerations are on the pod and should match the settings on the worker node.

Affinities specify properties for node scheduling and execution to the control plane. For example, instance types or availability zones for Amazon Web Services.

The DaemonSet is very similar to Deployment without a ReplicaSet. Log collector is a popular use case of the DaemonSet.

# Control Plane vs Data Plane

Kubernetes nodes is divided into two types: a control plane and a data plane (see Figure 4-2). The difference is in the nodes used to manage your Kubernetes cluster (control plane) and the ones used to execute the user requests (data plane).

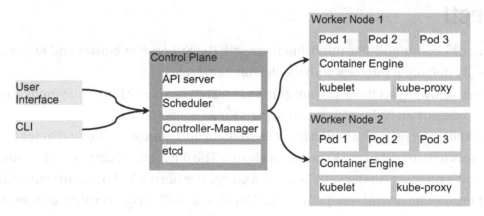

***Figure 4-2.*** *Control plane vs data plane*

The Kubernetes Control Plane has at least two API server nodes and three etcd nodes. Kubernetes automatically detects and repairs unhealthy control plane nodes in order to guarantee the continuity of the service. The data plane is a fleet of worker nodes where you can allocate your Kubernetes resources. The worker nodes are often called only *nodes*.

The Controller Manager (running inside the control plane) runs all the time in the Kubernetes cluster because it maintains the cluster in the desired status. Every time you send a command to Kubernetes, you express an intent or a wish to the Controller Manager and check if you are allowed and if there are enough resources to perform the action. The Cloud Controller translates your wish into a request for each cloud provider. The scheduler specifies where to allocate resources for your Kubernetes resources. The commands are performed via restful API.

The cluster can execute your container using a large variety of container runtime engines. The most commonly used are Docker and Podman, but your setup might vary according to your use cases.

The kubelet is a vital process that connects directly to the API server of the control plane nodes in the worker node.

Kubernetes operators enable you to specify custom resource manifests for your cluster.

# kubectl

The kubectl command-line utility interacts with the Kubernetes cluster and Kubernetes objects. By default, it interacts with the default namespace.

In the following sections, you are going to create a simple nginx deployment and service to deploy an Nginx web server in your Kubernetes cluster.

The kubeconfig configuration file is the default authentication method to read the parameters to connect to the Kubernetes cluster. The file is called config and is stored in the .kube directory under your home directory. The file is a YAML document with the Kubernetes hostname, endpoint of the Kubernetes API server, certificate authority data, username, and authentication method. Your Kubernetes administrator team usually provides this configuration file. More details are in the "Ansible Troubleshooting" section.

**Note**   You can also investigate inside your pod running the shell (usually bash for Linux) using this command:

```
$ kubectl exec -it nginx-pod -n ansible-examples -- /bin/bash
```

Where `nginx-pod` is the pod name and `ansible-examples` is the namespace name. After running the command, you obtain a root shell inside the contained confirmed by the # of the command-line output, similar to this: `bash-5.0#`

# GitOps Continuous Deployment

Developers worldwide recognize the advantage of testing the codebase early as a DevOps principle. It's a common practice to launch a test suite to test your code each time it is sent to the server. Behind the scenes, a pipeline of code is created to launch the testing at every submission of code (`commit`) in the SCN repository, usually Git.

A more modern approach uses Pipeline as Code to define deployment pipelines through source code.

The Pipelines as Code model, like all the "as code" models, has a lot of benefits:

- **Version tracking**: Changes are tracked and teams can use the current version or roll back to previous configurations versions

- **Audit trails**: Transparency is the key advantage for all the stakeholders, external auditors, and developers; it shows every change made to the code and by whom.

- **Ease of collaboration**: The code is the source of truth, all the stakeholders can suggest changes, improvements, updates, or deletes.

- **Knowledge sharing**: Stakeholders share best practices, using templates and popular design patterns, and share code snippets so teams can learn from each other.

Continuous Integration (CI) enables the testing of the application in every change (every commit in Git). It's a common best practice enabled by using automatic pipelines triggered by hooks. Errors are detected and corrected as soon as possible, and increments are small and gradual.

Organizations can speed up the release process when any new code update or change is made through the rigorous automated test process.

After a successful Continuous Integration (CI) build, a test suite with a bunch of integration tests is executed. The next stage of software automation is Continuous Delivery (CD).

Continuous Delivery (CD) takes care of the release and deployment process. A fully automated CI/CD workflow enables a more frequent and reliable release process in your organization by taking advantage of the DevOps methodologies.

The conjunction with the Git repository, Kubernetes enables the GitOps use case. You can manage Kubernetes manifest files stored inside it. The main use case of the GitOps approach is to allow systems convergence when updating or installing new applications.

# Jenkins

Jenkins Pipeline is the most commonly used open-source option to integrate CI/CD and GitOps.

Jenkins Pipeline is a suite of plugins that allows a Jenkins user to define a Jenkins job in a Jenkinsfile. A *Jenkinsfile* is a text file that defines a Jenkins Pipeline and is checked into source control. In a Jenkins Pipeline, you can define a series of tasks, called *stages*, that are executed in a specific order. For example, you might have a stage that checks out code from a version control system, another stage that builds the code, and another stage that runs tests. Each stage consists of one or more steps, which are individual tasks that are executed in the context of the stage. One of the main advantages of a Jenkins Pipeline is that it is built for the Jenkins software in the Groovy programming language with declarative syntax in a Jenkinsfile. The declarative syntax is easier to read and write, but the scripted syntax provides more flexibility.

You can define the entire build process in a single Jenkinsfile, which can be version-controlled and shared among team members. This makes it easy to manage and track changes to the build process over time, and it allows you to automate the entire build and deployment process.

Developers and system administrators worldwide create Jenkinsfiles to automate their tasks every day, store them in a source control management system (SCM), and execute them via a Jenkins server. The Jenkinsfile is the single source of truth (SSOT) about how a deployment executes. The advantage of using a Jenkins Pipeline is the predictability of the workflow and the opportunity to share the result with all the relevant stakeholders.

# VMWare Tanzu Application Platform

The VMWare Tanzu Application Platform is a platform-as-a-service (PaaS) solution that enables organizations to develop, deploy, and manage applications on top of Kubernetes. It provides a set of tools and services that allow developers to focus on building their applications rather than worrying about the underlying infrastructure.

Here are some key features of the VMWare Tanzu Application Platform:

- It is created on the Kubernetes open-source platform, which makes it easy to manage and scale applications in a consistent way across environments.

- It provides a range of pre-built services and tools, such as databases, message queues, and monitoring, which can be easily integrated into applications.

- It includes a range of tools for developing, testing, and deploying applications, including an integrated development environment (IDE), a continuous integration/continuous delivery (CI/CD) platform, and a registry for storing and sharing Docker images.

- It provides a range of security and compliance features, encryption of data at rest and in transit, and the ability to enforce policies for access to resources.

Overall, the VMWare Tanzu Application Platform is designed for organizations to easily build, manage, and deploy applications in a cloud-native environment. Some organizations use the VMWare Tanzu Application Platform instead of Jenkins for their deployment.

# Set Up Your Laboratory

Creating a laboratory to experiment with the Kubernetes cluster is handy for testing code, creating a new configuration, or experimenting with an upgrade of the Kubernetes platform. The control plane coordinates all the activities of your cluster. A minimum of three nodes is generally recommended for a production Kubernetes cluster. If one goes down, the redundancy is compromised because the etcd and the control plane instance are lost. Developers usually add more control plane nodes to mitigate this risk.

Creating a Kubernetes cluster from scratch, even if possible, is a daunting task, and there are better ways to save time than reinventing the wheel. Minikube and Kubespray are convenient software ways to deploy Kubernetes clusters. The Minikube software is popular for non-production clusters for the laboratory, whereas Kubespray is focused more on deploying Kubernetes on cloud providers.

You can deploy your Kubernetes cluster on physical or virtual machines. If none of these is available, cloud providers have plenty of resources available at their fingertips, often for a free testing trial.

# Virtual Machines

In a home laboratory, you can use an old laptop of bare metal or some virtual machines. For managing virtual machines, there are many alternatives for the hypervisor software (also known as a virtual machine monitor, VMM, or virtualizer). This platform assigns physical resources to virtual machines (see Figure 4-3).

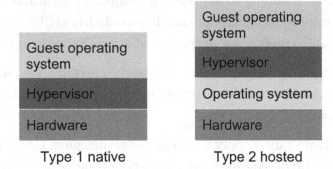

*Figure 4-3.* *Type 1 vs type 2 hypervisors*

A long list of hypervisor software is available in modern operating systems. The following names are likely familiar: Microsoft Hyper-V, Oracle Virtualbox, VMWare ESX(i), KVM, Xen, QEMU, LXC, Proxmox, and Parallels Desktop for Mac.

The procedure varies from software to software but involves the decision of how many physical resources are assigned to the virtual machine, creating a virtual machine ("guest" system), and running like a virtual computer. Once the operating system is installed, you can install all the Kubernetes components. This might be a long process because you need to manually download and install all the different open-source components from scratch and match the different versions. This task might be fun for some, but difficult for most. The following sections discuss some solutions that help you spin up a Kubernetes cluster in your laboratory or production without having to spend months building everything from scratch.

## Raspberry Pis

Raspberry Pi is a popular small single-board computer (SBCs) series. Raspberry Pi 4 Model B (see Figure 4-4) is the latest at the time of writing this book.

***Figure 4-4.*** *Raspberry Pi 4 Model B Attribution: Michael H. (Laserlicht) / Wikimedia Commons / CC BY-SA 4.0[1]*

It was developed by the Raspberry Pi Foundation in the United Kingdom in association with Broadcom. The original aim of the project was to teach computer science in schools and developing countries. The low cost (from $35) boosted the popularity of the original model. The key advantages are a modular, open design combined with the low energy consumption of the ARM processor. Some cutting-edge technologies are available as well: a fast ARM processor, memory from 1 GiB to 4 GiB, fast data transfer by USB 3.0 and Gigabit Ethernet, onboard wireless network connectivity, and Bluetooth 5.0, with support for two 4K HDMI displays. It is used for applications such as smart home hubs, game consoles, robot brains, media servers, VPN servers, home computers, and more.

It's possible and relatively affordable to buy a bunch of Raspberry Pi minicomputers and use them to create a home laboratory for experimentation. Nowadays, they are available in many variants (RAM, eMMC, wireless) that are shipped worldwide. It is very interesting to use the latest Raspberry Pi Compute Module 4 cluster board for the clustering experimentation, a stripped-down edition without any connectors available from $25. Recent years saw a rise in the popularity of some interesting motherboards

---

[1] https://commons.wikimedia.org/wiki/File:Raspberry_Pi_4_Model_B_-_Side.jpg

that plug in and use the Raspberry Pi Compute Module as a cluster or a server farm. Jeff Geerling has become popular on YouTube for testing and crowdsourcing cluster board projects. Installing Kubernetes software on the Raspberry Pi is usually via the SSH terminal interface. Remember that the Raspberry Pi processor uses the ARM processor architecture, which might differ from the one use in your main computer. There are many alternative ways to install Kubernetes on a single Raspberry Pi or a cluster of Raspberry Pis. It depends on your experience with Kubernetes; among all, the easiest is MicroK8s. It simply deploys using the `microk8s` snap with classic confinement and interacts using the `microk8s` command-line tool. You can start and stop the cluster, save batteries, and use the `microk8s start` and `microk8s stop` command-line. You can verify the status using the `microk8s status` command: `running` or `not running`. You can enable some Kubernetes features, for example, the Kubernetes Dashboard (see Figure 4-5), using the `microk8s enable dashboard` command. More features are also available: `rbac`, `dns`, `registry`, `istio`, `helm`, `ingress`, `prometheus`, `hostpath-storage`, and so on. Once enabled, the Kubernetes Dashboard is available using the `microk8s dashboard-proxy` command. Just remember to add the following line to the `/boot/firmware/cmdline.txt` file to enable the `cgroup` on kernel bootstrap, because it is disabled by default on the ARM platform:

```
cgroup_enable=memory cgroup_memory=1
```

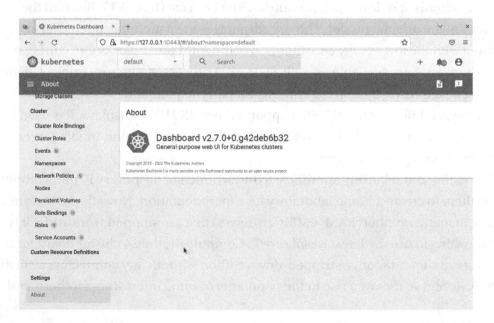

***Figure 4-5.***  *microk8s Kubernetes Dashboard*

# Kubespray

The Kubespray project focuses on deploying the Kubernetes platform on cloud providers: Amazon Web Services (AWS), Microsoft Azure, Google Cloud Platform (GCP), OpenStack, VMWare vSphere, Equinix Metal, Oracle Cloud Infrastructure (experimental), and bare metal. Kubespray is the preferred choice when you want to deploy a cluster and don't want to manually compile the entire Kubernetes ecosystem. Kubespray enables the deployment of a Kubernetes cluster using simple configuration management powered by Ansible (Playbooks and Inventory), provisioning tools, and platform knowledge.

The result is the following:

- Cluster high availability

- Modularity (choices between network plugins)

- Support for most popular Linux distributions, including Flatcar Container Linux by Kinvolk, Debian, Ubuntu LTS (16.04, 18.04, 20.04, 22.04), RHEL/CentOS/Oracle Linux (7, 8, 9), Fedora (CoreOS, 35, 36), openSUSE (Leap 15/Tumbleweed), Alma Linux/Rocky Linux (8, 9), Kylin Linux Advanced Server V10, and Amazon Linux 2

- Tested by CI/CD

- Kubernetes version 1.22+, Ansible v2.11+, Jinja 2.11+ and python-netaddr

The first step of the installation process is to set up the cluster IPs inside the inventory/mycluster file, as shown in Listing 4-1.

*Listing 4-1.* Kubespray inventory/mycluster File

```
node1 ip=10.3.0.1
node2 ip=10.3.0.2
node3 ip=10.3.0.3
[kube_control_plane]
node1
node2
[etcd]
```

```
node1
node2
[kube_node]
node2
node3
[k8s_cluster:children]
kube_node
kube_control_plane
```

You can customize the variables for the Ansible groups all and k8s_cluster using these files:

- inventory/mycluster/group_vars/all/all.yml

- inventory/mycluster/group_vars/k8s_cluster/k8s-cluster.yml

Once everything is configured, you can execute your playbook to set up your nodes:

```
$ ansible-playbook -i inventory/mycluster --become --become-user=root
cluster.yml
```

The output is long and the execution time depends on the performance of your hardware. A successful execution ends in a Kubernetes cluster that's ready to use.

## OpenShift Local

OpenShift Local (formerly CodeReady Containers) is an easy and fast way to deploy an OpenShift cluster for the laboratory in a virtual machine in minutes.

The purpose of the deployment is only local and for a laboratory, for testing purposes, because it's meant to be ephemeral. A control plane and the worker node are embedded in a single-node virtual machine. It supports many operating systems—Red Hat Enterprise Linux/CentOS x86_64 (7, 8, and 9) and two latest stable Fedora releases, Windows 10 x86_64 Fall Creators Update (version 1709+), and macOS (BigSug 11+ Intel Chip x86_64 or Apple Silicon arm64). The minimum resources required are four vCPU, 8 GiB memory, and 35 GiB of storage. A special edition base on Podman container runtime is designed for Apple Silicon arm64 SoC processors (M1, M1 Pro, M1 Max, M1 Ultra, M2, and so on) and requires two physical CPU cores, 2 GiB of available physical memory, and 35 GiB of storage space.

At the moment of writing this book, the latest release is version 2.12, based on using Red Hat OpenShift Container Platform 4. You should use the full OpenShift installer for other OpenShift Container Platform use cases, such as cloud, data center, headless, or multi-developer setups.

It is a stripped-down release of OpenShift with the following current limitations:

- Single node: Control plane and worker node

- Runs in a virtual machine: Different from external networking

- Upgrade path: It doesn't support an upgrade path other than downloading an updated, newer virtual machine

- Cluster monitoring operator: It is non-functional and disabled

You can start downloading the `crc` command-line tool via the official Red Hat website (`https://console.redhat.com/openshift/create/local`). On Windows and macOS, a guided installer is provided with an easy and straightforward process; just following the workflow, as shown in Figure 4-6.

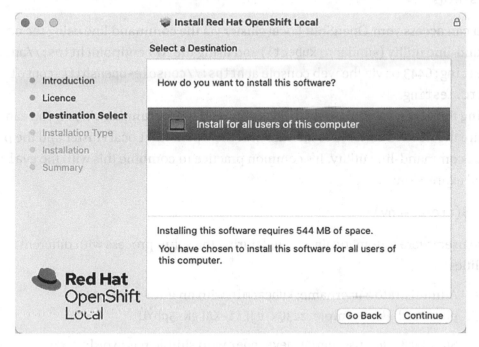

***Figure 4-6.***  *OpenShift Local guided install on macOS*

A successful installation allows you to run the crc command-line utility from your terminal and move forward with the OpenShift Local setup. You can download the latest version of the OpenShift Local virtual machine and store it under the current user's .crc directory. Then bootstrap with the following command:

```
$ crc setup
```

At the moment, the downloaded virtual machine is 3.09 GiB and requires 31 GiB storage once decompressed. After the successful download, you can start your environment. It creates the local-only *.crc.testing domain to provide an environment to test your containers using the local IPv4 address range starting with 172.x.y.z.

```
$ crc start
```

The first start requires more time because all the initialization utilities need to run as well as the Kubernetes Operators. You can verify the running status of the OpenShift Local cluster anytime using the status parameter:

```
$ crc status
```

You can access your OpenShift Local cluster via the command line using the oc command-line utility (similar to kubectl) and using the API endpoint https://api. crc.testing:6443 or via the web console at https://console-openshift-console. apps-crc.testing.

Using the oc-env parameter of the oc command with a running cluster, you can configure the needed variable to interact with the OpenShift Local cluster and the path of the oc command-line utility. It's common practice to combine this with the eval terminal expression:

```
$ eval $(crc oc-env)
```

Two users were automatically created during the setup process with different capabilities:

- Administrator: username: kubeadmin with an auto-generated password. For example, zc3Qx-ejEii-KALgK-5pbYU

- Standard user: username: developer with simple password: developer

To log in to your OpenShift Local cluster, just provide the desired username (-u parameter) and password (-p parameter):

```
$ oc login -u developer -p developer https://api.crc.testing:6443
```

Otherwise, you can use the token retrieved from the OpenShift console:

```
$ oc login --token=sha256~xxxxxx --server=https://api.crc.testing:6443
```

You can check which user you're logged in as using this command:

```
$ oc whoami
```

The OpenShift Local cluster has also a container image registry inside. With the same users, you can access the OpenShift Local Dashboard via the web address (shown in Figure 4-7). It's at https://console-openshift-console.apps-crc.testing.

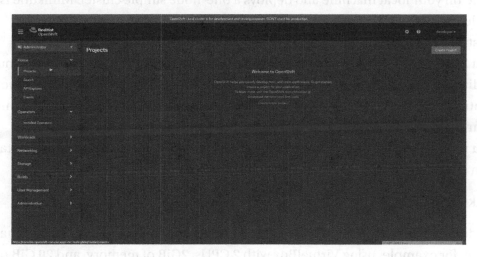

*Figure 4-7.  OpenShift Local console*

# hetzner-ocp4

When your target cloud provider is Hetzner, you can use the hetzner-ocp4 project by RedHat-EMEA-SSA-Team (https://github.com/RedHat-EMEA-SSA-Team/hetzner-ocp4). It deploys and consumes the Red Hat OpenShift Container Platform 4 environment as a sandpit in the CentOS Root Server bare metal servers from Hetzner. Currently, it supports CentOS Stream 8 and Red Hat Enterprise Linux 8 and 9.

The tool relies on Ansible to provision, install, start, stop, and delete the Red Hat OpenShift Container Platform 4 cluster, renew the SSL certificates using the "Let's Encrypt" project, and set up the public DNS records. Current tools allow the use of three out-of-the-box DNS providers (AWS Route53, Cloudflare, DigitalOcean, and GCP DNS) or setting a few environment variables (Azure, CloudFlare, Gandi, and TransIP).

# Create a Cluster with Minikube

The easiest and smallest Kubernetes cluster comprises only one node. Obviously, this setup is good enough for a workstation laboratory, but not for a production environment, which requires more nodes to guarantee high availability.

Minikube is a Go implementation of Kubernetes lightweight that creates one virtual machine on your local machine and deploys a one-node simple cluster. Minikube is available for the most recent operating systems—Linux, macOS, and Windows.

First of all, you need a fresh install of a modern operating system, for example, Ubuntu 22.04 LTS, for the official repository. During the setup, the configuration enables the additional packages openssh and docker. Make sure to enable the Allow Password Authentication over SSH command in the SSH Setup options. This simplifies the initial configuration, but feel free to move to the PKI authentication anytime.

You need to install the minikube command-line tool. Once it's successfully installed, you can start the minikube by typing the following:

```
$ minikube start
```

Underneath the tool, download the latest Kubernetes images and set up a virtual machine; for example, using VirtualBox with 2 CPUs, 2GiB of memory, and 20 GiB of storage. Inside the virtual machine, the tool downloads the Minikube ISO, sets up a virtual IP address, configures the Docker container runtime, downloads the kubelet and kubeadm, launches the Kubernetes cluster, configures the cluster permission, and verifies the component health.

You can also start the minikube with more or fewer resources by specifying the memory parameter with the desired amount of RAM in MiB and the amount of CPUs:

```
$ minikube start --memory=8192 --cpus 2
```

This will yield the output shown in Figure 4-8.

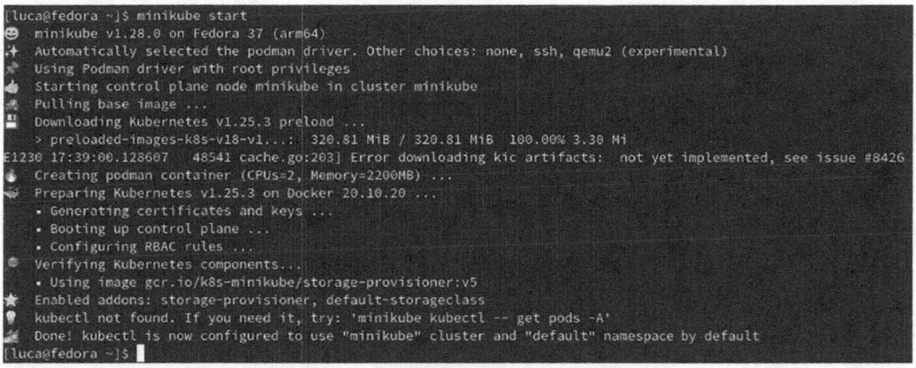

*Figure 4-8.* *minikube start command-line output*

Assigning more resources usually results in a faster environment and more space to experiment as a data plane. Still, you should compromise within the available physical resources. At least 1 GiB of RAM is recommended to handle operating system/virtual machine overhead. The minimum amount of memory required by Kubernetes is at least 2048 MiB of memory. Recommended setup requires four CPUs, 10 GiB of memory, and as much storage as needed.

Alternatively, you can set the memory and CPUs settings as a configuration as follows:

```
$ minikube stop
$ minikube config set memory 8192
$ minikube config set cpus 4
$ minikube start
```

Once started, you can start sending commands via the kubectl command to execute your Kubernetes Pods, Services, Deployment, and so on.

As you can see, all control planes and workers are running on the same machine. You can verify using the kubectl command and the get nodes parameter. The output shows only one node, called minikube, has a Ready status with control-plane,master roles and the Kubernetes running version.

Moreover, the minikube dashboard command enables the Kubernetes Dashboard and proxy and returns the URL for the connections.

The result is a dashboard opened in the current browser, as shown in Figure 4-9.

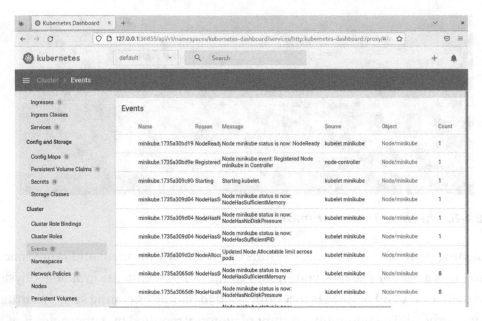

***Figure 4-9.*** *minikube Kubernetes Dashboard*

# Kubeadm

Kubeadm is a tool to build a Kubernetes cluster following the best-practice "fast paths" for creating domain knowledge of the clusters' lifecycle management, self-hosted layouts, dynamic discovery services, and so on.

It provides a simple `kubeadm` command-line utility with the following options:

- `init`, sets up the initial Kubernetes control-plane node.

- `join`, sets up a Kubernetes additional control plane node and joins it to the cluster or a worker node.

- `upgrade`, upgrades the Kubernetes cluster to a newer version.

- `reset`, reverts any changes by `init` or `join` made to the current host.

## K3s Lightweight Kubernetes

K3s is a CNCF sandbox project created in 2020 that was originally developed by Rancher Labs and packaged as a single binary with a very small footprint (<100 MB). It creates a Kubernetes cluster that's simple to install, run, and auto-update from Raspberry Pi to AWS a1.4x large 32 GB server. It is a good fit for Internet of Things (IoT), edge computing, and ARM processors. The lightweight storage backend is based on sqlite3 and extensible with etcd3, MySQL, and PostgreSQL. K3s can run in a container or as a native Linux service. With Rancher and K3s, you can manage more than 1,000 edge clusters using a GitOps Continuous Delivery pipeline.

When the cluster is up and running, you can interact with it using simple commands.

```
$ export KUBECONFIG=/etc/rancher/k3s/k3s.yaml
```

As usual, you can interact with the cluster using the kubectl command-line utility. For example, the following command displays all the pods in all the namespaces of the cluster:

```
$ kubectl get pods --all-namespaces
```

## Kubernetes Upgrade

Kubernetes has a vibrant community with four releases per year, so expect a new version every three months. At the moment of writing this book, the latest Kubernetes version is 1.26.1. In Kubernetes jargon, the values are Major 1, Minor 26 Patch 1. Major are versions with huge, with impacts that break compatibility with past releases. Minor versions introduce new features and deprecate some APIs. Patch versions are usually just bug-fixing releases and are automatically applied by the control plane every month. The Kubernetes lifecycle of version 1.26 was generally available and released on December 9, 2022, entered maintenance mode on December 28, 2023, and will enter its official end-of-life phase on February 24, 2024. See Figure 4-10.

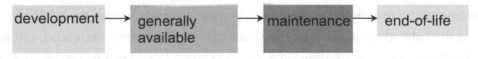

*Figure 4-10.* *Kubernetes releases lifecycle*

These constant upgrades guarantee bug fixing and the latest codebase and features on your cluster. You must proceed one minor version at a time. You can't jump by two versions. Note that you can't revert the upgrade process either.

Always plan for an upgrade. Read the documentation, the changelog, and the release notes carefully to understand if some API items are going to be deprecated. It's a best practice to create a checklist and identify which team performs the upgrade. Usually, security, operation, and infrastructure are involved in this operation. Define, test, and document upgrade procedures. Have a rollback/fallback plan in place and know how to process it. You need to assess the impact on your environment and test in Dev and UAT before promoting to production. Possible minor service interruptions might happen, so it's a good idea to notify your organization or your business continuity officer.

If an upgrade is unsatisfactory for your organization and you need the previous release, you need to start a new version and restore your data. Define what to do if there are some conflicts between versions of Kubernetes.

You should always begin the upgrade with the control plane, and only when it works fine, upgrade the data plane (when using managed workgroup). Nodes and add-ons can be upgraded after a successful upgrade of the control plane. A robust upgrade procedure identifies which team is responsible and which is tested in the test environment. Have a Plan B if something is not working as expected. A step-by-step documentation procedure is a good upgrade strategy to share with colleagues in your organization. A test of the main API used in your organization is always good for strategies. Identify downstream dependencies of the operators, services, and addons used in your Kubernetes cluster, determine the correct order to upgrade components (control plane first, data place second), and plan for API changes.

The following upgrade process is for a cluster installed using the `kubeadm` command-line tool. For Kubernetes clusters installed with other tools, the procedure is similar.

The plan begins with upgrading the control plane nodes. You need to set the `cordon` and `drain` node offline settings one by one, thus preventing scheduling and evicting any workloads, upgrade the `kubelet` and `kubectl` packages, restart the `kubelet` service, and bring the `uncordon` node back online.

After upgrading the control plane nodes, you can upgrade worker nodes. Begin by upgrading the `kubeadm` tool, executing the `kubeadm upgrade node` command, setting the node in `drain` mode, upgrading `kubelet` and `kubectl,` and restarting the `kubectl` process, then you `uncordon` the node.

# Create a Cluster with kOps

Kubernetes Operations (kOps) deploys a production-grade Kubernetes cluster. It provides installation, upgrades, and management, and enables you to be specific with your favorite cloud provider. kOps is tightly integrated with the unique features that your cloud provider supports, so it can be a better choice if you know that you will only be using one cloud provider platform in the foreseeable future.

kOps officially supports AWS (Amazon Web Services) and GCE (Google Cloud Platform); beta support is available for DigitalOcean, Hetzner, and OpenStack, and alpha support is available for Azure. The initial kOps command-line utility supports Linux, macOS, and Windows operating systems.

Its significant advantages are as follows:

- Supports dry-runs and automatic idempotency

- YAML manifest-based configuration

- Multi-architecture with ARM64 support

The installation procedure changes based on the target cloud provider platform, but involves the use of the `kops` command-line tool with some parameters. The `create cluster` parameter actually creates the Kubernetes cluster when the relevant variables are set for your environment. Some cloud providers require that you set permission to a service account beforehand. You can customize and update the cluster configuration as well as validate the configuration of the cluster to ensure your cluster is working as expected.

# Configure Ansible for Kubernetes

The good news is that an Ansible collection is designed to interact with any Kubernetes cluster. Under the hood, all these resources interact with the Kubernetes API and create Ansible resources through the Python programming language.

You can interact with the Kubernetes cluster using the `kubernetes.core` Ansible collection. At the moment of writing this book, these resources are available:

- `helm`: Add, update, and delete Kubernetes packages using the package manager Helm

- `helm_info`: Obtain information about a Helm package deployed into the Kubernetes cluster

- `helm_plugin`: Add, update, and delete Helm plugins

- `helm_plugin_info`: Obtain information about your Helm plugins

- `helm_repository`: Add, update, and delete Helm repositories

- `helm_template`: Render Helm chart templates

- `k8s`: Interact with the Kubernetes (K8s) objects

- `k8s_cluster_info`: Obtain Kubernetes clusters, any APIs available, and their respective versions

- `k8s_cp`: Copy files and directories to and from a pod

- `k8s_drain`: Set `drain`, `cordon`, or `uncordon` for a node in the Kubernetes cluster

- `k8s_exec`: Execute a command in a pod

- `k8s_info`: Obtain information about Kubernetes objects

- `k8s_json_patch`: Apply JSON patch operations to existing Kubernetes objects

- `k8s_log`: Fetch logs from a Kubernetes resource

- `K8s_rollback`: Roll back Kubernetes object deployments and DaemonSets

- `k8s_scale`: Set the scale parameter for a deployment, ReplicaSet, replication controller, or job

- `k8s_service`: Add, update, and delete services on Kubernetes

- `k8s_taint`: Set the taint attribute for a node in a Kubernetes cluster

- `kubectl`: Execute commands in Pods on a Kubernetes cluster (connection plugin)

- `k8s_config_resource_namer`: Generate resource names for the given resource of type ConfigMap, Secret (filter plugin)

- `k8s`: Fetch containers and services for one or more Kubernetes clusters and group by cluster name, namespace, namespace_ services, namespace_pods, and labels (inventory plugin)

- k8s: Provide access to the full range of Kubernetes APIs (lookup plugin)

- kustomize: Use the kustomization.yaml file to build a set of Kubernetes resources (lookup plugin)

Let me highlight the kubernetes.core.k8s module, as it is probably the most important of the Ansible collection.

The kubernetes.core collection is not included in the Ansible Core, which includes only the ansible.builtin collection. When you try to use a module that's not present in your system, you might end up with the following Ansible error:

```
ERROR! couldn't resolve module/action 'kubernetes.core.k8s'.
```

You can verify the presence of the kubernetes.core Ansible collection using the following ansible-galaxy command:

```
$ ansible-galaxy collection list
```

This command shows all the Ansible collections in your system with the relative version. The latest version of the kubernetes.core Ansible collection is 2.3.2 at the moment of writing this book.

The collection requires Python 3 installed in your system and the kubernetes Python library. If they are not present, you can install them manually using the PIP Python package manager. The pip utility is available for the most recent version of Linux, by installing the package python3-pip. The command for installing the PyYAML jsonpatch kubernetes Python libraries dependencies is as follows:

```
$ pip3 install PyYAML jsonpatch kubernetes
```

When you want to interact with the Helm package manager, you also need the helm Python library. However, it uses the legacy setup.py install method, which is discouraged by pip 23.1 and later. You can read more at https://github.com/pypa/pip/issues/8559; the workaround at the moment for the Helm package is to use the extra --use-pep517 parameter.

```
$ pip3 install --use-pep517 helm
```

When the Python dependencies are satisfied, you can install the Ansible collection manually or automatically using the ansible-galaxy command-line utility included in every Ansible installation.

- manual: Just type the action (collection install) followed by the collection name. The full command looks like this:

  ```
  $ ansible-galaxy collection install kubernetes.core
  ```

- automatic: Require creating a requirements.yml file, a particular YAML file with the list of all the Ansible collections to install in the target system. See Listing 4-2.

***Listing 4-2.***  The requirements.yml File

```
---
collections:
  - name: cloud.common
  - name: kubernetes.core
```

You can execute the requirements.yml file by specifying the -r parameter using the ansible-galaxy command-line tool:

```
$ ansible-galaxy install -r collections/requirements.yml
```

After the manual or automatic Ansible collection installation process, your system is configured to interact with the kubernetes.core Ansible collection.

---

**Tip**   The kubernetes.core Ansible collection supports the Ansible Turbo mode. By default, this feature is disabled. It requires an additional cloud.common Ansible collection installed.

The AnsibleTurboModule class is inherited from the standard AnsibleModule class, which spawns a little Python daemon, and the module logic runs inside this Python daemon. The result is a drastic improvement in performance because Python modules are loaded one time, and Ansible can reuse an existing authenticated session. The daemon run in a single process exposes a local UNIX socket for communication and kills itself after 15 seconds. You can set the ENABLE_TURBO_MODE variable to true or 1 using the environment statement in the Play section of the Ansible Playbooks.

---

Once you have successfully installed the Python and Ansible dependencies, you need to execute the authentication to your cluster in order to execute API requests via the command-line tool.

For the Kubernetes cluster, you need the kubectl command-line utility. Many options are available as binary or by using your favorite package managers. For example, in macOS, you can download it as a binary, use Macports, or use Homebrew (https://brew.sh/):

```
$ brew install kubernetes-cli
```

The kubectl Linux package is available in the DEB and RPM packages format or as a binary. In Windows, you can download and install the kubectl binary from the website or use the Chocolatey, Scoop, or "winget" package manager.

For the OpenShift cluster, the oc command-line utility is needed instead. In macOS with Homebrew, you can find in the package:

```
$ brew install openshift-cli
```

You don't need any modifications in the Ansible configuration file ansible.cfg to use Ansible with Kubernetes. This file allows you to fine-tune some settings and enables custom Ansible plugins. You can also customize directory paths in your system.

# Ansible Troubleshooting

Ansible troubleshooting can be difficult because more often than not, the fatal error root cause is related to a Kubernetes or Ansible configuration. The following errors might appear when you try to configure your environment to interact with a Kubernetes or OpenShift cluster.

# 401 unauthorized

Kubernetes authenticates the API requests using bearer tokens, client certificates, or an authentication proxy through authentication plugins.

You might obtain the Kubernetes 401 unauthorized fatal error message when you try to access your cluster when trying to execute some code without an authorization token or using an invalid token.

The root cause is related to Kubernetes authentication and not to Ansible Playbook or Ansible configuration. It could be because you are not authorized to access the namespace or resource or simply because you are not authenticated. Bear in mind that the authentication token expires after a specified amount of time, so you need to authenticate again in your Kubernetes cluster.

The full fatal error message looks similar to the following:

```
fatal: [localhost]: FAILED! => {"changed": false, "error": 401, "msg":
"Namespace example: Failed to retrieve requested object: b'{\"kind\":\"St
atus\",\"apiVersion\":\"v1\",\"metadata\":{},\"status\":\"Failure\",\"me
ssage\":\"Unauthorized\",\"reason\":\"Unauthorized\",\"code\":401}\\n'",
"reason": "Unauthorized", "status": 401}
```

# Kubernetes

In a Kubernetes cluster, obtaining a valid authentication token requires the setup of a context for your cluster with the `kubectrl` command-line utility.

You can obtain a valid Kubernetes authentication token by first entering the username and password and saving them as credentials using the following command:

```
$ kubectrl config set-credentials developer/foo.example.com
--username=developer --password=developer
```

With:

- `kubectrl`: Specifies the command-line tool to connect to the Kubernetes cluster

- `config`: Specifies the action to configure the cluster

- `set-credentials developer/foo.example.com` Creates a new credential named `developer/foo.example.com` (I prefer to use the same cluster name, but you can specify any name)

- `--username=developer`: Specifies the username for the login

- `--password=developer`: Specifies the password for the login

Then you need to configure the cluster connection server:

```
$ kubectl config set-cluster foo.example.com --insecure-skip-tls-
verify=true --server=https://foo.example.com
```

With:

- kubectrl: Specifies the command-line tool to connect to the Kubernetes cluster

- config: Specifies the action to configure the cluster

- set-cluster foo.example.com: Creates a new cluster named foo.example.com (you can specify any name)

- --insecure-skip-tls-verify=true: Skips TLS certificates validation

- --server=https://foo.example.com: Specifies the cluster URI

Then you can join in a context the cluster and credentials information:

```
$ kubectl config set-context default/foo.example.com/developer
--user=developer/foo.example.com --namespace=default --cluster=foo.example.com
```

With:

- kubectrl: Specifies the command-line tool to connect to the Kubernetes cluster

- config: Specifies the action to configure the cluster

- set-context default/foo.example.com/developer: Creates a new context named default/foo.example.com/developer (you can specify any name)

- --user=developer/foo.example.com: Skips TLS certificates validation

- ---namespace=default: Specifies the default namespace (in this case, default)

- --cluster=foo.example.com: Specifies the cluster configuration name

Than you can finally use this context and obtain the authentication token:

```
$ kubectl config use-context  default/foo.example.com/developer
```

From now on, all the commands are sent from within this context to the Kubernetes cluster that you configured.

# OpenShift

You can obtain the OpenShift cluster using the oc command and specifying the username and password:

```
$ oc login -u developer -p developer https://api.openshift.example.com:6443
```

With:

- oc: Specifies the command-line tool to interact with OpenShift cluster
- login: Specifies the action to authenticate in the cluster
- -u developer: Specifies the username for the login
- -p developer: Specifies the password for the login
- https://api.openshift.example.com:6443: Specifies the cluster URI and the port

As an alternative to a username and password, you can authenticate using a token obtained via the OpenShift console. After successfully logging in to the web user interface, just choose Copy Login Command under your username in the top-right menu area, as shown in Figure 4-11.

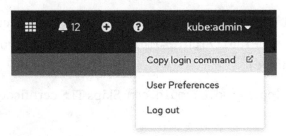

***Figure 4-11.***  *OpenShift console token generation*

The token is a SHA256 series of alphanumeric characters displayed in a new window on the screen, as shown in Figure 4-12.

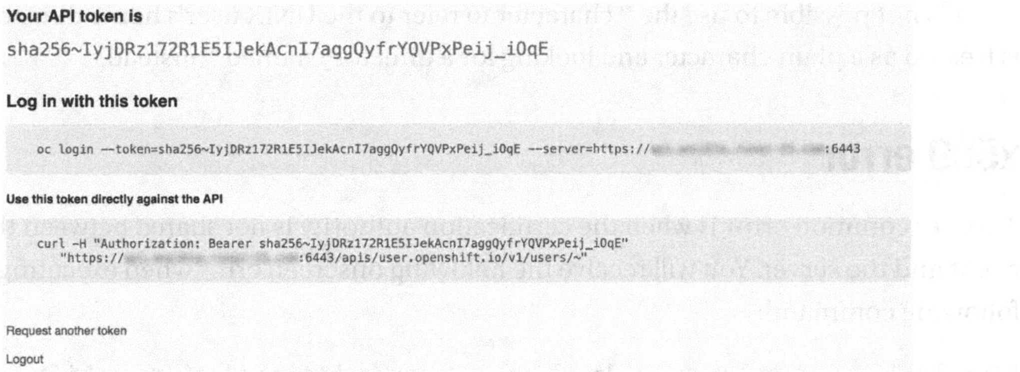

**Your API token is**

sha256~IyjDRz172R1E5IJekAcnI7aggQyfrYQVPxPeij_iOqE

**Log in with this token**

oc login --token=sha256~IyjDRz172R1E5IJekAcnI7aggQyfrYQVPxPeij_iOqE --server=https://                :6443

**Use this token directly against the API**

curl -H "Authorization: Bearer sha256~IyjDRz172R1E5IJekAcnI7aggQyfrYQVPxPeij_iOqE"
     "https://                :6443/apis/user.openshift.io/v1/users/~"

Request another token

Logout

*Figure 4-12.* *OpenShift console token example*

Once generated, the token is usable via the command-line oc command like the following:

```
$ oc login --token=sha256~xxxxxx --server=https://api.openshift.example.
com:6443
```

With:

- oc: Specifies the command-line tool to interact with OpenShift cluster

- login: Specifies the action to authenticate in the cluster

- --token=sha256~xxxxxx: Specifies the usage of the access token

- https://api.openshift.example.com:6443: Specifies the cluster URI and the port

After successfully authenticating, an authentication token is stored in the .kube directory under the config file on the local machine. You can customize the filename and path using the KUBECONFIG environment variable in the terminal.

```
$ export KUBECONFIG=/home/devops/.kube/config-developer
```

In the same way, you should instruct Ansible to read the environment variable by adding the following environment lines in the Play area of your Ansible Playbook:

```
[...]
environment:
  KUBECONFIG: "/home/devops/.kube/config-developer"
[...]
```

It is not possible to use the ~ character to refer to the UNIX user's home directory as is treated as a plain character and looking for a directory named ~ instead.

## x509 error

Another common error is when the certification authority is not shared between the client and the server. You will receive the following onscreen error when executing the following command:

```
$ oc login -u developer -p developer --server=https://api.openshift.
example.com:6443
```

The parameters were discussed in the previous section. The fatal error on the screen is as follows:

```
error: x509: "kube-apiserver-service-network-signer" certificate is
not trusted
```

You can solve adding the additional certification authority file with the --certificate-authority parameter followed by the path on disk of the certificate.

You can acquire more information by increasing the verbosity level to six, the highest available, with the --loglevel 6 parameter.

A successful login procedure can be verified using this OpenShift command:

```
$ oc whoami
developer
```

## kubeconfig

The kubectl command-line utility and the kubernetes.core Ansible collection both require a valid kubeconfig file with the authentication information to connect to the Kubernetes cluster. This book assumes that you have a valid kubeconfig file to connect to your Kubernetes cluster. The file contains the following key information:

- cluster-ca-cert: The Kubernetes cluster certification authority

- endpoint: Kubernetes cluster endpoint (IP or DNS of the master node)

- cluster-name: K8s cluster name

- cluster-username: Username or service account

- secret-token: A secret token of the username of the service account

This is a schematic of a typical kubeconfig file:

```
---
apiVersion: v1
kind: Config
current-context:  <cluster-name>
clusters:
- name: <cluster-name>
  cluster:
    certificate-authority-data: <cluster-ca-cert>
    server: <endpoint>
contexts:
- name: <cluster-name>
  context:
    cluster:  <cluster-name>
    user:  <cluster-username>
preferences: {}
users:
- name: <cluster-username>
  user:
    token: <secret-token>
```

The default path of this file is in the .kube user directory and is named config.

You can customize the path of the kubectl command-line utility using the
KUBECONFIG environment variable as follows:

```
$ export KUBECONFIG=$HOME/.kube/config
```

For Ansible code, you can specify a custom path by specifying the kubeconfig
module parameter or via the K8S_AUTH_KUBECONFIG environment variable. The code in
this book assumes that your kubeconfig file is stored under the ~/.kube/config path

119

(the default path), where the ~ (tilde symbol) indicates the home of your user. You can customize this path using the kubeconfig parameter for each Ansible module. The most common usage with the k8s Ansible module is as follows:

```
kubernetes.core.k8s:
  kubeconfig: '~/.kube/config'
```

# Configure a Python Virtual Environment

A Python Virtual Environment is a tool to keep your application environment separate from the system-wide environment. Ansible, like all Python applications, requires some Python libraries as dependencies. Maintaining up-to-date all the Python dependencies of Ansible and of the Ansible collection without interfering with your Linux system can be challenging without a Python Virtual Environment.

The first step is to create the virtual environment using the Python venv module, preceded by the -m parameter. In the following example, the virtual environment is named venv; feel free to customize it according to your needs:

```
$ python3 -m venv venv
```

After creating the venv virtual environment, you need to activate it using the script for your operating system activate for Linux/macOS e activate.bat for Windows. You can find the script in the directory named like your virtual environment (venv). You can return every time to this state using the activate script.

```
$ source venv/bin/activate
```

Once inside the venv virtual environment, prepend the prompt to the name (venv). It's a best practice to upgrade the package manager pip and setuptools to the latest versions:

```
(venv) $ pip3 install --upgrade pip setuptools
```

On some systems, the pip/pip3 command tool is not available out of the box. It might be necessary to install the python3-pip package or use following a manual installation process.

```
$ python -m ensurepip --upgrade
```

After upgrading the pip installed, you can install the Python PyYAML, jsonpatch and kubernetes dependency:

```
(venv) $ pip3 install PyYAML jsonpatch kubernetes
```

For Ansible modules that interact with the Helm package manager, the extra helm Python library is required with the --use-pep517 parameter workaround:

```
(venv) $ pip3 install --use-pep517 helm
```

You can save all the Python libraries and their dependencies using the pip3 freeze command and save the result to requirements.txt. Sharing this file with someone else or another system will result in the same configuration of this virtual environment.

```
(venv) $ pip3 freeze > requirements.txt
```

Listing 4-3 shows the contents of the requirements.txt at the time of writing this book; it includes the ansible-builder and ansible-runner utilities.

***Listing 4-3.*** The requirements.txt File

```
ansible-builder==1.2.0
ansible-runner==2.3.1
bindep==2.11.0
cachetools==5.2.0
certifi==2022.12.7
charset-normalizer==2.1.1
distro==1.8.0
docutils==0.19
google-auth==2.15.0
helm==0.4
idna==3.4
kubernetes==25.3.0
lockfile==0.12.2
oauthlib==3.2.2
packaging==22.0
Parsley==1.3
pbr==5.11.0
pexpect==4.8.0
```

```
ptyprocess==0.7.0
pyasn1==0.4.8
pyasn1-modules==0.2.8
python-daemon==2.3.2
python-dateutil==2.8.2
PyYAML==6.0
requests==2.28.1
requests-oauthlib==1.3.1
requirements-parser==0.5.0
rsa==4.9
six==1.16.0
types-setuptools==65.6.0.2
urllib3==1.26.13
websocket-client==1.4.2
```

If you want to use the Ansible Turbo feature, you must install the `cloud.common` Ansible collection using the `ansible-galaxy` command-line utility:

```
(venv) $ ansible-galaxy collection install cloud.common
```

The `kubernetes.core` Ansible collection is a must-have in your system to execute Kubernetes automation:

```
(venv) $ ansible-galaxy collection install kubernetes.core
```

You can deactivate your virtual environment at any time and return to your system console. You should activate the virtual environment every time you want to use it. The virtual environment preserves all installed libraries and collections.

```
$ deactivate
```

When you want to use your virtual environment, just execute the `activate` script again.

When the complexity of the Python Virtual Environment grows too much, it can become challenging to manage the Python library dependencies and Ansible module dependencies. You can use the Ansible Execution Environment instead.

# Configure an Ansible Execution Environment

The Ansible Execution Environment is a way to containerize the execution of the Ansible invented by Red Hat. It maintains archives of the separation of the operating system dependencies, Python dependencies, and Ansible collections without interfering with your Linux system. It's the evolution of Python Virtual Environment and can be executed natively in a Kubernetes cluster. It supersedes manual Python Virtual Environments, Ansible module dependencies, and Ansible Tower bubblewrap.

Ansible Execution Environment relies on the Ansible Builder, the `ansible-builder` command, to create an Ansible Execution Environment. Ansible Builder produces a directory with the build context for the container image. It contains the `Containerfile`, along with any other files that need to be added to the image.

The Ansible Runner, the `ansible-runner` command utility, executes the Ansible Playbook in an Ansible Execution Environment. The Ansible Runner enables you to run the Ansible Execution Environment as a container in the current machine.

You can install the `ansible-builder,` and `ansible-runner` command-line utilities via the DNF package manager (Fedora, CentOS, and Red Hat Enterprise Linux) or via the `pip` package manager:

```
$ pip3 install ansible-builder
$ pip3 install ansible-runner
```

Listing 4-4 creates a custom Ansible Execution Environment for Kubernetes called my_kube. The `execution-environment.yml` file contains the blueprint of the newest Execution Environment, specifying that you want to customize the operating system packages (`system: bindep.txt`), the Python libraries (`python: requirements.txt`), and the Ansible collections (`galaxy: requirements.yml`). See Listing 4-4. You're going to see these files one by one. Before the build step, you install and upgrade the `pip` and `setuptools`, and afterwards, you list the file in the root directory. The building process will not work in disconnected or "air-gapped" environments. Ensure that your systems are connected to the Internet because the process must download some resources in order to build the Ansible Execution Environment.

***Listing 4-4.*** The execution-environment.yml File

```
---
version: 1
dependencies:
  galaxy: requirements.yml
  python: requirements.txt
  system: bindep.txt
additional_build_steps:
  prepend: |
                RUN pip3 install --upgrade pip setuptools
  append:
    - RUN ls -al /
```

The append part is an optional additional step that demonstrates that you can run commands after building your Ansible Execution Environment.

As demonstrated in Listing 4-5, the requirements.yml file specifies the list of Ansible collections to download. In this case, cloud.common for Ansible Turbo and kubernetes. core for the Ansible resources for Kubernetes.

***Listing 4-5.*** The requirements.yml File

```
---
collections:
  - name: cloud.common
  - name: kubernetes.core
```

The requirements.txt file specifies the Python library dependencies, in that case, the JSONpatch, kubernetes, and PyYAML Python libraries, as shown in Listing 4-6.

***Listing 4-6.*** The requirements.txt File

```
kubernetes>=12.0.0
PyYAML>=3.11
jsonpatch
```

You can also specify some operating system package files, in this case, the git Source Code Management package for using the rpm and dpkg package installation methods, as shown in Listing 4-7.

***Listing 4-7.*** The bindep.txt File

```
git [platform:rpm]
git [platform:dpkg]
```

You can start building the `my_kube` Ansible Execution Environment using the `ansible-builder` command and specifying the `build` parameter with the name of the newest Ansible Execution Environment after the `-t` parameter. Optionally, you can obtain the output in verbose mode using the `-v 3` parameter. The full command is like the following:

```
$ ansible-builder build -t my_kube -v 3
```

The command requires connecting to the Container Registry to download the base image and the Ansible Builder image. When you use it in an enterprise environment, type the following command to authenticate to the Red Hat Container Registry with your Red Hat Portal username and password:

```
$ podman login registry.redhat.io
```

Once the Ansible Builder has completed the execution successfully, a `context/Containerfile` file is created. You can build your image using this command:

```
$ podman build -f context/Containerfile -t my_kube context
```

The Ansible Runner enables you to run the Ansible Execution Environment as a container in the current machine. The syntax resembles the `ansible-playbook` command-line utility, specifying the name of the Ansible Execution Environment:

```
$ ansible-runner run -p ping.yml --inventory inventory --container-
image=my_kube .
```

This uses the simplest Ansible INI `inventory` file against the `localhost` and using the local connection (instead of the SSH connection):

```
localhost ansible_connection=local
```

The Ansible Playbook shown in Listing 4-8 uses the popular `ansible.builtin.ping` Ansible module to test the successful connection to the target node. The `ping` module executes a connection to the target node and executes some sample Python code. In this way, you can test the connection and the ability of the Python interpreter to listen and execute code on the target node.

125

***Listing 4-8.*** The ping.yml Ansible Playbook File

```
---
- name: test
  hosts: all
  tasks:
    - name: test connection
      ansible.builtin.ping:
```

In this section, you learned how to create a custom my_kube Ansible Execution Environment with the Ansible Builder and how to execute an Ansible Paybook inside of it using the Ansible Runner command-line tools. Since it's a container, you can deploy your Ansible Environment in your Container Registry. You can execute your Ansible Playbook scripts in the local machine or in a Kubernetes cluster.

---

**Tip**    The Ansible Automation Platform easily manages the Ansible Execution Environments and the execution against any Kubernetes and OpenShift cluster. Under the Ansible Controller, you can create a container group specifying a namespace, a service account with roles that allow to launch and manage pods in the namespace, the OpenShift or Kubernetes bearer token, and the SSL certification authority certificate associated with the cluster.

---

# Create a Namespace

You can automate the creation of the ansible-examples namespace in Kubernetes or project in OpenShift. You just need a few parameters for the kubernetes.core.k8s Ansible module. The k8s Ansible module is part of the kubernetes.core collection; it's very powerful and allows you to interact with the Kubernetes API like the kubectl or oc command-line utilities. The name parameter specifies the namespace that you want to create or verify if present. The api_version parameter specifies the Kubernetes API version; the default is v1 for version 1. The kind parameter specifies an object model, which is namespace for this use case. As with other modules, the state parameter determines if an object should be created (the - present option), updated (the - patched option), or deleted (the - absent option). You can customize the myproject variable with your namespace in the code or via an Ansible extra variable.

The full Ansible Playbook is shown in Listing 4-9.

***Listing 4-9.*** The ns_create.yml Ansible Playbook File

```
---
- name: k8s ns
  hosts: all
  vars:
    myproject: "ansible-examples"
  tasks:
    - name: namespace present
      kubernetes.core.k8s:
        api_version: v1
        kind: Namespace
        name: "{{ myproject }}"
        state: present
```

You are going to execute the playbook in the current Ansible Controller so you can use the localhost in the inventory with a local connection, as shown in Listing 4-10.

***Listing 4-10.*** The Inventory File

```
localhost ansible_connection=local
```

The code executes the ansible-playbook command. The full command is as follows:

```
$ ansible-playbook -i inventory ns_create.yml
```

A successful execution output includes the following:

- Managed host: localhost

- Play recap status: ok=2 changed=1

- Task status:

```
TASK [namespace ansible-examples present]
changed: [localhost]
```

You receive the changed status when the namespace is successfully created in the Kubernetes cluster, whereas you receive the ok status when the namespace was already present in the cluster (Ansible idempotency property).

You can verify that the namespace list uses the kubectl command-line utility:

```
$ kubectl get namespace | grep ansible-examples
ansible-examples      Active  10m
```

Instead, OpenShift calls namespace as a project but the result is similar to the previous:

```
$ oc projects | grep ansible-examples
   ansible-examples
```

The previous Ansible Playbook supposes that you perform the authentication in the Ansible Controller outside the Ansible Playbook using the kubectl for Kubernetes or oc for OpenShift command. It's also possible to perform the authentication step in the Ansible Playbook using the k8s_auth Ansible module, which is part of the kubernetes. core Ansible collection. If you want to execute the authentication directly in the Ansible Playbook, you need to add a task before executing any command to the cluster. The get access token task connects to the host address with the specified username and password credentials and saves the result in the k8s_auth_results runtime variable. The variable contains the token under the k8s_auth.api_key variable. Every time you use the k8s module, the extra parameter api_key is specified with the value of the token registered from the previous task. Listing 4-11 shows the full Ansible Playbook.

**Listing 4-11.** The ns_create_auth.yml Ansible Playbook File

```
---
- name: k8s ns
  hosts: all
  vars:
    myproject: "ansible-examples"
    k8s_username: "kubeadmin"
    k8s_password: "password"
    k8s_host: "https://api.k8s:6443"
    k8s_validate: true
```

```
tasks:
  - name: get access token
    kubernetes.core.k8s_auth:
      username: "{{ k8s_username }}"
      password: "{{ k8s_password }}"
      host: "{{ k8s_host }}"
      validate_certs: "{{ k8s_validate }}"
    register: k8s_auth_results

  - name: namespace present
    kubernetes.core.k8s:
      api_key: "{{ k8s_auth_results.k8s_auth.api_key }}"
      api_version: v1
      kind: Namespace
      name: "{{ myproject }}"
      state: present
```

In the real world, it's better to store any variables with sensitive data (beginning with k8s_ of the previous Ansible Playbook) in an Ansible vault that's encrypted and protected. For OpenShift authentication, use the community.okd.openshift_auth Ansible module in the first task.

# Report Namespaces

Kubernetes cluster administrators often need to list all the namespaces (*projects* in OpenShift jargon). Reporting is a simple, repetitive, and boring task that can be automated with Ansible. This can be easily achieved using Ansible Playbook with two tasks. The first task uses the Ansible query lookup plugin and invokes the Ansible kubernetes.core.k8s module to interact with the Kubernetes API and return a list of all the namespaces in the cluster. The result of the Ansible lookup plugin is saved in the projects runtime variable using the ansible.builtin.set_fact Ansible module. You can use this variable to perform further tasks, such as print the result onscreen using the ansible.builtin.debug Ansible module. Listing 4-12 shows the full ns_list.yml Ansible Playbook file.

***Listing 4-12.*** The ns_list.yml Ansible Playbook File

```
---
- name: k8s ns
  hosts: all
  tasks:
    - name: list all namespaces
      ansible.builtin.set_fact:
        projects: "{{ query('kubernetes.core.k8s', api_version='v1',
        kind='Namespace') }}"

    - name: display the result
      ansible.builtin.debug:
        msg: "{{ projects }}"
```

The easier execution is locally in the Ansible Controller, specifying the `localhost` in the inventory, as shown in Listing 4-13.

***Listing 4-13.*** The Inventory File

```
localhost ansible_connection=local
```

The Ansible code can be executed using the `ansible-playbook` command included in every Ansible installation. A successful execution output includes the following:

- Managed host: `localhost`

- Play recap status: `ok=3 changed=0`

- Task status:

```
TASK [print]
ok: [localhost] => {
    "msg": [
        {
            "apiVersion": "v1",
            "kind": "Namespace",
[...]
```

You receive the ok statuses for the two tasks and a long JSON file containing the list of all the namespaces in the Kubernetes cluster. To filter the output in a more synthetic and useful way, see the next section about using the `community.general.json_query` filter plugin and JMESPath.

# Report Deployments in Namespace

Reporting deployments in namespaces is another repetitive and useful task for a Kubernetes user or administrator. First of all, you need to create a deployment in order to list them in the Kubernetes/OpenShift cluster.

The Kubernetes Deployment is a central object that allows you to specify the number of replicas of your pods. The pod definition is inside the Deployment YAML manifest document in the following example. The `deployment.yaml` document is a simple Deployment YAML file that deploys the latest tag of the container named `nginx` with two replicas listening on port TCP 3000 under the `ansible-examples` namespace, as shown in Listing 4-14.

*Listing 4-14.* The deployment.yaml Kubernetes File

```
---
apiVersion: apps/v1
kind: Deployment
metadata:
  name: nginx
  namespace: ansible-examples
spec:
  replicas: 2
  selector:
    matchLabels:
      app: nginx
  template:
    metadata:
      labels:
        app: nginx
    spec:
      containers:
```

131

```
        - name: nginx
          image: nginx:1.22
          imagePullPolicy: Always
        ports:
          - containerPort: 3000
```

You can apply your deployment to the Kubernetes cluster manually using the kubectl command-line utility or via the kubernetes.core.k8s Ansible module:

```
$ kubectl apply -f deployment.yaml
```

A successful execution of the kubectl command returns the following message:

```
deployment.apps/nginx created
```

You can check the status of the nginx deployment using the following command:

```
$ kubectl get deployment nginx
```

The output confirms that your nginx deployment has been running for three minutes (under the AGE column):

```
NAME          READY    UP-TO-DATE    AVAILABLE    AGE
nginx         2/2      1             1            3m
```

You can also check your Kubernetes resources such as the pods allocated by your deployment using this command:

```
$ kubectl get pods
```

If you don't specify the kubectl namespace, try to list the resources of the default namespace. You should always specify the namespace (the -n ansible-examples parameter) in order to obtain the full list of pods. If you see the following message on the screen, it means you forgot to specify your namespace:

```
No resources found in the default namespace.
$ kubectl get pods -n ansible-examples
```

The output confirms your nginx pod, plus a random identifier inside the ansible-examples namespace:

```
NAME                              READY    STATUS     RESTARTS    AGE
nginx-98fabf9-pvw89               2/2      Running    0           5m
```

As you can see, the pod had 2 replicas and the status is Running for 5 minutes.

---

**Note**    When Kubernetes cannot download the Container Image from the Container Registry; it reports the statuses ImagePullBackOff and CrashLoopBackOff. These two statuses are connected, meaning that the Kubernetes cluster tried to download the image from the registry but without success. The full workflow is from ErrImagePull, then ImagePullBackOff, and then keep trying. The root cause could be a misspelled image name or tag, a registry issue, a rate limit in the registry (see Free vs. Pro accounts in Docker Hub), a private registry without specifying the Secret for the Pod, or simply a bit of bad luck about connectivity.

---

You can automate the application of your Kubernetes deployment.yaml file using the following Ansible Playbook and the k8s module, as demonstrated in Listing 4-15.

*Listing 4-15.* The deployment.yml Ansible Playbook File

```
---
- name: k8s deployment
  hosts: all
  vars:
    myproject: "ansible-examples"
  tasks:
    - name: namespace present
      kubernetes.core.k8s:
        api_version: v1
        kind: Namespace
        name: "{{ myproject }}"
        state: present

    - name: deployment present
      kubernetes.core.k8s:
        src: deployment.yaml
        namespace: "{{ myproject }}"
        state: present
```

Now execute your code in the Ansible Controller machine using the inventory, as shown in Listing 4-16.

***Listing 4-16.*** The Inventory File

```
localhost ansible_connection=local
```

A successful execution using the `ansible-playbook` command output includes the following:

- Managed host: `localhost`

- Play recap status: `ok=3 changed=2`

- Task status:

```
TASK [namespace ansible-examples present]
changed: [localhost]
TASK [deployment present]
changed: [localhost]
```

You receive the two `changed` statuses for the two tasks, which means the deployment request was successfully sent to the Kubernetes cluster API and executed. The two `changed` statuses mean that the namespace and the deployment were created. If one of the two is already present, you receive an ok status.

```
TASK [deployment present]
ok: [localhost]
```

**Note**   You'll receive a Kubernetes return code 404 error when the namespace is not present and a 403 error when the namespace is terminated.

The following code lists all the deployments in the specified namespace. As you explored in the previous section, the Ansible `query` lookup plugin invokes the `kubernetes.core.k8s` module to interact with the Kubernetes API and return a list of all the deployments in the cluster. The `query` lookup plugin (sometimes shortened as `q`) invokes the `kubernetes.core.k8s` module, specifying the deployment as the `kind` parameter and `ansible-examples` as a `namespace` parameter. You can list other

Kubernetes objects by changing the kind parameter value or other namespaces by changing the namespace parameter value. The lookup plug returns the full JSON received from the Kubernetes cluster.

You need to filter the output to extract a single element: the name of the deployment in the namespace. The most useful Ansible filter plugin to extract a single element is the Ansible json_query filter plugin. It's specifically designed to select a single element or a data structure from a JSON output. Its full name is community.general.json_query, which means that you need the additional community.general Ansible collection installed in your system. The community.general.json_query.

You can install the collection using the ansible-galaxy command-line tool:

```
$ ansible-galaxy collection install community.general
```

See Chapter 2 when you want to automate this process using a requirements. yml file. The Ansible module requires the Python jmespath library to be installed in the system:

```
$ pip3 install jmespath
```

Follow the guidance of the previous section about how to install these dependency resources manually or automatically. With the Ansible json_query filter plugin, you can use the JMESPath popular query language for JSON. Considering the Kubernetes output, you apply the [*].metadata.name filter pattern which means extracting for each element of the list (the star between brackets [*]) the key metadata, and displaying the subkey name specified using the dot notation. The result of the Ansible lookup plugin and the Ansible filter is saved in the deployments runtime variable using the ansible.builtin. set_fact Ansible module. It's displayed onscreen using the Ansible debug module.

Listing 4-17 shows the full Ansible Playbook code.

*Listing 4-17.* The deployment_list.yml File

```
---
- name: k8s deployments
  hosts: all
  tasks:
    - name: list all deployments
      ansible.builtin.set_fact:
```

```
    deployments: "{{ query('kubernetes.core.k8s', kind='Deployment',
    namespace='ansible-examples') | community.general.json_query('[*].
    metadata.name') }}"

- name: display the result
  ansible.builtin.debug:
    msg: "{{ deployments }}"
```

You can execute the `ansible-playbook` command on the Ansible Controller machine using the inventory, as shown in Listing 4-18.

***Listing 4-18.*** The Inventory File

```
localhost ansible_connection=local
```

A successful execution output includes the following:

- Managed host: `localhost`

- Play recap status: `ok=3`

- Task status:

```
TASK [display the result]
ok: [localhost] => {
    "msg": [
        "nginx"
    ]
}
```

# Create a Pod

A *pod* is an atomic unit that deploys one or more containers in a Kubernetes cluster. You can automate the creation of the `nginx` pod in the `ansible-example` namespace with Ansible module k8s in your Kubernetes/OpenShift cluster. The k8s Ansible module is part of the `kubernetes.core` collection and manages Kubernetes objects by applying a YAML object manifest to the `src` parameter. You also specify the namespace in the `namespace` parameter; it refers to the Ansible variable `myproject` defined in the Play area of the Playbook. The present state indicates the final result of the execution to create the object if not present or to verify its existence if it's already present in the Kubernetes cluster.

The Ansible Playbook shown in Listing 4-19 executes the Kubernetes pod.yaml manifest file to create the pod in the desired namespace.

***Listing 4-19.*** The pod.yml Ansible Playbook File

```
---
- name: k8s pod
  hosts: all
  vars:
    myproject: "ansible-examples"
  tasks:
    - name: namespace present
      kubernetes.core.k8s:
        api_version: v1
        kind: Namespace
        name: "{{ myproject }}"
        state: present

    - name: pod present
      kubernetes.core.k8s:
        src: pod.yaml
        namespace: "{{ myproject }}"
        state: present
```

The full Kubernetes YAML manifest file is shown in Listing 4-20.

***Listing 4-20.*** The pod.yaml Kubernetes File

```
---
apiVersion: v1
kind: Pod
metadata:
  name: nginx
spec:
```

```
containers:
  - name: nginx
    image: nginx:latest
    ports:
      - containerPort: 80
```

As usual, execute the playbook code in your Ansible Controller with the `localhost` in the inventory, as demonstrated in Listing 4-21.

***Listing 4-21.*** The Inventory

```
localhost ansible_connection=local
```

A successful execution using the `ansible-playbook` command output includes the following:

- Managed host: `localhost`

- Play recap status: `ok=2 changed=1`

- Task status:

---

```
TASK [pod present]
changed: [localhost]
```

---

You can check the `nginx` pod running as a result of the operation using the Kubernetes `kubectl` command-line utility for a Kubernetes cluster:

```
$ kubectl get pods -n ansible-examples
```

In a similar way, you can list the pods in a namespace in an OpenShift cluster with the `oc` command line:

```
$ oc get pods -n ansible-examples
```

The output displays the pod name, the number of pods (also called the *replica count* 1/1), the current status (`Running`), and the number of restarts:

| NAME | READY | STATUS | RESTARTS | AGE |
|------|-------|--------|----------|-----|
| nginx | 1/1 | Running | 0 | 2m |

# Create a Secret

Secrets are not encrypted; they are encoded in base64 and stored in etcd on an encrypted volume. Note that when you decide to encrypt your data, you can't return to the non-encrypted status.

Listing 4-22 shows you how to automate the creation of the mysecret Kubernetes secret in the ansible-examples namespace in the Kubernetes/OpenShift cluster using the Ansible module k8s.

***Listing 4-22.*** The secret.yml Ansible Playbook File

```
---
- name: k8s secret
  hosts: all
  tasks:
    - name: namespace present
      kubernetes.core.k8s:
        api_version: v1
        kind: Namespace
        name: "{{ myproject }}"
        state: present

    - name: secret present
      kubernetes.core.k8s:
        src: secret.yaml
        state: present
```

You can create two data fields: username and password, with the value. The value must be encoded as base64. Many encoders and decoders exist for the base64 encodings. In Listing 4-23, the following key and values are used:

- username = admin

- password - mysupersecretpassword

***Listing 4-23.*** The secret.yaml Kubernetes File

```
---
apiVersion: v1
kind: Secret
metadata:
  name: mysecret
  namespace: ansible-examples
type: Opaque
data:
  username: YWRtaW4=
  password: bXlzdXBlcnNlY3JldHBhc3N3b3Jk
```

You can execute this code locally in your Ansible Controller machine using the inventory, as shown in Listing 4-24.

***Listing 4-24.*** The Inventory File

```
localhost ansible_connection=local
```

A successful execution using the `ansible-playbook` command output includes the following:

- Managed host: `localhost`

- Play recap status: `ok=2  changed=1`

- Task status:

---

```
TASK [secret present]
changed: [localhost]
```

---

After execution, you can list the secrets in the `ansible-examples` namespace using the `kubectl` command-line utility for a Kubernetes cluster:

```
$ kubectl get secrets -n ansible-examples
```

You get the same command and output for the OpenShift cluster using the `oc` command-line utility:

```
$ oc get secrets -n ansible-examples
```

The output displays the secret name, the secret type (Opaque), the amount of fields (2), and the age of creation (2m54s):

```
NAME            TYPE                    DATA    AGE
mysecret        Opaque                  2       2m54s
```

# Use a Service to Expose Your App

The Kubernetes Service exposes your application to stakeholders without worrying about the internal IP addresses of pods. Your customers need to be able to connect to your Kubernetes pods in order to access a service or application. Now that you understand that pods can be ephemeral, it makes no sense to rely on the pod IP address for your services.

Instead, the best way is to use a Kubernetes Service that is designed to take care of this use case. The Kubernetes Service is continuously updated by the pod statuses with of healthy pods. The Kubernetes Service provides a constant IP address and port that act as an entry point to a group of pods. This information doesn't change for as long as the service exists. Internal and external clients can reach your application running in a group of pods by connecting to the service IP and ports. These connections are routed to one of the pods behind the Kubernetes Service.

The service.yaml document is a simple Deployment YAML file that deploys your service, exposing the internal port TCP 3000 of your application named nginx-example to the external TCP 80 (HTTP protocol), as shown in Listing 4-25.

*Listing 4-25.* The service.yaml Kubernetes File

```
---
apiVersion: v1
kind: Service
metadata:
  name: nginx-example
spec:
  selector:
    app: nginx-example
  ports:
```

```
    - protocol: TCP
      port: 80
      targetPort: 3000
```

You can create your `nginx-example` service by applying the `service.yaml` Service YAML file to the Kubernetes cluster with the `kubectl` command or via the `kubernetes.core.k8s` Ansible module:

```
$ kubectl apply -f service.yaml
```

Successful execution of the `kubectl` command returns the following message:

```
service/nginx-example created
```

You can also list the service `nginx-example` in your cluster with the following `kubectl` command:

```
$ kubectl get service nginx-example -n ansible-examples
NAME            TYPE        CLUSTER-IP      EXTERNAL-IP    PORT(S)   AGE
nginx-service   ClusterIP   172.30.112.45   <none>         80/TCP    4m
```

The output confirms that your `nginx-example` service has been running for four minutes; it listens on port 80/TCP at the `172.30.112.45` Cluster IP and has no external IP associated with it.

For reference, the following command operates in the OpenShift cluster:

```
$ oc get services -n ansible-examples
```

The Ansible Playbook shown in Listing 4-26 automates the execution of the `service.yaml` Kubernetes YAML manifest file using the k8s module.

***Listing 4-26.*** The service.yml Ansible Playbook File

```
---
- name: k8s service
  hosts: all
  vars:
    myproject: "ansible-examples"
  tasks:
    - name: k8s service
      kubernetes.core.k8s:
```

```
        src: service.yaml
        namespace: "{{ myproject }}"
        state: present
```

Execute your code using the `ansible-playbook` command on your Ansible Controller machine using the inventory file, as shown in Listing 4-27.

***Listing 4-27.*** The Inventory File

```
localhost ansible_connection=local
```

Successful execution using the `ansible-playbook` command output includes the following:

- Managed host: `localhost`

- Play recap status: `ok=2 changed=1`

- Task status:

---

```
TASK [k8s service]
changed: [localhost]
```

---

You can verify the result using the `kubectl` command-line utility for a Kubernetes cluster and the `oc` command-line utility for the OpenShift cluster.

## Kubernetes Networking

Kubernetes uses five techniques to track pod status and direct traffic to the appropriate pods:

- **ClusterIP**: Accessible only internally within the cluster.

- **NodePort**: Exposes a static port (the NodePort) on each node's IP that can be accessed from outside the cluster by the address `NodeIP:NodePort`. The NodePort service connects to a ClusterIP service that is created automatically for your NodePort.

- **LoadBalancer**: Exposes a load balancer externally. The LoadBalancer service connects to the NodePort and ClusterIP, automatically created.

- **Ingress**: Reduces the amount of load balancer for HTTP and HTTPS defining traffic routes.

- **ExternalName**: Maps to a DNS name. It returns a `CNAME` record with its value.

The simplest network configuration is the `ClusterIP` service type. This is accessible from within the cluster only. A `ClusterIP` service IP address is assigned from the cluster range. The ClusterIP service routes the traffic to the nodes. Behind the scene, each node runs a `kube-proxy` container for this task. The `kube-proxy` container creates the appropriate IPtables firewall rules to redirect the ClusterIP traffic to the appropriate Pod IP address. This type of service is used by frontend pods to redirect traffic to the backend pods or to act like load balancers.

In the Kubernetes YAML for `ClusterIP` service, the most important field is the `selector`. It determines which pods serve as endpoints for this service (see Listing 4-28).

***Listing 4-28.*** The ClusterIP.yaml Kubernetes File

```
---
apiVersion: v1
kind: Service
metadata:
  name: "nginx-example"
  namespace: "mynamespace"
spec:
  type: ClusterIP
  selector:
    app: "nginx"
  ports:
    - name: http
      protocol: TCP
      port: 80
      targetPort: 9376
```

The `NodePortservice` type is similar to a `ClusterIP` service, but it also opens a port on each node. Opening a port allows access to the service from inside the cluster (using the ClusterIP). External users can connect directly to the node on the `NodePort`.

A random port is opened on the local node for each service unless the nodeport property specifies a specific port (see Listing 4-29). The kube-proxy container forwards traffic from the port to the service's cluster IP and then to the pod that's updating the IPtable rules.

***Listing 4-29.*** The NodePort.yaml Kubernetes File

```
---
apiVersion: v1
kind: Service
metadata:
  name: "nginx-example"
  namespace: "mynamespace"
spec:
  type: NodePort
  selector:
    app: "nginx"
  ports:
    - name: http
      protocol: TCP
      port: 80
      targetPort: 9376
      nodeport: 25000
```

The LoadBalancer service type extends the NodePort service type by adding a load balancer in front of all nodes. This means Kubernetes requests a load balancer and registers all the nodes. The load balancer doesn't detect where the pods for a specific service are running. Consequently, the load balancer adds all worker nodes as backend instances. The Load Balancer service type uses the classic load balancers by default. This means there is a classic load balancer in front of all instances listening to your requests. The load balancer routes the requests to the nodes through an exposed port. You can also use the network load balancer instead of the classic load balancer.

The classic load balancer processes the requests one by one when they arrive from the Internet. It then forwards the request to one of the Kubernetes instances on a specific port. When there is a service listening to a specific port, it acts like a second-layer load balancer for the backend pods that handle the requests. Listing 4-30 illustrates this.

***Listing 4-30.*** The LoadBalancer.yaml Kubernetes File

```
---
apiVersion: v1
kind: Service
metadata:
  name: "nginx-example"
  namespace: "mynamespace"
spec:
  type: LoadBalancer
  selector:
    app: "nginx"
  ports:
    - name: http
      port: 80
      targetPort: 9376
```

You can reduce the number of load balancers using the Kubernetes ingress object. An ingress object exposes HTTP and HTTPS routes outside the cluster and routes traffic to your services according to defined traffic rules. Ingress objects use ingress controllers, which fulfill the ingress rules and requests (usually using a load balancer). Using the ingress objects and controllers, you can transition from one load balancing per service to one load balancer per ingress and route to multiple services. Traffic can be routed to the proper service using path-based routing. When using Kubernetes, you have many ingress controller options, for example, Envoy Controllers and NIGNX controllers.

The load balancer picks the proper target group based on the path. The load balancer then forwards the request to one of the Kubernetes instances on the application ports. The service listens at a specific port and balances the requests to one of the pods of the application or service, as demonstrated in Listing 4-31.

***Listing 4-31.*** The Ingress.yaml Kubernetes File

```
---
apiVersion: networking.k8s.io/v1
kind: Ingress
metadata:
  name: "nginx-example"
```

```
      namespace: "mynamespace"
      annotations:
        nginx.ingress.kubernetes.io/rewrite-target: /
spec:
  ingressClassName: nginx-example
  rules:
    - http:
        paths:
          - path: /webapp
            backend:
              service:
                serviceName: webapp
                servicePort: 9376
```

The ExternalName service type is used to connect to a resource outside of the cluster. For example, this could be a database or file system resource that is in the network outside the cluster. The pods that require access to the external resource service require access to the resource to connect to the resource service, which returns the external resource endpoints. This type of service is helpful when you decide to migrate the external resource to the Kubernetes cluster.

When the resource is deployed in the cluster, you can update the service type to ClusterIP. The application can continue to use the same resource endpoint.

The most important property in the YAML manifest is the externalName field, which specifies where the service maps to (see Listing 4-32).

***Listing 4-32.*** The ExternalName.yaml Kubernetes File

```
---
apiVersion: v1
kind: Service
metadata:
  name: "nginx-example"
  namespace: "mynamespace"
spec:
  type: ExternalName
  externalName: mydb.example.com
```

You can apply all your network YAML files in this section to the Kubernetes cluster using the `kubectl` command-line utility or via the `kubernetes.core.k8s` Ansible module:

```
$ kubectl apply -f ClusterIP.yaml
```

Substitute the name of the YAML file with the relevant code in this section: `ClusterIP.yaml`, `NodePort.yaml`, `LoadBalancer.yaml`, `Ingress.yaml`, or `ExternalName.yaml`.

# Scale Your App

Resilience is an important property that you want to achieve from your services or applications. Containers enable you to achieve this property by running multiple replicas of the same pod. Cost optimization involves running the minimum available pods (a minimum of two) when there is low traffic and being able to scale up or down following the traffic needs.

Some business-critical services must be designed with high availability and fault tolerance. Your application must be created to be cloud-ready or, even better, cloud-native in order to unlock the full potential of cloud computing.

Imagine a service scenario created by two pods. If there is a failure of one container or the infrastructure under the container, the service can survive one container failure.

In high availability (HA), the application survives the failure, but the traffic is impacted by poor performance. Even if the service survived failure, it withstands failure.

To be fault tolerant (FT), your application needs two instances in order to operate at its full potential. The service needs to be designed in order to recover at least the minimum amount of pods.

Since Kubernetes version 1.21, `PodDisruptionBudget` (PDB) is a way to limit the number of concurrent disruptions that your application experiences, thus allowing for high availability. Meanwhile, it allows the cluster administrator to manage the nodes of the cluster by manually draining a node or preventing an upgrade from taking too many copies of the application offline. PDB allows you to specify and overprovision in order to guarantee the high availability of your service. PDB is different from auto-scaling because it overprovisions the application on purpose. For full disclosure, if there is a failure in the production infrastructure and you need to have a Disaster Recovery (DR) infrastructure.

Scaling is the best feature of the Kubernetes platform and allows you to match customer demands with resources. You can scale up (increase) your deployment using the `scale` parameter of the `kubectl` command or using the `kubernetes.core.k8s_scale` Ansible module in order to change the number of replicas from the current number to three of your `nginx` deployment:

```
$ kubectl scale deployment nginx --replicas=3
```

The output confirms your `nginx` deployment was successfully scaled:

```
deployment.apps/nginx scaled
```

To check the number of replicas, you need to use the `get` parameter of the `kubectl` command:

```
$ kubectl get deployments
```

As you can see in the output, the `nginx` is now running on three replicas confirmed by the 3/3 in the READY column:

```
NAME                READY   UP-TO-DATE   AVAILABLE   AGE
nginx               3/3     3            3           125m
```

In the same way, you can scale down (reduce) your deployment using the `scale` parameter of the `kubectl` command. You do this in order to change the number or replicas of your deployment from the current number to one of your deployment:

```
$ kubectl scale deployment nginx --replicas=1
```

The output confirms your `nginx` deployment was successfully scaled:

```
deployment.apps/nginx scaled
```

To check the number of replicas, you need to use the `get` parameter of the `kubectl` command:

```
$ kubectl get deployments
```

As you can see in the output, the nginx is now running on one replica confirmed by the 1/1 in the READY column:

```
NAME        READY    UP-TO-DATE    AVAILABLE    AGE
nginx       1/1      1             1            31m
```

With Ansible, you can scale a deployment, ReplicaSet, replication controller, and job using the kubernetes.core.k8s_scale Ansible module. The k8s_scale Ansible module is part of the kubernetes.core collection and it interacts with the Kubernetes API like the kubectl or oc command-line utilities.

For example, let's suppose you want to increase the pod count for your nginx deployment inside the ansible-examples namespace. Figure 4-13 gives a clear overview of the result of the scale-up operation in your Kubernetes cluster dashboard. Note the pod count from two to ten. Consequently, all the other resources are increased as well.

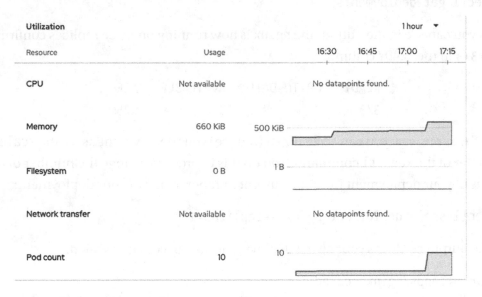

*Figure 4-13.* *Kubernetes pod resource utilization*

The Ansible Playbook shown in Listing 4-33 changes the replica count to ten of the deployment nginx in the namespace ansible-examples. The Ansible Playbook waits for a timeout maximum of 120 seconds (two minutes) for the operation to complete.

***Listing 4-33.*** The scale_up.yml Ansible Playbook File

```
---
- name: k8s scale
  hosts: all
  vars:
    myproject: "ansible-examples"
    mydeployment: "nginx"
    myreplica: 10
    mytimeout: 120
  tasks:
    - name: scale Deployment
      kubernetes.core.k8s_scale:
        api_version: v1
        kind: Deployment
        name: "{{ mydeployment }}"
        namespace: "{{ myproject }}"
        replicas: "{{ myreplica }}"
        wait_timeout: "{{ mytimeout }}"
```

Execute your code in the Ansible Controller machine using the inventory, as shown in Listing 4-34.

***Listing 4-34.*** The Inventory File

```
localhost ansible_connection=local
```

Successful execution using the `ansible-playbook` command output includes the following:

- Managed host: `localhost`

- Play recap status: `ok=2  changed=1`

- Task status:

```
TASK [scale up]
changed: [localhost]
```

The changed status means the deployment changed the replica count from the Kubernetes cluster API. If the replica count already matches the current pod count, you would obtain the ok status.

When the pod count is changed by a big number and the time is not sufficient, you might receive a failed status with the following message on the screen: Resource scaling timed out. This simply means that the Kubernetes cluster is taking longer than expected to execute the operation; it's not a failure message. A more deep analysis of the fatal error message, for example, reveals the operation in progress:

```
"message": "ReplicaSet \"nginx-689b466988\" is progressing."
```

Ansible allows you to scale your replica count when you reach a specific number of pods. The Ansible Playbook shown in Listing 4-35 reduces the pod count from 10 to 5 of the deployment nginx in the namespace ansible-examples.

***Listing 4-35.*** The scale_down.yml Ansible Playbook File

```
---
- name: k8s scale
  hosts: all
  vars:
    myproject: "ansible-examples"
    mydeployment: "nginx"
    curr_replica: 10
    myreplica: 5
  tasks:
    - name: scale down
      kubernetes.core.k8s_scale:
        api_version: v1
        kind: Deployment
        name: "{{ mydeployment }}"
        namespace: "{{ myproject }}"
        current_replicas: "{{ curr_replica }}"
        replicas: "{{ myreplica }}"
```

The outcome is similar to the previous Ansible Playbook, except that Kubernetes is going to reduce the replica count from 10 to 5 pods when the `current_replicas` parameter is reached. This playbook is helpful for performing the scale operation when the threshold is reached.

# Auto-scaling

The next level is to use metrics to automatically scale your cluster.

- Horizontal scaling adds/remove pods of the same size capacity.

- Vertical scaling keeps the same number of pods, but you change the size of capacity.

Kubernetes Cluster Autoscaler (CA) allocates the right amount of resources to guarantee that your application meets the demands of the traffic. The change is performed for your pods in the auto-scale group in your cluster in order to enable Horizontal Pod Autoscaler (HPA) or Vertical Pod Autoscaler (VPA).

Kubernetes Cluster Autoscaler can be deployed, but it requires permission to interact with your cluster. The Kubernetes Cluster Autoscaler needs a service account to interact with the auto-scaling group.

Table 4-1 lists the necessary configuration parameters in your Kubernetes cluster.

***Table 4-1.***  *Auto-Scaling API Endpoints*

| Key | Value |
| --- | --- |
| `k8s.io/cluster-autoscaler/my-cluster` | Owned |
| `k8s.io/cluster-autoscaler/enabled` | True |

You can download the Cluster Autoscaler via the `kubernetes/autoscaler` GitHub repository. The installation process might vary, but it's relatively simple and usually involves a YAML manifest file, according to the Kubernetes release version or cloud provider. For the Amazon Web Services (AWS) provider, you just need to download and install the `cluster-autoscaler-autodiscover.yaml` YAML manifest file.

After a successful download, you can apply it to your Kubernetes cluster:

```
$ kubectl apply -f cluster-autoscaler-autodiscover.yaml
```

You can also tune some parameters in the `kube-system` namespace:

```
$ kubectl -n kube-system edit deployment.apps/cluster-autoscaler
```

Set the appropriate Kubernetes version to the Cluster Autoscaler image tag with the following command. Replace `1.21` with your Kubernetes version value.

```
$ kubectl set image deployment cluster-autoscaler \
  -n kube-system \
  cluster-autoscaler=k8s.gcr.io/autoscaling/cluster-autoscaler:v1.21
```

Pods status pile up in a `Pending` status and they transition to `Ready` when they can handle the traffic.

The Vertical Pod Autoscaler has three working modes:

- `Off`: Recommended only for simulations

- `Initial`: Initialization only

- `Auto`: Performing the action on your cluster

It's always a good practice to start with the `Off` mode and increase the more you have data about your traffic and usage. The wrong combination of horizontal and vertical Autoscaler can be difficult to troubleshoot and not obtain the desired result.

---

**Tip**  The `k8s.gcr.io` registry is frozen and considered an "old" registry since April, 2023; no further images for Kubernetes and related subprojects are pushed in it. The `registry.k8s.io` is the community-owned image onward.

---

# Update Your App

This is the most controversial topic because users expect to access the application or service all the time. Instead, the development team wants to deploy new versions as fast as possible. Sometimes the release process happens several times a day, with continuous delivery. The rolling update is the solution in the Kubernetes world, as shown in Figure 4-14.

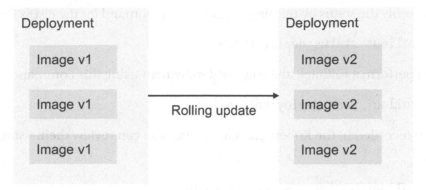

***Figure 4-14.*** *Kubernetes rolling update*

The Kubernetes rolling update enables you to update an application while the users are connected to it. Under the hood, Kubernetes updates pod instances with a new one performing a zero downtime deployment update on nodes with enough available resources. The mechanism behind it is similar to the scale mechanism. Like in application scaling, when a deployment is publicly exposed, the service load balances the traffic on the available pods during the update. Having more than one copy of the pods ensures the high availability of the application while the update is in progress. The rolling update mechanism also offers a rollback option if something goes wrong during the update process; you can simply return to the previous version of the pod anytime.

---

**Note**    Using the latest tag is discouraged because it fails when rolling an update from image:latest to a new image:latest, even when the image tag has been updated. The latest tag is identical from the Kubernetes point of view to the current value.

---

Suppose you are currently running a Nginx web server using the nginx:1.22 (image nginx tag 1.22) in the nginx deployment. The following command changes the image of the nginx deployment to the nginx:1.23 (image nginx tag 1.23). Manually, you can specify the set image parameter for deployment to set a new image or a new image tag to deploy.

```
$ kubectl set image deployments/nginx=nginx:1.23
```

The command tells the Kubernetes nginx deployment to use a different image and initialize a rolling update process to deploy the image nginx with tag 1.23.

You can verify the status by running the following command for the `nginx` deployment:

```
$ kubectl rollout status deployment nginx
```

You can perform a rollback in the `nginx` deployment using this command:

```
$ kubectl rollout undo deployments nginx
```

Logs are recorded in the Kubernetes cluster and you can review them using this command:

```
$ kubectl rollout history deployment nginx
```

You can automate the rolling update of the deployment using the Ansible k8s module and specifying a new deployment YAML manifest file.

The Kubernetes `nginx` deployment manifest file uses the following image definition `image: nginx:1.22`. The updated `nginx` deployment manifest file reports the new image and tag `image: nginx:1.23`.

The full Kubernetes updated YAML deployment manifest file is shown in Listing 4-36.

***Listing 4-36.*** The deployment2.yml Kubernetes Manifest File

```
---
apiVersion: apps/v1
kind: Deployment
metadata:
  name: nginx
  namespace: ansible-examples
spec:
  replicas: 2
  selector:
    matchLabels:
      app: nginx
  template:
    metadata:
      labels:
        app: nginx
    spec:
      containers:
```

```
- name: nginx
  image: nginx:1.23
  imagePullPolicy: Always
  ports:
    - containerPort: 3000
```

You can automate the application of your Kubernetes `deployment.yaml` file using the `deployment.yml`—the same Ansible Playbook that you used in the "Report Deployments in Namespace" section. You just need to change the value of the `src` parameters for the module, specifying the newest deployment manifest filename. Line 16 changes from `src: deployment.yaml` to `src: deployment2.yaml`.

Successful execution using the `ansible-playbook` command output includes the following:

- Managed host: `localhost`

- Play recap status: `ok=3 changed=1`

- Task status:

```
TASK [namespace ansible-examples present]
ok: [localhost]
TASK [deployment present]
changed: [localhost]
```

You received the `changed` statuses for the two tasks, which means the deployment request was sent to the Kubernetes cluster API and the rolling update process is ongoing.

# Assign Resources to Kubernetes K8s Pods

Out of the box, a Kubernetes cluster is configured to allow the usage of as many resources as available in the nodes. This behavior is understandable and potentially allows a Kubernetes service to serve many customers using all the cluster resources. On the other end, excessive resource consumption from a resource leak or an unstable or rogue pod could consume all the resources and not allow other pods to use them. Imagine how dangerous it could be if a program gets out of control and consumes all the available CPU. The root cause may a bad developer, bad code, or simply bad luck—the most important thing is being in control of your Kubernetes clusters. You can apply CPU and memory resource limitations to your Kubernetes cluster to prevent this possible harmful scenario.

Observability is the pillar of every successful service. Predicting trends and obtaining meaningful information from the data is more important than ever.

# Metrics

In order to guarantee a healthy Kubernetes cluster, the Cluster Administrator Team and the Service Reliability Team must acquire some data and perform some predictions. Managing metrics and logs in your Kubernetes cluster is the way to guarantee the business continuity of your application. The OpenTelemetry (`https://opentelemetry.io/`) project is trying to standardize metrics all over the world. The project delivers tools, a Software Development Kit, and an API to be instrumental in the generation, collection, and export of telemetry data (logs, metrics, and traces). They help you analyze the performance and behavior of your software. Prometheus metrics store the data inside Prometheus. PromQL is the query language to search across the data.

Control planes and data planes create metrics in the Prometheus format. You can see them in the RAW format (JSON) via the command-line command:

```
$ kubectrl get -raw /metrics
```

You can represent them in a graphical way from a Grafana dashboard. Performance monitoring, setting alarms, and acquiring insights from the logs and metrics are all of great value for making decisions in your organization.

# CPU Resources

Kubernetes CPU resources are defined in millicores. You can specify any integer value by adding the letter m to the end. Each virtual CPU core has a value of 1000m. If you want to specify 50 percent of a CPU core, you use the value 500m, whereas for two full CPU cores, you use the value 2000m.

Set a limitation on the usage of the CPU for your containers. A container is guaranteed to be allocated as much CPU as it requests when the cluster has enough capacity available. To specify a soft limitation, use the CPU request for a container using the `resources:requests` field in the container resource manifest. To specify a hard limitation, use the CPU limit, also including the `resources:limits`.

The `vish/stress` container image is a famous CPU stress test that allows you to test your cluster, set some limits and requests, and then see the results. You can find it in many Container Registries, such as Docker Hub (`https://hub.docker.com/r/vish/stress`).

Listing 4-37's Playbook executes the CPU stress test `cpu-demo-pod` in the `cpu-example` namespace, setting some CPU limits and requests.

***Listing 4-37.*** The cpu.yml Ansible Playbook File

```
---
- name: k8s cpu
  hosts: all
  vars:
    myproject: "cpu-example"
  tasks:
    - name: namespace present
      kubernetes.core.k8s:
        kind: Namespace
        name: "{{ myproject }}"
        state: present
        api_version: v1
    - name: cpu pod
      kubernetes.core.k8s:
        state: present
        definition:
          apiVersion: v1
          kind: Pod
          metadata:
            name: cpu-demo
            namespace: "{{ myproject }}"
          spec:
            containers:
              - name: cpu-demo-pod
                image: vish/stress
                resources:
```

```
            limits:
                cpu: "1"
            requests:
                cpu: "0.5"
        args:
            - -cpus
            - "2"
```

As usual, you execute the code in your Ansible Controller with the localhost in the inventory, as shown in Listing 4-38.

***Listing 4-38.*** The Inventory File

```
localhost ansible_connection=local
```

You can execute the cpu.yml playbook using the ansible-playbook command-line tool:

```
$ ansible-playbook -i inventory cpu.yml
```

Note that the Kubernetes cluster in this stress test respects the 0.5 CPU request (soft limitation) with a maximum of 1.0 CPU request (hard limitation), despite the process asking for more resources and 2.0 CPUs. You can verify this behavior using the kubect command line and specifying the cpu-example namespace and the cpu-demo pod name:

```
$ kubect get pod cpu-demo --namespace=cpu-example --output=yaml
[...]
    resources:
      limits:
        cpu: "1"
      requests:
        cpu: 500m
[...]
```

You can use the cpu.yaml playbook, changing the pod name to set CPU limits and requests to any pod in your Kubernetes cluster.

# Memory Resources

Kubernetes memory resources are defined in bytes and multiples. A mebibyte value for memory is commonly used, following the two powers 1024 KiB instead of the thousands 1000 kB.

You can limit the memory usage for pods to prevent dangerous memory leaks. The Kubernetes cluster honors the limits and requests specified by the user. To specify a memory request for a container, include the `resources:requests` field in the container resource manifest. To specify a memory limit, specify `resources:limits`.

The `polinux/stress` container image is a famous memory stress test that allows you to test your cluster and set some limits and requests about RAM usage. You can find the image on the most popular Container Registry, for example, Docker Hub (`https://hub. docker.com/r/polinux/stress`).

The playbook in Listing 4-39 executes the memory demo application `memory-demo-pod` in the `mem-example` namespace, thus setting some memory limits and requests.

***Listing 4-39.*** The ram.yml Ansible Playbook File

```
---
- name: k8s memory
  hosts: all
  vars:
    myproject: "mem-example"
  tasks:
    - name: namespace present
      kubernetes.core.k8s:
        kind: Namespace
        name: "{{ myproject }}"
        state: present
        api_version: v1
    - name: memory pod
      kubernetes.core.k8s:
        state: present
        definition:
          apiVersion: v1
```

```
        kind: Pod
        metadata:
          name: memory-demo
          namespace: "{{ myproject }}"
        spec:
          containers:
            - name: memory-demo-pod
              image: polinux/stress
              resources:
                requests:
                  memory: "100Mi"
                limits:
                  memory: "200Mi"
              command: ["stress"]
              args: ["--vm", "1", "--vm-bytes", "500M", "--vm-hang", "1"]
```

As you can see, the pod has set a memory request of 100 MiB and a memory limit of 200 MiB. During execution, the pod attempts to allocate 500 MiB of memory, which is not allowed.

You can verify the successful application of a pod limitation using the following command:

```
$ kubect get pod memory-demo --namespace=mem-example --output=yaml
[...]
    resources:
      limits:
        memory: 200Mi
      requests:
        memory: 100Mi
[...]
```

# Namespace Resources

Assigning resources per pod is very granular but might be daunting. A more durable approach is to define resource needs at a namespace level.

After creating a namespace, you can add a `ResourceQuotas` Kubernetes object that defines the CPU and memory limits and requests for each namespace. A more powerful Kubernetes object is `LimitRange`. Unlike the `ResourceQuotas` Kubernetes object, which looks at the namespace as a whole, a `LimitRange` Kubernetes object applies to an individual pod.

## GPU Resources

At the moment, Kubernetes doesn't provide a native tool to manage the Graphics Processing Units (GPU) resources of the cluster. The GPUs are a critical component in order to build and train deep learning (DL) and machine learning (ML) algorithms and bring artificial intelligence (AI) initiatives to production. At the moment, it's possible to allocate the GPU resources in a static way and only on the worker node of your pod. The Run:AI startup from Tel Aviv, Israel created the Atlas AI Orchestration Platform to pool the available GPU resources, efficiently optimize the scheduling, distribute the workload, and set a prioritization schedule in your cluster. More details are available on the official website at `https://www.run.ai`.

## Configure a Pod to Use a Volume for Storage

A pod is ephemeral; the file system of a pod lives only as long as the pod does. Therefore, when a pod terminates or restarts, any file system changes are lost. Volumes allow you to assign more consistent storage, independent from the pod's lifecycle. This is especially important for stateful applications, data lakes (structured, semi-structured, and unstructured data), and databases.

For example, let's suppose you want to execute a Redis server. Redis is a popular BSD open-source license, in-memory data structure store used as a NoSQL database, cache, and message broker. The Ansible Playbook shown in Listing 4-40 creates the `volume-example` namespace with a pod from the `redis` container image. It also has a `redis-storage` storage that stores the data created in your application.

***Listing 4-40.*** The storage.yml Ansible Playbook File

```
---
- name: k8s volume
  hosts: localhost
  gather_facts: false
  connection: local
  vars:
    myproject: "volume-example"
  tasks:
    - name: create namespace
      kubernetes.core.k8s:
        kind: Namespace
        name: "{{ myproject }}"
        state: present
        api_version: v1

    - name: pod with storage
      kubernetes.core.k8s:
        state: present
        namespace: "{{ myproject }}"
        definition:
          apiVersion: v1
          kind: Pod
          metadata:
            name: redis
          spec:
            containers:
              - name: redis
                image: redis
                volumeMounts:
                  - name: redis-storage
                    mountPath: /data/redis
            volumes:
              - name: redis-storage
                emptyDir: {}
```

The inventory file in Listing 4-41 executes the Ansible Playbook in the current Ansible Controller with a local connection.

***Listing 4-41.*** The Inventory File

```
localhost ansible_connection=local
```

Successful execution using the `ansible-playbook` command output includes the following:

- Managed host: `localhost`
- Play recap status: `ok=2 changed=2`
- Task status:

```
TASK [create volume-example namespace]
changed: [localhost]
TASK [pod with storage]
changed: [localhost]
```

You receive the changed status when the namespace was successfully created in the Kubernetes cluster and the pod was successfully created. Otherwise, you'll receive the ok status when the namespace or the pod was already present in the cluster (Ansible idempotency property). You can verify the successful operation via the command line or via the dashboard, like the one shown in Figure 4-15.

***Figure 4-15.*** *Storage pod in the OpenShift console*

# Apply Multiple YAML Files at Once on Kubernetes

Deploying complex applications or services with Kubernetes requires many objects (namespaces, pods, services, deployments, and so on) in a precise order. Especially with the fast deploying applications, this task might need to be repeated often. If you perform manually or in a deployment pipeline, the following code is beneficial.

Ansible module k8s and the Ansible lookup plugin `fileglob` (both included in all the installations) enable you to list files to match a pattern. The `fileglob` lookup plugin is distributed as `ansible.builtin.fileglob`. You can specify the following parameter:

```
- "./defs/*.yaml"
```

The `*.yaml` command list all the files with the `yaml` extension under the `defs` directory on the target node. Obviously, the `*.yaml` YAML text files are assumed to be Kubernetes object manifest files. Ansible will process them in alphabetical order. Some services require a precise order, and a list of files becomes handy in this use case. The following Ansible list deploys a namespace, a pod, and a service, in this order:

```
- "./defs/namespace.yaml"
- "./defs/pod.yaml"
- "./defs/service.yaml"
```

Ansible processes each manifest file using the k8s module (full name `kubernetes.core.k8s`), which you read about in previous sections. You are going to use the `template` lookup plugin to read the contents of each manifest file. The plugin is very powerful because it enables retrieval of the contents of the file and template with the Jinja2 programming language. Jinja is a web template engine for the Python programming language.

The full Ansible Playbook is shown in Listing 4-42.

*Listing 4-42.* The multiple.yml Ansible Playbook File

```
---
- name: k8s multiple
  hosts: all
  tasks:
    - name: k8s resources
      kubernetes.core.k8s:
```

```
      definition: "{{ lookup('template', '{{ item }}') | from_yaml }}"
   with_fileglob:
   - "./defs/namespace.yaml"
   - "./defs/pod.yaml"
   - "./defs/service.yaml"
```

The following `inventory` file executes the Ansible Playbook in the current Ansible Controller with a local connection. See Listing 4-43.

***Listing 4-43.*** The Inventory File

```
localhost ansible_connection=local
```

The YAML manifest files are already included in the book in the previous sections.

Make sure that the YAML manifest files exist in the target node before launching the code. If a YAML manifest file is not found, Ansible proceeds to the next file without performing the Kubernetes requests. Successful execution using the `ansible-playbook` command output includes the following:

- Managed host: `localhost`

- Play recap status: `ok=2 changed=1`

- Task status:

```
TASK [k8s resources]
changed: [localhost] => (item=./defs/namespace.yaml)
changed: [localhost] => (item=./defs/pod.yaml)
changed: [localhost] => (item=./defs/service.yaml)
```

When the objects are already present in the Kubernetes cluster, you obtain an `ok: [localhost]` status.

# Key Takeaways

In this chapter, you learned how to install a Kubernetes cluster and how to create the objects inside of it. Kubernetes is an amazing technology that enables and simplifies the execution of world-scale applications and services with many features. Under the hood, it uses a lot of objects for services, deployment, and networking. This chapter explored the main components and explained how to deploy your Hello application and service. You can take advantage of the combination of Kubernetes for orchestration with Ansible automation to simplify the software lifecycle of your cluster and the application running inside of it. From installation to the deployment of applications, Ansible is the Swiss Army Knife kit. In the next chapters, you are going to dip your toes into the use cases of software deployment and cluster management, and you'll explore the most popular Kubernetes cloud providers.

# CHAPTER 5

# Ansible for K8s Data Plane

Ansible is a valuable tool for all IT professionals, DevOps personnel, application developers, site reliability engineers (SREs), and IT operations teams worldwide. This chapter explores some exciting use cases for the modern development team. Applying Agile methodologies and continuous integration, as well as quickly deploying applications to customers, is critical in today's fast-paced world. Software development teams in many organizations have embraced the software development lifecycle (SDLC) methodology (see Figure 5-1).

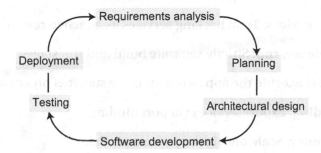

*Figure 5-1.* *The SDLC model*

The following stages apply to the SDLC methodology:

1. **Requirements analysis**: Identify the problems and use cases.

2. **Planning**: Define the costs and resources needed.

3. **Architecture design**: Determine the design specification requirements.

4. **Software development**: Build the software.

© Luca Berton 2023
L. Berton, *Ansible for Kubernetes by Example*, https://doi.org/10.1007/978-1-4842-9285-3_5

5. **Testing**: Test for defects and deficiencies and verify the meeting of the specifications.

6. **Deployment**: Launch the product to the customer and get feedback.

As you can notice, the SDLC methodology is a cyclical process that uses the Agile methodology. For example, in a sprint timeframe, you must release a minimum viable product (MVP) and enrich its features. Other methodologies that can be used are the waterfall model, the spiral model, extreme programming (XP), and so on.

The twelve-factor application[1] is an important methodology for building software-as-a-service (SaaS) applications that can be applied to any programming language with any combination of backing services (database, queue, memory cache, and so on). The twelve factors are based on the experience of development, operation, and scaling of hundreds of thousands of applications on the Heroku platform:

1. **Codebase**: Create one codebase tracked in revision control, many deploys.

2. **Dependencies**: Explicitly declare and isolate dependencies.

3. **Config**: Store the config in the environment.

4. **Backing services**: Treat backing services as attached resources.

5. **Build, release, run**: Strictly separate build and run stages.

6. **Processes**: Execute the app as one or more stateless processes.

7. **Port binding**: Export services via port binding.

8. **Concurrency**: Scale out via the process model.

9. **Disposability**: Maximize robustness with fast startup and graceful shutdown processes.

10. **Dev/prod parity**: Keep development, staging, and production as similar as possible.

11. **Logs**: Treat logs as event streams.

12. **Admin processes**: Run admin/management tasks as one-off processes.

---

[1] https://12factor.net/

The twelve-factor application principles lay the groundwork for developing scalable, resilient, and maintainable applications that can operate on any cloud platform. A good understanding of the twelve-factor application methodology is an indispensable requirement for constructing cloud-native applications that capitalize on the advanced functionalities of Kubernetes.

The Kubernetes data plane is populated by the cloud-native applications that your development team creates to satisfy the needs of your target customers and stakeholders. You can take advantage of Ansible in order to increase the velocity of deploying your software.

# Configuring a Java Microservice

Configuring a Java microservice consists of several steps. First, a cloud-native application follows the architecture design pattern and the structure of a set of loosely coupled, collaborating microservices. This will enable continuous integration and continuous delivery, as well as make the application easier to scale.

Next, you need to create three classes: configuration, application, and main. The configuration class defines the beans and their dependencies, while the application class sets up the application context, and the main class is used to run the application. You should also create a build file to specify how the application should be built and configured (often a Jenkinsfile).

Finally, you need to configure the external services, such as databases and messaging systems, that the microservice might use to store or process data. This involves setting up the appropriate connection parameters and security protocols. Once all of this is done, you can deploy the microservice and start using it.

To configure a Java microservice with Kubernetes, you first need to set up the Kubernetes cluster and create the necessary resources, such as deployments and services. After the cluster is set up, you create the configuration file that defines the application components and their dependencies, such as databases and messaging systems. This configuration file will be used by Kubernetes to create the application pods and services. After this is done, you need to deploy the application to the cluster using a deployment tool such as Kubernetes or Docker. Once the application runs, you need to configure the Kubernetes resources to ensure that the application is secure and performs optimally. Finally, you need to monitor the application to ensure it runs correctly and is not wasting your resources (memory leaks, CPU throttling, and so on).

As an example, evaluate the Quarkus project, a Java framework distributed under the open-source Apache License 2.0 by Red Hat, as a runtime environment. Its popular Kubernetes Native Java stack is perfectly tailored for OpenJDK HotSpot and GraalVM, with a small footprint. It's compatible with the most famous Java libraries and standards. The major benefits are a millisecond startup, low memory utilization, and a smaller container image compared to the traditional JVM execution stack.

A popular framework for creating Java microservices applications is Spring Boot. At the moment of writing this book, Spring Boot is the world's most popular Java framework and is supported by a great community of developers worldwide. The Spring Initializr enables you to start your projects and quickly package then as JARs.

There are multiple options for containerizing a Spring Boot application. Since you are already building a Spring Boot JAR file, you only need to call the plugin directly. The most common build automation tools are Maven and Gradle command-line utilities:

- Apache Maven: `$ mvn spring-boot:build-image`

- Gradle: `$ gradle bootBuildImage`

For the Windows platform, use the `gladlew` and `mvnw` commands instead.

# The Demo Java Web Application

The following example shows how you can build web and RESTful applications using Spring Web integrated on Spring MVC and distribute them as an embedded containers powered by Apache Tomcat. This is a pure Java application that creates a simple RESTful API interface.

The first step is to start with Spring Initializr from the website at `https://start.spring.io/`. Then select either Gradle or Maven and the Java language that you want to use. Then specify in the Dependencies Spring Web. When you're ready, choose the Generate button to download the sample ZIP file archive with the web application already configured. The final selection with Gradle build tool, Java language, and Spring Boot with Spring Web is shown in Figure 5-2.

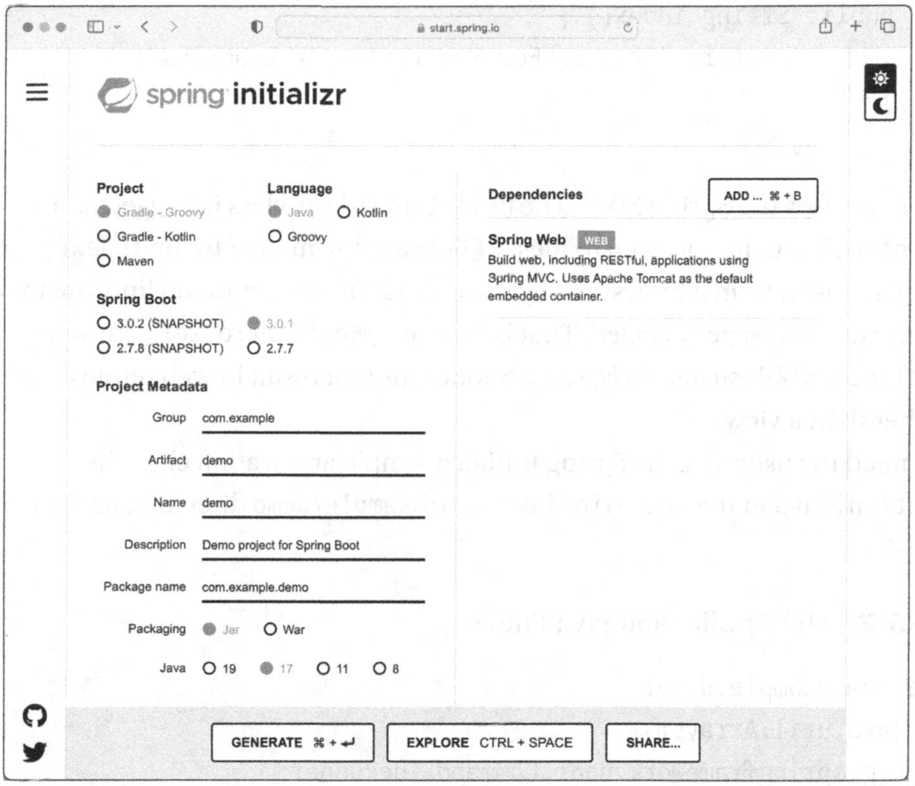

***Figure 5-2.*** *Spring Initializr for the Spring Web project*

The web-generated ZIP file archive contains the boilerplate for your web application using the Spring framework. Once it's downloaded and extracted from the ZIP file archive, remove the sample file called `Application.java` from the `src/main/java/com/example/demo` directory and create the `HelloController.java` file in the same directory with the code shown in Listing 5-1.

***Listing 5-1.*** The HelloController.java File

```
package com.example.demo;

import org.springframework.web.bind.annotation.GetMapping;
import org.springframework.web.bind.annotation.RestController;

@RestController
public class HelloController {
        @GetMapping("/")
```

```
        public String index() {
                return "Ansible For Kubernetes By Examples";
        }
}
```

The code uses the Spring MVC. The HelloController class is flagged as a
@RestController to handle web requests. @GetMapping maps / to the index() method.

When invoked from a browser or by using curl on the command line, the method
returns the text message specified. That is because @RestController combines
@Controller and @ResponseBody, two annotations that result in web requests returning
data rather than a view.

You need to customize the Spring Initializr simple application class file
Application.java in the src/main/java/com/example/demo directory, as shown in
Listing 5-2.

***Listing 5-2.*** The Application.java File

```
package com.example.demo;
import java.util.Arrays;
import org.springframework.boot.CommandLineRunner;
import org.springframework.boot.SpringApplication;
import org.springframework.boot.autoconfigure.SpringBootApplication;
import org.springframework.context.ApplicationContext;
import org.springframework.context.annotation.Bean;

@SpringBootApplication
public class Application {
        public static void main(String[] args) {
                SpringApplication.run(Application.class, args);
        }
        @Bean
        public CommandLineRunner commandLineRunner(ApplicationCont
        ext ctx) {
                return args -> {
                        String[] beanNames = ctx.getBeanDefinitionNames();
                        Arrays.sort(beanNames);
                        for (String beanName : beanNames) {
```

```
        System.out.println(beanName);
    }
};
}
}
```

Note that the main() method, the first method invoked by the Java interpreter, launches the application using Spring Boot. You can run your application using the following command in your favorite terminal:

```
$ gradle bootRun
```

If you use Maven, run the following command in a terminal window (in the complete) directory:

```
$ mvn spring-boot:run
```

The results are shown in Figure 5-3.

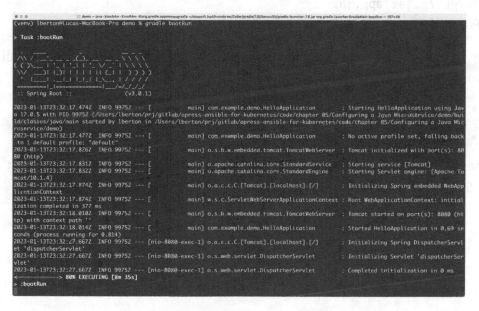

***Figure 5-3.*** *Executing the Gradle build tool*

You can easily test your application running locally in your workstation and accessing your API interface connecting via the localhost:8080 interface, as shown in Figure 5-4.

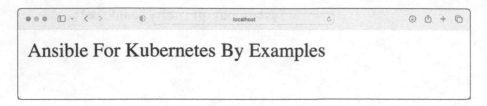

**Figure 5-4.** *Output of the Hello application*

When your application is packaged as a JAR file, you can use the Containerfile shown in Listing 5-3 to deploy as a container image copying all the content of the target/*.jar directory in the image.

**Listing 5-3.** The Containerfile

```
FROM openjdk:21
VOLUME /tmp
ARG JAR_FILE
COPY target/*.jar app.jar
ENTRYPOINT ["java","-jar","/app.jar"]
```

You can now compile your application as a container using the Maven or Gradle build tool:

- Maven: $ mvn spring-boot:build-image

- Gradle: $ gradle bootBuildImage

The output of the container build process looks similar to the output shown in Figure 5-5 provided by the Gradle build tool.

```
[creator]        spring-boot-loader (269.4 KB)
[creator]        snapshot-dependencies (0.0 B)
[creator]        application (31.1 KB)
[creator]    Launch Helper: Reusing cached layer
[creator]    Spring Cloud Bindings 1.11.0: Reusing cached layer
[creator]    Web Application Type: Reusing cached layer
[creator]    4 application slices
[creator]    Image labels:
[creator]        org.springframework.boot.version
[creator]    ===> EXPORTING
[creator]    Reusing layer 'paketo-buildpacks/ca-certificates:helper'
[creator]    Reusing layer 'paketo-buildpacks/bellsoft-liberica:helper'
[creator]    Reusing layer 'paketo-buildpacks/bellsoft-liberica:java-security-properties'
[creator]    Reusing layer 'paketo-buildpacks/bellsoft-liberica:jre'
[creator]    Reusing layer 'paketo-buildpacks/executable-jar:classpath'
[creator]    Reusing layer 'paketo-buildpacks/spring-boot:helper'
[creator]    Reusing layer 'paketo-buildpacks/spring-boot:spring-cloud-bindings'
[creator]    Reusing layer 'paketo-buildpacks/spring-boot:web-application-type'
[creator]    Reusing layer 'launch.sbom'
[creator]    Reusing 5/5 app layer(s)
[creator]    Reusing layer 'launcher'
[creator]    Reusing layer 'config'
[creator]    Reusing layer 'process-types'
[creator]    Adding label 'io.buildpacks.lifecycle.metadata'
[creator]    Adding label 'io.buildpacks.build.metadata'
[creator]    Adding label 'io.buildpacks.project.metadata'
[creator]    Adding label 'org.springframework.boot.version'
[creator]    Setting default process type 'web'
[creator]    Saving docker.io/library/demo:0.0.1-SNAPSHOT...
[creator]    *** Images (5994fbaab413):
[creator]        docker.io/library/demo:0.0.1-SNAPSHOT
[creator]    Reusing cache layer 'paketo-buildpacks/syft:syft'
[creator]    Reusing cache layer 'cache.sbom'

Successfully built image 'docker.io/library/demo:0.0.1-SNAPSHOT'

BUILD SUCCESSFUL in 22s
5 actionable tasks: 1 executed, 4 up-to-date
```

***Figure 5-5.*** *Output of the Hello application*

At the end of the process, the demo image with 0.0.1-SNAPSHOT tag is available in your workstation. You can analyze the resulting image with Docker Desktop, as shown in Figure 5-6.

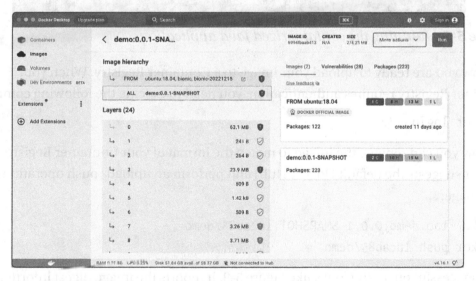

***Figure 5-6.*** *Hello container with your application*

Once the container image is built, you can execute locally using the Docker command (similar to the command for Podman):

```
$ docker run --name=demo demo:0.0.1-SNAPSHOT
```

The execution starts the container with the JVM and the Tomcat web server inside and produces the output shown in Figure 5-7.

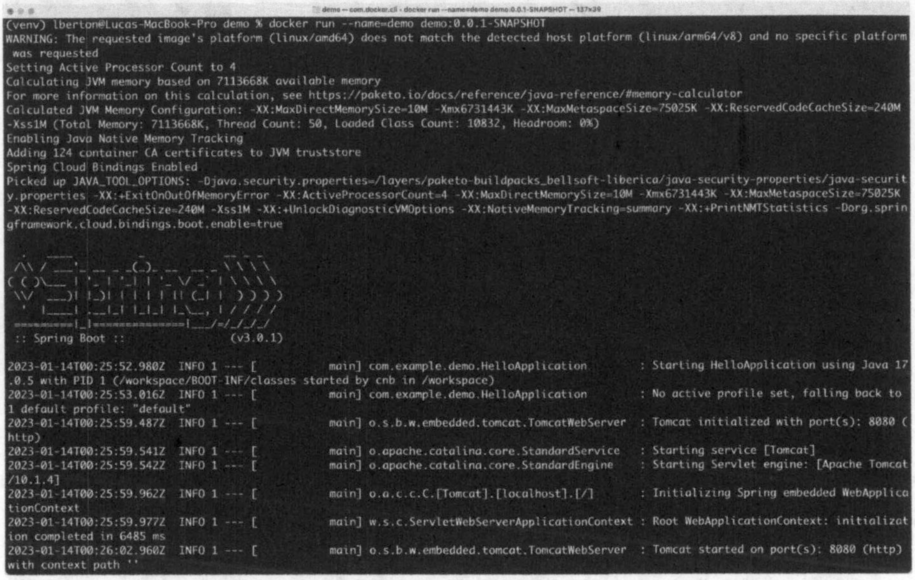

***Figure 5-7.*** *Running the containerized Java application*

Now you are ready to upload your image to a Container Registry. When your Container Registry requires authentication, you need to execute the following command:

```
$ docker login
```

Now you can rename the image to match the format of your Container Registry (Docker suggests the default Docker Hub) and perform an upload (push operation) of your image:

```
$ docker tag demo:0.0.1-SNAPSHOT lucab85/demo
$ docker push lucab85/demo
```

A successful operation looks like Figure 5-8. It reports the image digest information on the screen:

```
latest: digest: sha256:2b07da21327fc17f9a93f789d4dd1e0b859bab126c91b5b044
af97356772e816 size: 5325
```

```
(venv) lberton@Lucas-MacBook-Pro demo % docker login
Authenticating with existing credentials...
Login Succeeded

Logging in with your password grants your terminal complete access to your account.
For better security, log in with a limited-privilege personal access token. Learn more at https://docs.docker.com/go/access-tokens/
(venv) lberton@Lucas-MacBook-Pro demo % docker tag demo:0.0.1-SNAPSHOT lucab85/demo
(venv) lberton@Lucas-MacBook-Pro demo % docker push lucab85/demo
Using default tag: latest
The push refers to repository [docker.io/lucab85/demo]
1dc94a70dbaa: Pushed
7228e7d75f85: Pushed
b0ab7e0bbf67: Pushed
5f70bf18a086: Pushed
340afaf8b9b1: Pushed
c228c1bcc9a8: Pushed
536c412c7173: Pushing [===========================>    ] 17.33MB/18.35MB
f57c19ae0606: Pushed
fcc507beb4cc: Pushed
30a03cb7ff3f: Pushed
7039cb19c7da: Pushed
7fbc97c38fad: Pushed
67e5f2974521: Pushing [=========>                      ] 29.92MB/157.4MB
ec0381c8f321: Pushed
e6aa48c81965: Pushed
9651e85005c8: Pushed
308b4b02dd9a: Pushed
be948c2f3324: Pushed
d88b70389417: Pushed
0e974cc1d198: Pushing [=========================>      ] 25.91MB
dc622bd7e11b: Pushed
16dcc2eadf63: Pushed
101b05ef38e1: Pushing [===========================>    ] 33.02MB/63.15MB
```

***Figure 5-8.*** *Upload the container image to Container Registry*

After successfully uploading to the Container Registry, you can execute a Kubernetes deployment of this application. The Kubernetes deployment shown in Listing 5-4 is needed.

***Listing 5-4.*** The hello-deployment.yaml Manifest

```
apiVersion: apps/v1
kind: Deployment
metadata:
  name: ansiblebyexamples
spec:
  replicas: 2
  selector:
    matchLabels:
      app: ansiblebyexamples
  template:
    metadata:
      labels:
        app: ansiblebyexamples
    spec:
      containers:
```

```
    - name: ansiblebyexamples
      image: demo:0.0.1-SNAPSHOT
      ports:
        - containerPort: 8080
      imagePullPolicy: Always
```

***Listing 5-5.*** The hello-service.yaml Manifest

```
apiVersion: v1
kind: Service
metadata:
  name: ansiblebyexamples
spec:
  selector:
    app: ansiblebyexamples
  ports:
    - port: 80
      targetPort: 8080
  type: LoadBalancer
```

You can execute the Kubernetes YAML manifest file manually via the Ansible Playbook.

```
$ kubectl apply -f hello-deployment.yaml
```

# Stateless: Deploying PHP Guestbook Application with Redis

Every stateless application is perfectly scalable in Kubernetes. Stateless means that an instance can be stopped, restarted, or duplicated at any time without any data loss or inconsistent behavior. You can use the Redis database to store your data structure. Redis is a well-known key-value database, with in-memory cache and a message broker. The data durability is optional. Figure 5-9 illustrates the architecture of the Guestbook application you'll be deploying using Redis.

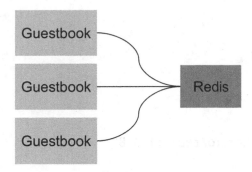

***Figure 5-9.***  *Architecture of the Guestbook application*

To deploy a PHP Guestbook application with Redis, you first need to set up a Redis database server to store the application data. After this is done, you can deploy three replicas of the frontend Guestbook application in the Kubernetes cluster. Once the application has been deployed, it can be tested and used by your users.

First of all, you need a Redis leader deployment to store your data using the latest version (7.0.8) of the official redis image from the Docker Hub Container Registry. This should run with one replica and listen on the network port 6379.

***Listing 5-6.***  The redis-deployment.yaml Manifest File

```
apiVersion: apps/v1
kind: Deployment
metadata:
  name: redis-db
  labels:
    app: redis
    role: db
    tier: backend
spec:
  replicas: 1
  selector:
    matchLabels:
      app: redis
  template:
    metadata:
      labels:
```

```
      app: redis
      role: db
      tier: backend
  spec:
    containers:
      - name: leader
        image: "docker.io/redis:7.0.8"
        resources:
          requests:
            cpu: 100m
            memory: 100Mi
        ports:
          - containerPort: 6379
```

The Redis Service YAML file is shown in Listing 5-7.

***Listing 5-7.*** The redis-service.yaml Manifest File

```
apiVersion: v1
kind: Service
metadata:
  name: redis-db
  labels:
    app: redis
    role: db
    tier: backend
spec:
  ports:
    - port: 6379
      targetPort: 6379
  selector:
    app: redis
    role: db
    tier: backend
```

You also need to create a configuration file that defines the application components and their dependencies, such as databases and messaging systems. Kubernetes will use this configuration file to create the application pods and services. Once the cluster is set up and the configuration file is created, you can deploy the application using a deployment tool such as Kubernetes or Docker. See Listing 5-8.

***Listing 5-8.*** The frontend-deployment.yaml Manifest File

```yaml
apiVersion: apps/v1
kind: Deployment
metadata:
  name: frontend
spec:
  replicas: 3
  selector:
    matchLabels:
      app: guestbook
      tier: frontend
  template:
    metadata:
      labels:
        app: guestbook
        tier: frontend
    spec:
      containers:
        - name: php-redis
          image: gcr.io/google_samples/gb-frontend:v5
          env:
            - name: GET_HOSTS_FROM
              value: "dns"
          resources:
            requests:
              cpu: 100m
              memory: 100Mi
          ports:
            - containerPort: 80
```

The Guestbook application service looks like Listing 5-9.

***Listing 5-9.*** The frontend-service.yaml Manifest File

```
apiVersion: v1
kind: Service
metadata:
  name: frontend
  labels:
    app: guestbook
    tier: frontend
spec:
  type: LoadBalancer
  ports:
    - port: 80
  selector:
    app: guestbook
    tier: frontend
```

Once the application has been deployed, you can test and use it. Finally, you need to configure the Kubernetes resources to ensure that the application is secure and performs optimally. One improvement to the architecture is to use some Redis "followers" nodes between the Redis database and the frontend. With the "followers" improvement, you can implement the high availability for the single replica Redis database (also called the "leader").

You can easily deploy your stateless Guestbook application using the "Apply Multiple YAML Files at Once on Kubernetes" Ansible Playbook; for more details, see Chapter 4.

# Kustomize: Do More with Less

Kustomize is a fantastic tool for generating Kubernetes YAML resources. It saves time creating usable resource artifacts for your use cases. It creates Kubernetes objects from a special "kustomization" file. It provides a way to define multiple objects in a single manifest file, as well as options to customize and override settings on existing objects. Kustomize also allows you to leverage the power of templating and variables, making it easier to customize and deploy objects to Kubernetes clusters. Kustomize can be used to manage multiple environments, create complex deployments, and manage resources across multiple namespaces. You are going to use Kustomize in the following section. The Kustomize tool has been supported since Kubernetes version 1.14 (kustomize build flow version 2.0.3).

You can view the resources found in a directory containing a kustomization file by running the following command:

```
$ kubectl kustomize <directory>
```

To apply the resources in your Kubernetes cluster, use the `--kustomize` or `-k` parameter of the `kubectl` command:

```
$ kubectl apply –kustomize <directory>
```

Ansible supports the `kubernetes.core.kustomize` lookup plugin to execute the Kustomization directory. The Ansible Playbook shown in Listing 5-10 executes the customization in the `kustomization` directory, in the namespace specified in the `myproject` variable.

***Listing 5-10.*** The kustomization.yml File

```
---
- name: k8s ns
  hosts: all
  vars:
    myproject: "ansible-examples"
    kustomize_dir: "kustomization"
  tasks:
    - name: namespace {{ myproject }} present
      kubernetes.core.k8s:
        api_version: v1
        kind: Namespace
        name: "{{ myproject }}"
        state: present
    - name: create kubernetes resource using lookup plugin
      kubernetes.core.k8s:
        namespace: "{{ myproject }}"
        definition: "{{ lookup('kubernetes.core.kustomize',
        dir=kustomize_dir) }}"
```

185

# Stateful: Deploying WordPress and MySQL with Persistent Volumes

A stateful application requires the persistence of data, contrary to stateless, which doesn't. A simple example is the common application based on the web framework WordPress deployed on top of a MySQL database. To deploy WordPress and MySQL with Kubernetes, you need persistent volumes to store the database and the application data. First, you have to create a Kubernetes cluster and configure the necessary resources. This will enable you to deploy WordPress and MySQL as two separate services. You need a PersistentVolume to store data with PersistentVolumeClaims declared at the deployment level. Figure 5-10 illustrates this architecture.

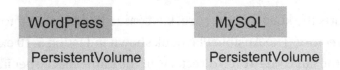

***Figure 5-10.*** *Architecture of WordPress with the MySQL application*

Next, you create the configuration file for each service. They define the components of the application and their dependencies, such as databases and messaging systems. Once the configuration files are created, you can deploy the application to Kubernetes using a customization file (see Listing 5-11) that links to the Deployment, Service, and PersistentVolume Kubernetes resources needed by your application (see Listings 5-12 and 5-13).

***Listing 5-11.*** The kustomization.yaml File

```
secretGenerator:
  - name: mysql-pass
    literals:
      - password=YOUR_PASSWORD
resources:
  - mysql.yaml
  - wordpress.yaml
```

***Listing 5-12.***  The mysql.yaml File

```
apiVersion: v1
kind: Service
metadata:
  name: wordpress-mysql
  labels:
    app: wordpress
spec:
  ports:
    - port: 3306
  selector:
    app: wordpress
    tier: mysql
  clusterIP: None
---
apiVersion: v1
kind: PersistentVolumeClaim
metadata:
  name: mysql-pv-claim
  labels:
    app: wordpress
spec:
  accessModes:
    - ReadWriteOnce
  resources:
    requests:
      storage: 20Gi
---
apiVersion: apps/v1
kind: Deployment
metadata:
  name: wordpress-mysql
  labels:
    app: wordpress
```

```yaml
spec:
  selector:
    matchLabels:
      app: wordpress
      tier: mysql
  strategy:
    type: Recreate
  template:
    metadata:
      labels:
        app: wordpress
        tier: mysql
    spec:
      containers:
        - image: mysql:5.7.41
          name: mysql
          env:
            - name: MYSQL_ROOT_PASSWORD
              valueFrom:
                secretKeyRef:
                  name: mysql-pass
                  key: password
          ports:
            - containerPort: 3306
              name: mysql
          volumeMounts:
            - name: mysql-persistent-storage
              mountPath: /var/lib/mysql
      volumes:
        - name: mysql-persistent-storage
          persistentVolumeClaim:
            claimName: mysql-pv-claim
```

***Listing 5-13.*** The wordpress.yaml File

```
apiVersion: v1
kind: Service
metadata:
  name: wordpress
  labels:
    app: wordpress
spec:
  ports:
    - port: 80
  selector:
    app: wordpress
    tier: frontend
  type: LoadBalancer
---
apiVersion: v1
kind: PersistentVolumeClaim
metadata:
  name: wp-pv-claim
  labels:
    app: wordpress
spec:
  accessModes:
    - ReadWriteOnce
  resources:
    requests:
      storage: 20Gi
---
apiVersion: apps/v1
kind: Deployment
metadata:
  name: wordpress
  labels:
    app: wordpress
```

```
spec:
  selector:
    matchLabels:
      app: wordpress
      tier: frontend
  strategy:
    type: Recreate
  template:
    metadata:
      labels:
        app: wordpress
        tier: frontend
    spec:
      containers:
        - image: wordpress:6.1.1-apache
          name: wordpress
          env:
            - name: WORDPRESS_DB_HOST
              value: wordpress-mysql
            - name: WORDPRESS_DB_PASSWORD
              valueFrom:
                secretKeyRef:
                  name: mysql-pass
                  key: password
          ports:
            - containerPort: 80
              name: wordpress
          volumeMounts:
            - name: wordpress-persistent-storage
              mountPath: /var/www/html
      volumes:
        - name: wordpress-persistent-storage
          persistentVolumeClaim:
            claimName: wp-pv-claim
```

You can apply the resources in your Kubernetes cluster by manually executing this command:

```
$ kubectl apply -k ./
```

Or you can automate with Ansible using the `kubernetes.core.kustomize` lookup plugin to execute the Kustomization directory described in the previous section.

Kubernetes operators often manage complex stateful applications on Kubernetes. Writing an operator is often a full-fledged software project, using low-level APIs and writing boilerplate code. The Operator SDK uses the Kubernetes controller-runtime library to make writing operators easier by providing a high-level API, tools for scaffolding and code generation, and extensions for use cases. The Operator SDK can generate the boilerplate for an Ansible Operator but also for Golang and Helm.

# Security Namespace (Pod Security Admission)

Enforcing proper Kubernetes security can save you time and protect your organization from unexpected behavior. The best practice of pod security is useful to apply pod security standards (pod security policy) at the namespace level. This can be a simple warning message, or you can't deny the deployment when the containers don't meet the acceptance criteria. You implement the policy at the namespace level. This policy defines the security rules for the namespace, including who can access what resources and the types of traffic that are allowed. Previously, the Pod Security Policy was configured to ensure that the security rules are enforced for the pods within the namespace. `PodSecurityPolicy` was previously deprecated in Kubernetes version 1.21 and removed from Kubernetes in version 1.25. Kubernetes implements role-based access control (RBAC). You can configure RBAC to ensure that only authorized users can access the resources in the namespace. Once this is done, the Pod Security Standards will be applied at the Namespace Level. Since Kubernetes version 1.23, Pod Security Admission (PSA) has been enabled in Kubernetes per cluster and namespace lever by default. It enables you to use these built-in Pod Security Standards modes:

- `enforce (baseline)`
- `audit (restricted)`
- `warn (restricted)`

Using Kubernetes labels of the built-in Pod Security Admission, it is possible to enable pod security standards at the namespace level. You can use the following label to set the pod security standard policy:

```
pod-security.kubernetes.io/<MODE>: <LEVEL>
```

- MODE sets the pod security standard modes: enforce, audit, warn
- LEVEL sets the pod security standard levels: privileged, baseline, or restricted

The following command enables the "warn" pod security standard on the baseline each time you try to retrieve the "latest" tag:

```
$ kubectl label --overwrite ns example pod-security.kubernetes.io/
warn=baseline pod-security.kubernetes.io/warn-version=latest
```

From now on, whenever you try to retrieve a "latest" tag for a pod, you will receive a warning on output that warns you about the policy violation:

```
violate PodSecurity "restricted:latest"
```

The warning message reminds you about the best practices of Kubernetes to specify a specific tag instead of using the "latest" tag.

# Security Pod Resources (AppArmor)

AppArmor is a Linux security tool that works by granting access first rather than applying restrictions. Sometimes AppArmor is confused with SELinux; the main differences are listed in Table 5-1.

**Table 5-1.** *AppArmor vs SELinux*

| Feature | AppArmor | SELinux |
|---|---|---|
| Access control | Security profiles based on paths | Security policies based on file labels |
| Linux distributions | Mainly used on SUSE and Ubuntu | Primarily used on RHEL/Fedora systems |
| Level of control | Medium | High |

Kubernetes has supported AppArmor since version 1.4. At the moment of writing this book, Kubernetes' annotation is the way to use the feature. When promoted to General Availability (GA), each annotation will be a Kubernetes Object field. AppArmor is used to restrict a container's access to resources; you need to create an AppArmor profile for the container. This profile will define the security rules for the containers, such as which files and directories it can access, which system calls it can make, and which other containers or processes it can interact with. Additionally, you need to configure the container runtime to ensure that the AppArmor profile is applied when the container is started. Kubernetes-supported container runtimes that support AppArmor technology are Docker, CRI-O, and containerd. Once this is done, the container will be restricted to the access rules defined in the AppArmor profile.

AppArmor profiles are specified per pod by adding the following annotation:

```
container.apparmor.security.beta.kubernetes.io/<container_name>:
<profile_ref>
```

You can deploy an application protected with AppArmor using the `kubectl` or Ansible `kubernetes.core.k8s` module. There is no native Kubernetes way to load AppArmor profiles onto nodes. However, you can use Ansible as an initialization script to enable it.

# Security Pod Syscalls (seccomp)

A system call, or *syscall*, is a direct request from your application to the operating system where it is executed. The typical use case is accessing hardware resources, launching threads, communicating with other processes, and interacting with internal kernel services.

You can use the Linux secure computing mode, called `seccomp`, to enable a "secure" state one-way transition, where it is possible to use only `exit`, `sigreturn`, `read`, and `write` on an already-open file descriptor system call. Of course, you can restrict the syscalls of the container creating a seccomp profile for the container. A profile defines a sandbox of the privileges of a process, restricting the call from the userspace to the kernel. This profile will define the syscalls that the container can make, as well as the parameters and arguments that can be used when making the syscalls.

Additionally, you need to configure the container runtime at bootstrap to ensure that the seccomp profile is applied. Once you do this, the container will be restricted to the syscalls defined in the seccomp profile. Seccomp requires at least Linux kernel 2.6 and Kubernetes version 1.19. The SCMP_ACT_LOG seccomp profile logs all system calls.

The snippet of a Kubernetes spec YAML manifest shown in Listing 5-14 enables the seccomp profile audit.json file defined in the localhost node.

***Listing 5-14.*** The seccomp.yaml Manifest File

```
[...]
  securityContext:
    seccompProfile:
      type: localhost
      localhostProfile: profiles/audit.json
[...]
```

***Listing 5-15.*** The audit.json seccomp Profile File

```
{
    "defaultAction": "SCMP_ACT_LOG"
}
```

# Ansible Dynamic Inventory

Ansible Dynamic Inventory enables you to generate Ansible Inventories automatically. The information is read from external sources such as cloud providers, CMDBs, and inventory management systems. This allows users to deploy infrastructure and applications dynamically and automate them quickly. The inventory is stored in a YAML file, which is then used by Ansible to determine which hosts to target for tasks. Ansible Dynamic Inventory can be used for several different use cases, such as dynamic scaling, provisioning, and application deployment.

---

**Tip**    Ansible can also use multiple inventory sources at the same time. You can mix and match dynamic and statically managed inventory sources in the same Ansible run.

---

Additionally, Ansible Dynamic Inventory can be used to manage multiple environments and ensure that the right resources are allocated for each environment. See Listing 5-16.

***Listing 5-16.*** The ansible.cfg File

```
[inventory]
enable_plugins = kubernetes.core.k8s
```

The Ansible plugin kubernetes.core.k8s searches for all files with the .k8s.yml or .k8s.yaml suffixes in the current working directory, as demonstrated in Listing 5-17.

***Listing 5-17.*** The inventory.k8s.yml File

```
plugin: kubernetes.core.k8s
connections:
 - namespaces:
    - ansible-examples
```

You can list all the containers in the namespace ansible-examples using the inventory.k8s.yml file and the ansible-inventory command:

```
$ ansible-inventory -i inventory.k8s.yml --list
```

If the location is given to the -i parameter in Ansible, it's a directory (or as so configured in the ansible.cfg file).

The output of the ansible-inventory command displays a JSON file with all the pods in the specified namespace (or projects when run in OpenShift).

- Namespace: ansible-examples

- list view

---

```
            "nginx-689b466988-4z9qq_nginx": {
[...]
                "ansible_kubectl_namespace": "ansible examples",
                "ansible_kubectl_pod": "nginx-689b466988-4z9qq",
                "container_image": "nginx",
                "container_name": "nginx",
                "container_ready": false,
                "container_state": "Waiting",
```

```
            "labels": {
                "app": "nginx",
                "pod-template-hash": "689b466988"
            },
            "object_type": "pod",
            "pod_host_ip": "192.168.50.15",
            "pod_ip": "10.131.0.3",
            "pod_name": null,
            "pod_node_name": "compute-2",
            "pod_phase": "Running",
            "pod_resource_version": "15542143",
            "pod_uid": "2994bacc-28b0-47fa-b44e-4b28f9ea7d5b"
[...]
```

The graph view is helpful for displaying in a graph style the pod in the selected namespaces (or projects when in OpenShift):

```
$ ansible-inventory -i inventory.k8s.yml --graph
```

The output of the execution of the ansible-inventory command with the graph parameter displays a tree style output with all the pods in the specified namespace (or projects when run in OpenShift).

- Namespace: ansible-examples

- graph view

```
@all:
  |--@console-openshift-ansiblepilot-com_6443:
  |  |--@namespace_ansible-examples:
  |  |  |--@namespace_ansible-examples_pods:
  |  |  |  |--nginx-689b466988-4z9qq_nginx
  |  |  |  |--nginx-689b466988-55jnd_nginx
  |  |  |  |--nginx_nginx
  |  |  |--@namespace_ansible-examples_services:
  |  |  |  |--nginx-service
[...]
```

You can execute an Ansible Playbook, for example for remediation in the inventory, that's dynamically generated by Ansible Dynamic Inventory.

The easiest Ansible Playbook is `ping.yml` (see Listing 5-18), which tests the connection between the Ansible controller and the target nodes.

***Listing 5-18.*** The ping.yml File

```
---
- name: test
  hosts: all
  gather_facts: false
  tasks:
    - name: test connection
      ansible.builtin.ping:
```

You can execute the code using the `ansible-playbook` command combined with the Ansible Dynamic Inventory configuration file for the `ansible-examples` namespace:

```
$ ansible-playbook -i inventory.k8s.yml ping.yml
```

Successful execution using the `ansible-playbook` command output includes the following:

- Play recap status: `ok=1 changed=0`

- Task status:

```
TASK [test connection]
ok: [nginx-689b466988-4z9qq_nginx]
ok: [nginx-689b466988-55jnd_nginx]
```

You might incur the "`Failed to create temporary directory`" error message when you try to connect to the remote pods. It is a permission error: "`In some cases, you may have been able to authenticate and did not have permissions on the target directory`". The message is trying to point out a possible solution: `Consider changing the remote tmp path in ansible.cfg to a path rooted in "/tmp"`. The root cause could be in the authentication phase or could be a lack of permission to create temporary files by the connection user. See Figure 5-11.

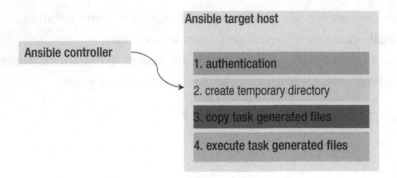

*Figure 5-11.* *Architecture of the Ansible connection*

The default behavior for Ansible to connect to any target hosts is to execute the authentication phase and then copy a file generated by every single task of your Ansible Playbook. Ansible connects to remote servers and executes code with the same username. You can specify the connection username with the `ansible_user` variable on the inventory. You can change the running user by specifying `remote_user` in the playbook or globally in the `ansible.cfg` file. After a successful connection, Ansible tries to create a temporary directory in the home of the user of the connection, where it copies the task files if they doesn't already exist. If Ansible is unable to create the temporary directory, if that user does not have a home directory, or if their home directory permissions do not allow them to write access, you can customize the path of the temporary directory via the `ansible.cfg` file. For example, you can use the following path in the `/tmp` directory:

```
remote_tmp     = /tmp/.ansible-${USER}/tmp
```

Ansible pipelining executes the Ansible modules on the target directly without the prior file transfer, consequently reducing the network operations. Another pleasant side-effect is the increase in performance when enabled. By default, Ansible pipelining is disabled. You can enable it using the `ANSIBLE_PIPELINING=True` environment variable or setting the `pipelining=true` key in the `[connection]` and `[defaults]` sections of the `ansible.cfg` file.

# Key Takeaways

You can develop the application of tomorrow by applying Agile methodologies. Similarly, you can deploy modern cloud-native applications in the Kubernetes cluster to obtain a faster workflow and more reliable applications or services for your customers. You can also mix and match stateless and stateful applications and apply security policies to the pod as desired. Some applications require a simple microservice architecture, whereas others require a more complex design. Using Kubernetes, you can focus on the high availability, scale your workflow, and increase the velocity with Ansible.

# CHAPTER 6

# Ansible for K8s Management

Ansible for Kubernetes helps organizations reduce operational costs by automating many manual processes associated with deploying and managing large-scale distributed systems like those used in modern production environments. This includes tasks such as provisioning nodes, configuring network settings, and setting up storage volumes for persistent data stores across multiple nodes in a cluster environment.

All this can be accomplished quickly using Ansible's easy-to-use playbooks written in the YAML format. Overall, Ansible provides great advantages when implementing Kubernetes in an organization's IT architecture, due to its ease of use combined with advanced capabilities. It allows developers and system administrators alike to create complex configurations quickly while ensuring consistency across different infrastructures regardless of whether they are located locally or remotely hosted in public clouds providers such Amazon Web Services (AWS) EC2 instances or other cloud providers running Linux operating system distributions like Ubuntu LTS Server Edition. Modern cloud-native applications embrace the workflow shown in Figure 6-1.

***Figure 6-1.*** *The DEV, SIT, UAT, and PROD workflow*

- DEV: Development (software development team)
- SIT: System Integration Test (software developer and QA engineer)
- UAT: User Acceptance Test (selected clients)
- PROD: Production (public users)

© Luca Berton 2023
L. Berton, *Ansible for Kubernetes by Example*, https://doi.org/10.1007/978-1-4842-9285-3_6

Organizations embrace the DEV, SIT, UAT, and PROD workflow in order to take advantage of automating tasks using the Ansible technology and to have a consistent environment at every stage of the execution and save time.

Managing multiple Kubernetes clusters to create the four environments needed for DEV, SIT, UAT, and PROD workflow can be a daunting process that burns IT resources in your IT department. Automating the process with Ansible enables you to have a consistent environment between the four stages and focus on the distribution of cloud-native applications to your target audience and stakeholders.

# The Helm Package Manager

The Helm Package Manager, originally created by Microsoft and written in the GO language, is available as an open-source project and has become the most convenient way to package and distribute applications for Kubernetes. A package includes all the necessary objects for a Kubernetes application to run. Helm is a graduate project of the Cloud Native Computing Foundation.

Helm is constantly used for installing, upgrading, and publishing packages in the Kubernetes cluster. The major advantages of the Helm software are as follows:

- Create standard and reusable templates

- Eliminate deploy errors

You can easily search for all the available Helm packages using the directory called Artifact Hub https://artifactshub.io/ (there are 9161 results at the moment of writing this book). Helm retrieves software from packages called "charts" in Helm slang. The packages are distributed in repositories.

To use Helm, you must install the helm command-line tool in your workstation. You can find that tool on the official website https://helm.sh/. Helm is available for most modern operating systems: Linux (i386, amd64, arm, arm64,ppc64le, and s390x), macOS (Intel and Apple Silicon), and Windows (amd64). It's also possible to install Helm using the most common package managers: Homebrew, Chocolatey, Scoop, GoFish, and Snap.

To report the Helm packages deployed inside the cluster, you can use the manual helm list command. This command displays all the Helm packages installed in the current namespace, as well as their versions and other information.

You can also use the `helm status` command to get detailed information about a specific package, such as its deployed version, release history, and a list of resources that were created when the package was deployed.

Additionally, you can use the `helm history` command to view a list of the releases that were installed or deleted in the current namespace. Additionally, the `helm search` command can be used to search for packages in the repositories that are currently configured.

The `kubernetes.core` Ansible collection enables you to automate the execution of tasks in Helm and obtain the same information in the Ansible way. The following modules are specific to Helm-related tasks:

- `helm`: Add, update, and delete Kubernetes packages using the package manager Helm

- `helm_info`: Obtain information about a Helm package deployed into the Kubernetes cluster

- `helm_plugin`: Add, update, and delete Helm plugins

- `helm_plugin_info`: Obtain information about your Helm plugins

- `helm_repository`: Add, update and delete Helm repositories

- `helm_template`: Render Helm chart templates

In the following section, you are going to apply the Ansible modules to some practical examples.

Ansible Helm modules rely on the `helm` command-line utility that should be installed in your system. When Ansible is unable to use the `helm` utility, the execution of the code terminates with the following fatal runtime error:

```
"msg": "Failure when executing Helm command. Exited 1
```

In most cases, it's simply necessary to install the `helm` utility. When some dependencies are missing, the message on the screen shows the exact library missing:

```
/bin/helm\", line 24, in <module>\n    import glib\nModuleNotFoundError: No
module named 'glib'\n"
```

The message points out that the `glib` Python library is missing on your system. You could install the following:

```
$ pip install glib
```

# Helm Repositories

A Helm repository enables you to simply install packages ("charts" in Helm slang) just as a package manager does in an operating system. The repository is a web server that houses an `index.yaml` file and some packaged charts. To manage Helm repositories, you can use the manual `helm repo` command or the Ansible `kubernetes.core.helm_repository` module. This command and the Ansible module allow you to add, remove, and list Helm repositories.

The most famous and widely used repository is the *Bitnami* repository. Bitnami is famous for the library of installers and software packages for web applications and software stacks, as well as virtual appliances, acquired by VMWare in May, 2019. The Bitnami repository hosts packages like Redis, PostgreSQL, MySQL, ExternalDNS, RabbitMQ, Apache Kafka, Keycloak, MongoDB, MiniO, Metrics Server, WordPress, Thanos, MariaDB, NGINX, ElasticSearch, MetailLB, InfluxDB, Apache ZooKeeper, Fluentd, Prometheus, Cassandra, Grafana, Harbor, Apache Spark, MariaDB Galera, Kibana, Odoo, Drupal, Contour, Memcached, Apache Tomcat, Apache AirFlow, Jenkins, Redmine, JupyterHub, Apache, Argo CD, HashiCorp Consul, MediaWiki, Moodle, Logstash, PyTorch, DokuWiki, Magento, Matomo, Prestashop, Apache Solr, ASP .NET Core, Kong, Apache MXNet, Parse, SonarQube, Joomla, EJBCA, HAProxy, OpenCart, phpBB, TensorFlow, Appsmith, Jaeger, Gitea, Pinniped, and more.

## Add Helm Repository

You can add a new Helm repository manually by using the `helm repo` command:

```
$ helm repo add <repo-name> <repo-url>
```

You can automate the Helm repository management using the `kubernetes.core.helm_repository` Ansible module.

The following `helm_repo_present.yml` Ansible Playbook adds the Bitnami repository to your cluster or verifies that it is already present. When you are dealing with a private repository, you can also specify the path of a Certification Authority certificate (`ca_cert` parameter) and the API key (`api_key` parameter), enable the domain credentials (`pass_credentials` parameter), and specify basic authentication (`repo_username` and `repo_password` parameters) or a specific path for the Helm binary

(binary_path parameter). The full Ansible Playbook looks like the following for the bitnami public Helm repository. Simply customize the helm_chart_name and helm_ chart_url variables for another Helm repository, as demonstrated in Listing 6-1.

***Listing 6-1.*** The helm_repo_present.yml File

```
---
- name: k8s helm repo
  hosts: all
  vars:
    helm_chart_name: "bitnami"
    helm_chart_url: "https://charts.bitnami.com/bitnami"
  tasks:
    - name: helm repo present
      kubernetes.core.helm_repository:
        name: "{{ helm_chart_name }}"
        repo_url: "{{ helm_chart_url }}"
        repo_state: present
```

You can execute the code using the ansible-playbook command and specifying the inventory file and the playbook filename:

```
$ ansible-playbook -i inventory helm_repo_present.yml
```

When you want to execute the Playbook code in your Ansible Controller, you specify the localhost in the inventory, as shown in Listing 6-2.

***Listing 6-2.*** Inventory

```
localhost ansible_connection=local
```

A successful execution using the ansible-playbook command output includes the following:

- Play recap status: ok=2  changed=1

- Task status:

```
TASK [helm repo present]
changed: [localhost]
```

After executing the Ansible Playbook, your Kubernetes cluster has the `bitnami` repository in place. You can confirm this using the manual `helm` command:

```
$ helm repo list
```

The report shows you the name and URL of the installed Helm repository in the Kubernetes cluster.

# Remove Helm Repository

To remove a repository, you can use the manual `helm repo` command:

```
$ helm repo remove <repo-name>
```

Otherwise, you can automate this process using the Ansible Playbook in your Kubernetes cluster. The `helm_repo_absent.yml` Ansible Playbook shown in Listing 6-3 removes the `bitnami` Helm repository from the Kubernetes cluster.

***Listing 6-3.*** The helm_repo_absent.yml File

```
---
- name: k8s helm repo
  hosts: all
  vars:
    helm_chart_name: "bitnami"
  tasks:
    - name: helm repo removed
      kubernetes.core.helm_repository:
        name: "{{ helm_chart_name }}"
        repo_state: absent
```

You can execute this in your Ansible Controller, specifying the `localhost` in the inventory (see Listing 6-4).

***Listing 6-4.*** Inventory

```
localhost ansible_connection=local
```

You can execute the code using the `ansible-playbook` command and specifying the `-i` parameter for the inventory file and the playbook filename:

```
$ ansible-playbook -i inventory helm_repo_absent.yml
```

A successful execution using the `ansible-playbook` command output includes the following:

- Play recap status: ok=2 changed=1

- Task status:

---

```
TASK [helm repo removed]
changed: [localhost]
```

---

After successful execution of the Ansible Playbook, your Kubernetes cluster has removed the `bitnami` repository. You can confirm this using the manual `helm` command:

```
$ helm repo list
```

The output of the command shows the name and URL of the installed Helm repositories in your Kubernetes cluster.

# Helm Packages

When a Helm repository is configured in your Kubernetes cluster, you can install any Helm packages you need. Many Helm charts are available worldwide. The Helm packages are also called "charts". You can use the manual `helm` command or the Ansible `kubernetes.core.helm` module.

## Install Helm Package

The following Ansible Playbook installs the popular NGINX web server using the `nginx` charts from the Bitnami repository. You can enable this repository using the code in the previous section. Feel free to customize the variable with the one in your Kubernetes cluster:

- `chart_name`: The name of the chart to install (`nginx-server`)

- `chart_ref`: The name of the repository to retrieve the chart (`bitnami/nginx`)

- `myproject`: The name of the target Kubernetes namespace/ OpenShift Project (`ansible-examples`)

The full Ansible Playbook is shown in Listing 6-5.

***Listing 6-5.*** The helm_present.yml File

```
---
- name: k8s helm
  hosts: all
  vars:
    chart_name: "nginx-server"
    chart_ref: "bitnami/nginx"
    myproject: "ansible-examples"
  tasks:
    - name: helm chart present
      kubernetes.core.helm:
        name: "{{ chart_name }}"
        namespace: "{{ myproject }}"
        chart_ref: "{{ chart_ref }}"
        release_state: present
```

You can execute the code in your Ansible Controller using the localhost inventory, as demonstrated in Listing 6-6.

***Listing 6-6.*** Inventory

```
localhost ansible_connection=local
```

You can execute your helm_present.yml Ansible Playbook using the ansible-playbook command and specifying the -i parameter for the inventory file and the playbook filename:

```
$ ansible-playbook -i inventory helm_present.yml
```

A successful execution using the ansible-playbook command output includes the following:

- Play recap status: ok=2  changed=1
- Task status:

```
TASK [helm chart present]
changed: [localhost]
```

Taking advantage of the Ansible idempotency property when you execute your code with the desired state already present, the code returns only an ok status. You can verify the installed status of the Helm "chart" package in your Kubernetes cluster in the following section (see the Report Helm Package section).

## Remove Helm Package

In the same way as you install a Helm "chart" package, you can automate its removal using the Ansible Playbook in your Kubernetes cluster. Feel free to customize the variable with the one in your Kubernetes cluster:

- chart_name: The name of the chart to install (nginx-server)

- myproject: The name of the target Kubernetes namespace/ OpenShift Project (ansible-examples)

The full Ansible Playbook is shown in Listing 6-7.

***Listing 6-7.*** The helm_absent.yml File

```
---
- name: k8s helm
  hosts: all
  vars:
    chart_name: "nginx-server"
    myproject: "ansible-examples"
  tasks:
    - name: helm chart absent
      kubernetes.core.helm:
        name: "{{ chart_name }}"
        namespace: "{{ myproject }}"
        release_state: absent
```

When you execute the code in your Ansible Controller, you use the localhost inventory (see Listing 6-8).

***Listing 6-8.*** Inventory

```
localhost ansible_connection=local
```

The ansible-playbook command executes your code and specifies the -i parameter for the inventory file and the helm_absent.yml filename:

```
$ ansible-playbook -i inventory helm_absent.yml
```

A successful execution using the ansible-playbook command output includes the following:

- Play recap status: ok=2 changed=1
- Task status:

---

```
TASK [helm chart absent]
changed: [localhost]
```

---

You can verify the removed status of the Helm "chart" package in your Kubernetes cluster in the following section (see Report Helm Package).

## Report Helm Package

You can verify the status of the installed Helm "chart" packages using the manual helm command or the Ansible kubernetes.core.helm_info module. It might be useful to the release_state parameter (default to deployed and failed):

- all: Show all releases
- deployed: Show only deployed releases
- failed: Show only failed releases
- pending: Show only pending releases
- superseded: Show only superseded releases
- uninstalled: Show only uninstalled releases
- uninstalling: Show only releases that are currently being uninstalled

Feel free to customize the variable of the following code:

- chart_name: The name of the chart to install (nginx-server)

- myproject: The name of the target Kubernetes namespace/
  OpenShift Project (ansible-examples)

The full code of the Ansible Playbook shown in Listing 6-9 displays the Helm charts.

***Listing 6-9.*** The helm_info.yml File

```
---
- name: k8s helm
  hosts: all
  vars:
    chart_name: "nginx-server"
    myproject: "ansible-examples"
  tasks:
    - name: gather chart information
      kubernetes.core.helm_info:
        name: "{{ chart_name }}"
        release_namespace: "{{ myproject }}"
```

The localhost inventory shown in Listing 6-10 executes the code in the Ansible
Controller.

***Listing 6-10.*** Inventory

```
localhost ansible_connection=local
```

You can execute the code using the ansible-playbook command and specifying the
inventory file and the playbook filename:

```
$ ansible-playbook -i inventory helm_info.yml
```

A successful execution using the `ansible-playbook` command output includes the following:

- Play recap status: `ok=2 changed=1`

- Task status:

```
TASK [gather chart information]
changed: [localhost]
```

The output of the `helm_info.yml` playbook shows information about the installed "chart" packages: application version, chart version, revision, status, and updated date time.

# Helm Plugins

The Helm plugins are software add-ons that expand Helm's functionalities.

To report the Helm plugins deployed inside the cluster manually, you can use the `helm plugin list` command. This command will list all the plugins installed in the current namespace, as well as their versions and other information.

Additionally, you can use the `helm plugin install` command to install a plugin and the `helm plugin update` command to update a plugin. The `helm plugin uninstall` command can be used to uninstall a plugin. Finally, the `helm plugin status` command can be used to get detailed information about a specific plugin. You can automate Helm plugin management using the `kubernetes.core.helm_plugin` Ansible module.

## Install Helm Plugin

Many Helm plugins expand Helm functionality with new pieces of software. For example, the Helm plugin called `helm env` allows users to view the environment variables. The following Ansible Playbook downloads the latest release of the `helm env` plugin and installs it in your Kubernetes cluster. Feel free to customize the plugin path and the Kubernetes namespace/OpenShift project variables:

- `myplugin_name`: The name of the plugin to install (`env`)

- `myplugin_path`: The name of the repository to retrieve the plugin (`https://github.com/adamreese/helm-env`)

The full Ansible Playbook is shown in Listing 6-11.

***Listing 6-11.*** The helm_plugin_present.yml file

```
---
- name: k8s helm plugin
  hosts: all
  vars:
    myplugin_name: "env"
    myplugin_path: "https://github.com/adamreese/helm-env"

  tasks:
    - name: helm plugin present
      kubernetes.core.helm_plugin:
        plugin_name: "{{ myplugin_name }}"
        plugin_path: "{{ myplugin_path }}"

        state: present
```

The `localhost` inventory executes your code in the Ansible Controller
(see Listing 6-12).

***Listing 6-12.*** Inventory

```
localhost ansible_connection=local
```

You can execute the code with the `ansible-playbook` command:

```
$ ansible-playbook -i inventory helm_present.yml
```

A successful execution using the `ansible-playbook` command output includes the
following:

- Play recap status: `ok=2 changed=1`

- Task status:

---

```
TASK [helm plugin present]
changed: [localhost]
```

---

You can verify the installed Helm plugin in the following section (see Report Helm Plugin).

A possible improvement to the code is to use a list of namespaces and loop them with the Ansible Playbook.

## Remove Helm Plugin

When a plugin is not needed anymore in your Kubernetes cluster, you can automate the removal process using the kubernetes.core.helm_plugin Ansible module. The full Ansible Playbook is shown in Listing 6-13.

***Listing 6-13.*** The helm_plugin_absent.yml File

```
---
- name: k8s helm plugin
  hosts: all
  vars:
    myplugin_name: "env"

  tasks:
    - name: helm plugin absent
      kubernetes.core.helm_plugin:
        plugin_name: "{{ myplugin_name }}"

        state: absent
```

The localhost inventory executes your code in the Ansible Controller, as shown in Listing 6-14.

***Listing 6-14.*** Inventory

```
localhost ansible_connection=local
```

You can execute this code with the ansible-playbook command:

```
$ ansible-playbook -i inventory helm_absent.yml
```

A successful execution using the `ansible-playbook` command output includes the following:

- Play recap status: `ok=2 changed=1`

- Task status:

---

```
TASK [helm plugin absent]
changed: [localhost]
```

---

You can verify the installed Helm plugin in the following section (see Report Helm Plugin).

## Report Helm Plugin

You can use the `helm plugin list` manual command to report the Helm plugins deployed inside the cluster. This command lists all the plugins installed in the current namespace, as well as their versions and other information. You can automate this process using the `kubernetes.core.helm_plugin_info` Ansible module.

The Ansible Playbook shown in Listing 6-15 displays the version of the `env` plugin installed in the `ansible-examples` namespace.

***Listing 6-15.*** The helm_plugin_info.yml File

```
---
- name: k8s helm plugin
  hosts: all
  vars:
    myplugin_name: "env"
  tasks:
    - name: helm plugin info
      kubernetes.core.helm_plugin_info:
      register: output

    - name: print plugin version
      ansible.builtin.debug:
        msg: "{{ (output.plugin_list | selectattr('name', 'equalto',
        myplugin_name) | list)[0].version }}"
```

215

You can execute the code in your Ansible Controller using the localhost inventory, as shown in Listing 6-16.

***Listing 6-16.*** Inventory

```
localhost ansible_connection=local
```

You can execute your helm_present.yml Ansible Playbook using the ansible-playbook command and specifying the -i parameter for the inventory file and the playbook filename:

```
$ ansible-playbook -i inventory helm_plugin_info.yml
```

A successful execution using the ansible-playbook command output includes the following:

- Play recap status: ok=3 changed=0

- Task status:

```
TASK [helm plugin info]
ok: [localhost]
TASK [print plugin version]
ok: [localhost]
```

# Deploy a Monitoring Tool

Prometheus is a popular monitoring tool based on time series data. Under the hood, it streams timestamped values belonging to the same metric and the same set of labeled dimensions. One of the strengths of Prometheus is its deep integration with Kubernetes.

You can choose between several different ways to deploy a monitoring tool inside your Kubernetes clusters:

- Prometheus Operator and kube-prometheus

- Ansible role cloudalchemy.prometheus

- Helm chart

The Prometheus Operator is the Kubernetes-native solution that allows you to deploy and manage Prometheus and its components, such as Alertmanager and Grafana. It provides a declarative configuration that allows you to specify the desired state of your monitoring stack, and the operator will ensure that it is always kept up-to-date. In addition to deploying Prometheus, the operator can be used to configure monitoring rules, manage alerting rules, and set up dashboards. To deploy the Prometheus Operator, you can use different options, discussed next.

## kube-prometheus

The kube-prometheus project is the easiest way to install end-to-end Kubernetes cluster monitoring with Prometheus using the Prometheus Operator. It deploys the Prometheus Operator by deploying it as part of kube-prometheus. The kube-prometheus project deploys the Prometheus Operator and schedules a Prometheus job called prometheus-k8s with alerts and rules by default. The default deployment includes multiple Prometheus and Alertmanager instances, metric exporters such as node_exporter for gathering node metrics, scrape target configurations linking Prometheus to various metric endpoints, and example alerting rules for notification of potential issues in the cluster. The setup is performed in three manual steps:

1.  Download the kube-prometheus project:

    ```
    $ git clone https://github.com/prometheus-operator/
    kube-prometheus.git
    ```

2.  Deploy kube-prometheus:

    ```
    $ kubectl create -f manifests/setup
    $ kubectl create -f manifests/
    ```

3.  Forward the ports for Prometheus, Alertmanager, and Grafana:

    ```
    $ kubectl --namespace monitoring port-forward svc/
    prometheus-k8s 9090
    $ kubectl --namespace monitoring port-forward svc/
    prometheus-k8s 9090
    $ kubectl --namespace monitoring port-forward svc/
    alertmanager-main 9093
    $ kubectl --namespace monitoring port-forward svc/grafana 3000
    ```

# Ansible Collections

When you want to automate the installation of Prometheus, you can deploy it using Ansible. You need to acquire the Ansible Collection called prometheus.prometheus from the Ansible Galaxy repository. The collection requires the community.crypto collection to be installed (resolved by the ansible-galaxy tool). The Prometheus role inside the collection substitutes the previous cloudalchemy.prometheus Ansible role, which has been deprecated in Ansible Galaxy.

1. Install the collection manually:

```
$ ansible-galaxy collection install prometheus.prometheus
```

2. Install the collection via requirements.yml, as shown in Listing 6-17.

***Listing 6-17.*** The requirements.yml File

```
---
collections:
  - name: prometheus.prometheus
```

The role requires the jmespath Python library and gnu-tar when run on an Ansible Controller, as demonstrated in Listing 6-18.

***Listing 6-18.*** The prometheus.yml File

```
---
- name: install prometheus
  hosts: all
  roles:
    - prometheus.prometheus.prometheus
  vars:
    prometheus_targets:
      node:
        - targets:
            - k8s.ansiblepilot.com:9100
          labels:
            env: ansible-examples
```

The `localhost` inventory executes your code in the Ansible Controller (see Listing 6-19).

***Listing 6-19.*** Inventory

```
localhost ansible_connection=local
```

You can execute the code using the `ansible-playbook` command and specifying the inventory file and the playbook filename:

```
$ ansible-playbook -i inventory prometheus.yml
```

A successful execution using the `ansible-playbook` command output includes the following:

- Play recap status: `ok=2  changed=1`
- Many messages according to the `prometheus.prometheus.`
  `prometheus` role

# Helm Chart

Another way to install the Prometheus Operator is via a Helm Chart. You can reuse the Ansible Playbook seen in the previous section (see The Helm Package Manager) with different Ansible variables. You can specify the extra variables via the command line using the `-e` parameter of the `ansible-playbook` command. The extra variables override the values of the Ansible Playbooks.

Enable the Helm repository called `prometheus-community` by specifying the URL:

```
$ ansible-playbook -i inventory -e "helm_chart_name=prometheus-community"
-e "helm_chart_url=https://prometheus-community.github.io/helm-charts"
helm_repo_present.yml
```

Install the Helm chart package named `kube-prometheus-stack` from the `prometheus-community` Helm repository as follows:

```
$ ansible-playbook  i inventory -e "chart_name=kube-prometheus-stack" -e
"chart_ref=prometheus-community/kube-prometheus-stack" helm_present.yml
```

# Fetch Logs from Resources

To fetch logs manually from Kubernetes resources, you can use the `kubectl logs` command. This command allows you to view the logs of a container in a pod or to retrieve the logs of a resource such as a Deployment, StatefulSet, or CronJob. The syntax for the command is as follows:

```
$ kubectl logs <resource-name> [<container-name>]
```

If a container name is not provided, the logs of the first container in the pod will be fetched. For example, to view the logs of a Deployment, you can use the `kubectl logs my-deployment` command. This will show the logs for all of the pods in the Deployment. To view the logs of a specific container in a pod, you can use the `$ kubectl logs my-pod -c my-container` command.

The Ansible Playbook shown in Listing 6-20 obtains the log from the `ansible-examples` pod in the `ansible-examples` namespace.

***Listing 6-20.*** The log_pod.yml File

```
---
- name: k8s log
  hosts: all
  vars:
    myproject: "ansible-examples"
    pod_name: "nginx-server"
  tasks:
    - name: get log from pod
      kubernetes.core.k8s_log:
        name: "{{ pod_name }}"
        namespace: "{{ myproject }}"
      register: log

    - name: display log
      ansible.builtin.debug:
        var: log
```

Instead, the Ansible Playbook in Listing 6-21 can obtain logs from different resources: Deployment, DeploymentConfig, StatefulSet, and CronJob.

***Listing 6-21.*** The log_resource.yml File

```
---
- name: k8s log
  hosts: all
  vars:
    myproject: "ansible-examples"
    myname: "nginx-server"
    mykind: "Deployment"
  tasks:
    - name: get log from resource
      kubernetes.core.k8s_log:
        api_version: apps/v1
        kind: "{{ mykind }}"
        namespace: "{{ myproject }}"
        name: "{{ myname }}"
      register: log
    - name: display log
      ansible.builtin.debug:
        var: log
```

The localhost inventory executes your code in the Ansible Controller, as shown in Listing 6-22.

***Listing 6-22.*** The Inventory File

```
localhost ansible_connection=local
```

You can execute your code with the ansible-playbook command (specifying the log_pod.yml or log_resource.yml file):

```
$ ansible-playbook -i inventory log_pod.yml
```

Successful execution using the `ansible-playbook` command includes the following:

- Play recap status: ok=2  changed=1

- Log messages displayed onscreen

# Apply a JSON Patch Operation

JSON Patch is a format for describing changes to a JSON document. To apply JSON patch operations to existing Kubernetes objects manually, you can use the `kubectl patch` command. This command takes two arguments—the object name and a JSON patch file. The patch file should contain one or more operations, in either JSON or YAML format, that you want to apply to the object. For example, to add a new label to an existing pod, you can create a patch file containing the YAML shown in Listing 6-23.

***Listing 6-23.*** The patch-file.yaml File

```
- op: add
  path: /metadata/labels/new-label
  value: new-value
```

Then, you can apply this patch to the `nginx-server` pod object using the following command:

```
$ kubectl patch pod nginx-server --patch "$(cat patch-file.yaml)"
```

This will add the new label to the pod. You can use the same command with different patch files to make changes to other objects in the cluster.

You can also automate the previous operation using the Ansible Playbook shown in Listing 6-24.

***Listing 6-24.*** The patch.yml File

```
---
- name: k8s patch
  hosts: all
  vars:
    mypod: "nginx-server"
    myproject: "ansible-examples"
```

```
tasks:
  - name: patch a Pod
    kubernetes.core.k8s_json_patch:
      kind: Pod
      namespace: "{{ myproject }}"
      name: "{{ mypod }}"
      patch:
        - op: add
          path: /metadata/labels/new-label
          value: new-value
```

The localhost inventory executes this code in the Ansible Controller, as shown in Listing 6-25.

***Listing 6-25.*** The Inventory File

```
localhost ansible_connection=local
```

You can execute the patch.yml Ansible Playbook with the ansible-playbook command:

```
$ ansible-playbook -i inventory patch.yml
```

A successful execution using the ansible-playbook command output includes the following:

- Play recap status: ok=2 changed=1

- Task status:

```
TASK [patch a Pod]
changed: [localhost]
```

# Copy Files and Directories to and from a Pod

It's helpful to copy files and directories to and from a pod in Kubernetes, especially in the early stage of the development or for some investigations. For manual operations, you can use the `kubectl cp` command. This command allows you to copy files and directories between a pod and the local file system. The syntax for the command is `kubectl cp <source> <destination>`, where the source can be either a pod or the local file system, and the destination can be either a pod or the local file system. For example, to copy a file from a pod to the local file system, you can use this command:

```
$ kubectl cp <pod-name>:/path/to/file /local/destination/path
```

Similarly, to copy a file from the local file system to a pod, you can use this command:

```
$ kubectl cp /local/source/path <pod-name>:/path/to/destination
```

You can automate the operation using the `kubernetes.core.k8s_cp` Ansible module. The parameter state defines whether you want the default operation to copy data from local to pod (the to_pod option) or from pod to local (the `from_pod` option). The Ansible Playbook in Listing 6-26 copies data from the `/data` directory of the pod named `nginx-server` in the `ansible-examples` namespace to the local folder called `/tmp/data`.

***Listing 6-26.*** The cp.yml File

```
---
- name: k8s copy
  hosts: all
  vars:
    mypod: "nginx-server"
    myproject: "ansible-examples"
    remote_path: "/data"
    local_path: "/tmp/data"
    direction: "from_pod"
  tasks:
    - name: copy data
      kubernetes.core.k8s_cp:
```

```
namespace: "{{ myproject }}"
pod: "{{ mypod }}"
remote_path: "{{ remote_path }}"
local_path: "{{ local_path }}"
state: "{{ direction }}"
```

You can execute the code in your Ansible Controller using the localhost inventory, as shown in Listing 6-27.

***Listing 6-27.*** Inventory

```
localhost ansible_connection=local
```

You can execute your cp.yml Ansible Playbook by using the ansible-playbook command and specifying the -i parameter for the inventory file and the playbook filename:

```
$ ansible-playbook -i inventory cp.yml
```

A successful execution using the ansible-playbook command output includes the following:

- Play recap status: ok=2 changed=1

- Task status:

---

```
TASK [copy data]
changed: [localhost]
```

---

# Manage Services on Kubernetes

To manage services on Kubernetes, you can use the kubectl command-line tool. This tool lets you create, edit, delete, and view services in your Kubernetes cluster.

To create a service, you can use the kubectl expose command, which takes a deployment or a pod as an argument.

To edit a service, you can use the kubectl edit command, which will open the service definition in an editor.

To delete a service, you can use the kubectl delete command, which takes the service name and namespace as arguments.

To view a service, you can use the kubectl get command, which takes the service name and namespace as arguments.

You can also use the kubectl describe command to view detailed information about a service.

You can automate the managing of services on the Kubernetes cluster using the following Ansible Playbook (see Listing 6-28).

***Listing 6-28.*** The service.yml File

```
---
- name: k8s service
  hosts: all
  tasks:
    - name: expose https port with ClusterIP
      kubernetes.core.k8s_service:
        state: present
        name: port-https
        namespace: default
        ports:
          - port: 443
            protocol: TCP
            selector:
              key: special
```

You can execute the code in your Ansible Controller by specifying the localhost in the inventory, as shown in Listing 6-29.

***Listing 6-29.*** Inventory

```
localhost ansible_connection=local
```

You can execute the code using the ansible-playbook command and specifying the -i parameter for the inventory file and the playbook filename:

```
$ ansible-playbook -i inventory service.yml
```

A successful execution using the `ansible-playbook` command output includes the following:

- Play recap status: `ok=2 changed=1`

- Task status:

```
TASK [expose https port with ClusterIP]
changed: [localhost]
```

# Taint Nodes

Taints and tolerations are a flexible way to steer pods away from nodes or evict pods that shouldn't be running. A typical use case of the taint node is to take advantage of particular nodes with special hardware (such as GPUs) to run only pods that require the use of the specialized hardware and keep out the pods that don't require it. Moreover, you can use this tool when you need to execute maintenance in your Kubernetes cluster.

Kubernetes Taint is used to mark a node as unable to schedule any pods that do not tolerate the taint. This is useful when you need to perform maintenance on a node, as it ensures that any existing pods running on the node will remain running and any new pods will be rescheduled onto other nodes in the cluster. The `taint` command works by adding a label to the node, which is then used to identify which pods should not be scheduled onto the node. This label can be removed when the maintenance is complete, allowing the node to start accepting new pods again.

The Ansible Playbook in Listing 6-30 taints the node defined in the `mynode` variable and sets the `NoExecute` and `NoSchedule` attributes' keys and values. The playbook uses the `kubernetes.core.k8s_taint` Ansible module, introduced in version 2.3 of the `kubernetes.core` Ansible collection in March, 2022.

***Listing 6-30.*** The taint.yml File

```
---
- name: k8s taint
  hosts: all
  vars:
    mynode: "k8s.ansiblepilot.com"
```

```
tasks:
  - name: taint node
    kubernetes.core.k8s_taint:
      state: present
      name: "{{ mynode }}"
      taints:
        - effect: NoExecute
          key: "key1"
          value: "value1"
        - effect: NoSchedule
          key: "key1"
          value: "value1"
```

You can execute your Ansible Controller by specifying the localhost in the inventory, as shown in Listing 6-31.

***Listing 6-31.*** Inventory

```
localhost ansible_connection=local
```

You can execute the code using the ansible-playbook command and specifying the -i parameter for the inventory file and the playbook filename:

```
$ ansible-playbook -i inventory taint.yml
```

A successful execution using the ansible-playbook command output includes the following:

- Play recap status: ok=2  changed=1

- Task status:

---

```
TASK [taint node]
changed: [localhost]
```

---

# Drain, Cordon, or Uncordon Nodes

Kubernetes Drain is a tool used to safely evict all of the pods from a node before performing maintenance on the node. Note that it's always a good practice to have a planned maintenance window. The Drain operation is often combined with the Taint operation.

When you run the `drain` command, Kubernetes will attempt to delete all of the pods on the node except for mirror pods, which are created by replication controllers, jobs, or daemon sets. The `drain` command also allows you to specify a `PodDisruptionBudget`, which will ensure that the number of pods running on the node does not drop below the specified minimum during the eviction process. Once the eviction process is complete, you can then safely perform maintenance on the node, knowing that the pods will be safely relocated to other nodes in the cluster.

Kubernetes Cordon marks a node as "unschedulable," meaning that no new pods will be scheduled onto the node. This is useful when you need to perform maintenance on a node, as it ensures that any existing pods running on the node will remain running and any new pods will be rescheduled onto other nodes in the cluster. The `cordon` command works by setting the node's `unschedulable` flag to `true`, which will prevent the Kubernetes scheduler from placing any new pods on the node. Once the maintenance is complete, the `unschedulable` flag can be reset back to false, allowing the node to start accepting new pods again.

Kubernetes Uncordon is used to mark a node as `schedulable`, meaning that new pods can be scheduled onto the node. This is the opposite of the `kubectl cordon` command, which marks a node as `unschedulable`, thus preventing new pods from being scheduled onto that node. The `uncordon` command works by setting the node's `unschedulable` flag to `false`, allowing the Kubernetes scheduler to place new pods on the node. This is useful when maintenance has been completed on a node, and you want to allow new pods to start running on the node again.

The Ansible Playbook shown in Listing 6-32 sets a node in the `drain` state but aborts the operation if there are pods not managed by a ReplicationController, Job, or DaemonSet. It uses a grace period of ten minutes.

***Listing 6-32.***  The drain.yml File

```
---
- name: k8s drain
  hosts: all
  vars:
    mynode: "k8s.ansiblepilot.com"
    grace_period: 600
  tasks:
    - name: drain node
      kubernetes.core.k8s_drain:
        state: drain
        name: "{{ mynode }}"
        delete_options:
          terminate_grace_period: "{{ grace_period }}"
```

The Ansible Playbook in Listing 6-33 marks the specified node as `unschedulable` as part of the Cordon status.

***Listing 6-33.***  The cordon.yml File

```
---
- name: k8s cordon
  hosts: all
  vars:
    mynode: "k8s.ansiblepilot.com"
  tasks:
    - name: cordon node
      kubernetes.core.k8s_drain:
        state: cordon
        name: "{{ mynode }}"
```

In the same way, you can perform the `uncordon` operation to mark the selected node as schedulable in the Kubernetes cluster. The Ansible Playbook is shown in Listing 6-34.

***Listing 6-34.*** The uncordon.yml File

```
---
- name: k8s uncordon
  hosts: all
  vars:
    mynode: "k8s.ansiblepilot.com"
  tasks:
    - name: uncordon node
      kubernetes.core.k8s_drain:
        state: uncordon
        name: "{{ mynode }}"
```

The localhost inventory shown in Listing 6-35 executes the code in the Ansible Controller.

***Listing 6-35.*** Inventory

```
localhost ansible_connection=local
```

You can execute the code using the ansible-playbook command and specifying the inventory file and the playbook filename (drain.yml, cordon.yml, uncordon.yml):

```
$ ansible-playbook -i inventory drain.yml
```

A successful execution using the ansible-playbook command output includes the following:

- Play recap status: ok=2 changed=1

- Task status:

```
TASK [drain node]
changed: [localhost]
```

Many IT professionals chain the three Ansible Playbooks when they upgrade a new version of Kubernetes in their clusters or expand with a list of hostnames and loops between them.

# Kubernetes Dynamic Inventory

Ansible Dynamic Inventory is a feature of Ansible that allows you to automatically generate and update inventory information from external sources such as cloud providers, CMDBs, and inventory management systems. This allows users to deploy infrastructure and applications dynamically and automate them quickly. The inventory is stored in a YAML file, which is then used by Ansible to determine which hosts to target for tasks. Ansible Dynamic Inventory can be used for several different use cases, such as dynamic scaling, provisioning, and application deployment. It can be used to manage hybrid data center environments and ensure that the right resources are allocated for each environment. See the "Ansible Dynamic Inventory" section in Chapter 5 for a practical example.

# Roll Back Deployments and DaemonSets

Deployments can fail to deploy for a number of reasons. Your Plan B should be to execute a rollback of the previous working version of the application or service. You can execute this operation, thus triggering the rollback operation to the deployments and DaemonSets. The Ansible Playbook in Listing 6-36 starts a rollback on the `nginx-server` deployment in the `ansible-examples` namespace.

*Listing 6-36.* The rollback.yml File

```
---
- name: k8s rollback
  hosts: all
  vars:
    myproject: "ansible-examples"
    kind: "Deployment"
    name: "nginx-server"
  tasks:
    - name: rollback
      kubernetes.core.k8s_rollback:
        api_version: apps/v1
        kind: "{{ kind }}"
        name: "{{ name }}"
        namespace: "{{ myproject }}"
```

The `localhost` inventory shown in Listing 6-37 executes the code in the Ansible Controller.

***Listing 6-37.*** Inventory

```
localhost ansible_connection=local
```

You can execute the code using the `ansible-playbook` command and specifying the inventory file and the `playbook` filename:

```
$ ansible-playbook -i inventory rollback.yml
```

A successful execution using the `ansible-playbook` command output includes the following:

- Play recap status: `ok=2 changed=1`

- Task status:

```
TASK [rollback]
changed: [localhost]
```

# Set a New Size for a Deployment, ReplicaSet, Replication Controller, or Job

You can automate the setting of the number of replicas for a Deployment, ReplicaSet, or Replication Controller, or the parallelism attribute of a Job using the `kubernetes.core.k8s_scale` Ansible module. See the "Scale Your App" section in Chapter 4.

# Security

Security is a broad concept, especially when many components are interconnected, like in a Kubernetes cluster. The Linux kernel has a number of overlapping security extensions (capabilities, SELinux, AppArmor, and `seccomp-bpf`) that can be configured to provide the least privilege to programs.

The reference for Kubernetes in this field are the four Cs of cloud-native security:

- Cloud

- Cluster

- Container

- Code

To begin with, the *cloud infrastructure* that hosts your cluster needs to be adequately secured and enable access to ports on the cluster only by trusted networks. By default, Container Engines are open from anywhere. A network firewall could be helpful in mitigating this behavior. This prevents a potential attacker from running port scans to detect potential open ports in your systems and connect to them. This is the first "C" in cloud-native and it impacts the security of the entire infrastructure, even when the cluster is in a private or public cloud data center.

The next is *cluster security,* which involves the ability of a potential attacker to execute commands in your cluster. A potential attacker could have the ability to access running Container Engines such as Docker Daemons, exposed publicly, as well as the Kubernetes Dashboard without the proper authentication or authorization mechanism. This can be prevented by using network policies and security in ingress.

The next "C" is *containers*. A potential attacker can run any container of choice without restriction, even in privileged mode, no matter what repository it came from or what tag is used.

Moreover, the attacker can install any application when it can run a malicious container in your cluster without restriction. A few years ago, the Dirty Cow CVE-2016-5195 exploited a bug in the Linux kernel's memory subsystem copy-on-write (COW) to gain write access from the container to the host system, increasing the privileges.

You can prevent this behavior by enabling only running containers from a secure internal registry, disallowing running in privileged mode, and sandboxing isolating each other.

The best way to prevent supply chain attacks and minimize microservice vulnerability is acting in the *code*. Avoid hard-coding database credentials, thereby passing critical pieces of information through environment variables or exposing applications without TLS/SSL. These are bad coding practices.

The DevSecOps movement applies security as soon as possible in the code design phase of your development.

Another important tool is to scan for vulnerabilities as soon you create your container image, when you push to the container image. You must apply this methodology as soon as possible during the development process.

You can also reduce the attack surface of container images using the smallest images possible, removing all unnecessary binaries. Reducing the attack surface should be your mantra.

A good security practice is to build your images using scratch. Add a USER directive to run as a non-root user inside a container. You can sign your images in order to run only trusted containers. Most of the time, you derive your containers using the FROM directive.

The most secure way is to combine the scratch with a multi-stage build. In this way, you obtain a shirked image with only your application. This approach is demonstrated in Listing 6-38.

***Listing 6-38.*** The Containerfile File

```
FROM fedora:latest as build
COPY hello.go /app
WORKDIR /app/
RUN go build -o hello

FROM scratch
COPY -from=build /app/hello /app/
ENTRYPOINT ["/app/hello"]
```

The resulting container has only the executable /app/hello. Hence, it's super compact and very secure because it doesn't have unnecessary binaries and doesn't require all the unused libraries of the operating system.

# AAA

Every time you make a request, Kubernetes determines if it is allowed or denied using Authentication, Authorization, and Accounting (AAA). This is how your Kubernetes cluster verifies who you are and what you are authorized to execute. Policies define permissions according to role-based access control (RBAC) or attribute-based access control (ABAC). Associated policies define Kubernetes resources. Kubernetes RBAC is the most commonly used method to perform AAA tasks. Policies are in place to make decisions to allow or deny an action. The following acronyms are used in the AAA context:

- `authn`: Authentication (who are you?)
- `authz`: Authorization (what are you authorized to do?)
- `auth`: Accounting (what area are you authorized to access?)

You can use Kubernetes RBAC to provide authorization to resources in your Kubernetes cluster.

# OpenID Identity Provider

An *identity provider* stores and authenticates the identities of users, ensuring the validity of their login credentials across multiple platforms. In the past, Kerberos was the preferred authentication system, but it's sometimes complicated, so nowadays, especially for API authentication, other solutions are preferred.

OpenID Connector (OIDC) is an authentication layer on top of OAuth 2.0. It is a secure mechanism allowing an application to contact an identity service, retrieve user-specific data, and return some information to the application in a secure way. You can see this with Facebook and Google login buttons in many mobile apps and websites. They use the authentication information stored in your account, so you don't have to retype information into every service. GitHub, Microsoft, and Azure ID are other popular identity providers.

Kubernetes hosts a per-cluster, public OpenID Connect (OIDC) endpoint that contains signing keys for JSON web tokens allowing external systems, like Amazon IAM, to validate and accept the Kubernetes-issued OIDC tokens. OIDC federation access allows you to assume RBAC roles via the Secure Token Service (STS), enabling authentication with an OIDC provider and receiving a JSON Web Token (JWT), which is used to assume a role. OpenID Connect allows single sign-on (SSO) for logging into your Kubernetes cluster. You can use an existing public OpenID Connect Identity Provider (such as Google, GitHub, Microsoft, Amazon, and so on), or you can run your own identity providers, such as dex, Keycloak, CloudFoundry UAA, or Tremolo Security's OpenUnison.

## Calico

You can secure your network communications using Calico around your pod. Calico acts like a firewall in your pod. It enables you to use network policies within a pod and apply the zero-trust security model. This means that it considers all the traffic dangerous by default, and you need to manually set an allow list. The easiest way to install Calico is via the Tigera operator. The Tigera operator provides lifecycle management for Calico exposed via the Kubernetes API, defined as a custom resource definition.

## Key Takeaways

Automating the management of your Kubernetes clusters using Ansible technology enables a faster maintenance window and fewer human errors. You can apply the automation to small and large clusters and many use cases. Managing software with the Helm package manager simplifies the adoption of the standard software lifecycle maintenance process. Ansible reduces the cluster administration toil, automating every operation of cluster maintenance and software lifecycle management. Creating another cluster is becoming easy and very affordable nowadays, especially for Cloud providers (Amazon, Google, Azure, and so on). You explore Kubernetes and its cloud computing opportunities in the next chapter.

# CHAPTER 7

# Ansible for Kubernetes Cloud Providers

Cloud providers are a great resource for propelling your business to a new level. The need for more resources is just a few clicks away. Cloud computing is a commercial offer from a vendor that offers a pool of on-demand computing, storage, database, and network shared resources sold as a service that you can rapidly deploy at scale. In recent times also, Machine Learning and Artificial Intelligence resources are becoming popular.

Worldwide analysts see growth in the adoption of cloud provider services year after year. Forrester report predicts[1] that in 2023 cloud-native adoption will rise to 50 percent of worldwide enterprise organizations. The previous adoption rate was 42 percent in 2021 and 33 percent in 2020. Gartner forecasts[2] end-user spending on public cloud services of $591.8 Billion in 2023. The reason behind this is that maintaining on-premise infrastructure might drain a lot of resources from your IT department. An affordable Total Cost of Ownership (TCO) and the possibility of obtaining a fully managed service have attracted organizations in recent years to move their applications to cloud providers. From the application point of view, it changes nothing, as they perceive the underlying layer as platform-independent because they rely on container technology. You have the ability to run your pods in the Kubernetes cluster on-premise, via cloud computing, or via a hybrid infrastructure without any changes. Ansible Dynamic Inventories are very useful in conjunction with the cloud provider because the environment can be fast-paced. As the number of machines and systems under your control increases, you need a powerful tool to comply with regulations. Ansible Dynamic Inventories interact with the cloud provider API and retrieve identifiers and IP addresses

---

[1] https://www.forrester.com/report/predictions-2023-cloud-computing/RES178164
[2] https://www.gartner.com/en/newsroom/press-releases/2022-10-31-gartner-forecasts-worldwide-public-cloud-end-user-spending-to-reach-nearly-600-billion-in-2023

© Luca Berton 2023
L. Berton, *Ansible for Kubernetes by Example*, https://doi.org/10.1007/978-1-4842-9285-3_7

of the machines in the IT real estate. Ansible Dynamic Inventories are heavily used to query cloud providers or Kubernetes cluster infrastructures (see the "Ansible Dynamic Inventory" section in Chapter 5).

One of the main benefits of adopting cloud computing in your organization is that you are outsourcing the management of the Kubernetes control plane because the vendor manages it. Adopting the shared responsibility model displayed in Table 7-1, this complies with the most up-to-date international security and process management standards. Usually, you need to set up the network configuration for your applications or services. After the initial configuration, you can spin up global-scale cloud-native applications in minutes.

***Table 7-1.*** *Cloud Computing Shared Responsibility Model*

| Responsibility | On-premise | IaaS | PaaS | SaaS |
|---|---|---|---|---|
| Application configuration | Customer | Customer | Customer | Customer |
| Identity and access control | Customer | Customer | Shared | Shared |
| Application data storage | Customer | Customer | Shared | Vendor |
| Application | Customer | Customer | Customer | Vendor |
| Operating system | Customer | Customer | Vendor | Vendor |
| Network flow control | Customer | Shared | Vendor | Vendor |
| Host infrastructure | Customer | Vendor | Vendor | Vendor |
| Physical security | Customer | Vendor | Vendor | Vendor |

Like everything in life, you can't apply a "one size fits all" approach. Cloud computing is a great tool that you can apply to your IT infrastructure when the on-premises resources are not enough, your stakeholders are located worldwide, or you need to handle a temporary spike of traffic. In this context, a hybrid deployment makes much more sense. On the other hand, complexity arises because you need to interconnect your local on-premise infrastructure with infrastructure, machines, applications, and cloud-based resources. This context is where the Ansible automation tool shines!

# Cloud Architecture

Cloud providers organize their data center architecture in regions and availability zones. Figure 7-1 shows the Amazon Web Services (AWS) global infrastructure map, currently divided into 99 availability zones within 31 geographic regions worldwide at the moment of writing this book. A region directly impacts the performance and services of the final users. When your users are in only one part of the world, reducing the latency for the final user deploying compute and storing the data as closely as possible is more convenient. A region is a set of data centers connected to a low-latency network. Each region has more than a data center. An availability zone is a data center independent in the region. You need to distribute between more availability zones to implement a high availability and redundant application. Implementing this application architecture makes the service more reliable and tolerant of some resources or availability zone failures.

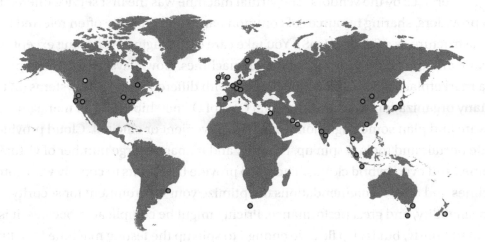

**Figure 7-1.** The Amazon Web Services (AWS) global infrastructure map

The availability zone is a totally independent data center within the region, with its electric system, cooling system, and network devices. Each region has at least two availability zones. Multiple availability zones protect from data center failures. Services for redundant zone storage automatically replicate your data and services across zones.

Note that some features might not be available in all regions. Review your cloud provider documentation when you need a specific feature. You need the least amount of latency as possible, so the data will be sent as fast as possible to your final users. Usually, the price of services varies from region to region.

Most providers provide a paired region in the same country. For example, us-west-1 and us-west-2. This guarantees that if your primary choice region fails because of an outage, the second region will fail over the workload. If the outage affects multiple regions, the vendor will prioritize at least one region per area for repair. Planned maintenance is always scheduled in one region at a time. Service replication is often provided in the paired region as well.

There are three architectural approaches in the cloud providers:

- Infrastructure as a Service (IaaS)

- Platform as a Service (PaaS)

- Software as a Service (SaaS)

Virtual machines are the building blocks inside cloud providers. They have different names, but the concept is the same and sometimes hidden behind totally managed services by the vendors. The virtual machine was the first service offered by cloud providers, sharing resources of common hardware. They are often referred to by Infrastructure as a Service (IaaS). You take care of managing everything except the hardware and the networking for the virtual machines. Nowadays, all the cloud providers offer a marketplace of virtual machine images with different operating systems on them.

Many organizations calculate the Total Cost of Ownership (TCO) of managing the hardware and plan some migration when it is convenient or efficient. Cloud providers provide portals and tools to spin up, monitor, and manage a large number of virtual machines and even hybrid clouds. They also provide blueprints to comply with company guidelines and offer recommendations to optimize your environment for security, high availability, and great performance. Pricing might be complicated because it is calculated hourly, but is also flexible enough to spin up the testing machine for a limited amount of time. The maintenance of virtual machines (operating system updates, patches, security, storage, and so on) might impact your IT department and you might decide to move to a completely managed service offered by the cloud providers. These types of services are called Platform as a Services (PaaS) because you delegate the management of the resources to the vendor and take care only of the application to deliver to your audience. This model is also sometimes called a fully managed platform.

Containers are an important part of modern cloud computing. The major benefits of containers are their self-contained dependency, which increases portability between operating systems and hardware platforms and increases efficiency. Containers reduce the overhead related to maintenance.

Most of the vendors offer a PaaS service to spin up a limited amount of containers via the Portal, API, and CLI via client SDK. When the number of containers increases, you need Kubernetes.

Kubernetes is the common ground for deploying containers in the cloud because it is widely deployed and adopted by all modern vendors. Containers standardized the experience between different suppliers, enabled hybrid cloud IT data centers, and enabled a consistent user experience between vendors. When the number of containers increases, you need a system to keep track of the moving parts, as well as to make sure that containers are configured correctly, the file system is consistent, and works together. As you learned in the previous chapters, Kubernetes takes care of the automatic application deployment and automatic scaling to meet the load and the customer traffic demand. It's battle-tested by Google and many worldwide organizations.

The third architectural design is called Software as a Service (SaaS). Some vendors also refer to this category as "serverless" or "functions." It's the smallest computing service and can be triggered via a standard web address (URL). It executes once and then stops. It's a *serverless* computing service because you don't need to worry about virtual machine toil, maintenance, or processes to manage; you just focus on the functionality. The most famous serverless services are Amazon Lambda and Azure Function. This architectural design enables great growth and great flexibility and saves money because it reduces wasted resources when nobody is using them.

Storing secrets is another important task in a modern IT infrastructure. The most convenient way is to use external services such as AWS Key Management Service (AWS KMS), Google Cloud Key Management Service (Cloud KMS), Azure Key Vault, or Vault by Hashicorp. These types of services help store and retrieve Kubernetes secrets. Keys are stored in a customer-owned key vault customer-managed key (CMK) or a hardware security module (HSM).

The Envelope Encryption technique (or Digital Envelope) allows you to store keys inside an external service and use them using a double encryption mechanism. Using this method, only the provider can read the envelope, and only the customer can read the content of the message. You need to encrypt the encryption key with the key stored in the Key Management Service. Key rotation is also good advice in order to maintain a high-security level.

You can grant temporary access to keys; this feature is helpful for audit account use cases.

# Amazon Web Services (AWS)

Amazon Web Services is probably the biggest cloud provider on the market at the moment, according to international analysts. Amazon Web Services spans 31 regions with 99 availability zones and is available for users of 245 countries and territories. Amazon Elastic Compute Cloud (EC2) provides Infrastructure as a Service (IaaS), many options for Platform as a Service (PaaS), and serverless options with the Amazon Lambda service.

The network is managed by Virtual Private Clouds (VPC) that you can configure as public and private segments, and traffic between is regulated by gateways. There are multiple storage services (detailed in Table 7-2). The most famous is Elastic Block Storage (EBS), which offers persistent block-level storage and the flexibility to attach from one instance of EC2 to another. Amazon Simple Storage Service (S3) instead is an object storage service designed to provide 99.999999999 percent durability, 99.99 percent availability, and incredible scalability and security.

***Table 7-2.*** *Amazon Web Services IaaS, PaaS, SaaS Services*

| IaaS | PaaS | SaaS |
|---|---|---|
| Amazon Elastic Compute Cloud (AWS EC2) | Amazon Elastic Kubernetes Service (EKS) Amazon Elastic Container Service (ECS) | AWS Fargate |

You can try the Amazon Web Services with a one-year trial, which includes some resources for the most popular products, like 750 hours per month of Linux, Red Hat Enterprise Linux (RHEL), or SUSE Linux Enterprise Server (SLES), t2.micro or t3.micro EC2, and RDS instances (managed Relational Database Service for MySQL, PostgreSQL, MariaDB, or SQL Server).

You can generate an Ansible Dynamic Inventory of the resources in your Amazon Web Services infrastructure. The `aws_ec2` inventory plugin is included in the `amazon.aws` collection. You can also interact with Amazon Web Services and create inventory groups automatically with your machines inside based on Amazon EC2 instance metadata (see the section in Chapter 5 titled "Ansible Dynamic Inventory"). First of all, you need to install the `amazon.aws` collection in your Ansible Controller. If it's not already installed, you can proceed using the `ansible-galaxy` command included in all the Ansible installations:

```
$ ansible-galaxy collection install amazon.aws
```

You can verify the successful installation of the `amazon.aws` collection using the same command with the `list` option:

```
$ ansible-galaxy collection list amazon.aws
```

The `amazon.aws` collection requires the `botocore` and `boto3` Python libraries to be installed:

```
$ pip3 install botocore boto3
```

The minimal parameter of the `aws_ec2` inventory plugin is the "regions" that specify which regions to query in AWS. The most powerful feature is the ability to create dynamic groups. This feature reads the host variables according to the `keyed_groups` option. The `keyed_groups` option also defines the prefix and a key format. The full inventory configuration file of the plugin is shown in Listing 7-1.

***Listing 7-1.*** The inventory.aws_ec2.yml File

```
plugin: amazon.aws.aws_ec2
regions:
  - us-east-1
filters:
  tag:env: ansible-examples
keyed_groups:
  - key: 'architecture'
    prefix: arch
  - key: instance_type
    prefix: instance_type
  - key: tags.type
    prefix: tag_type
hostnames:
  - ip-address
```

You need to enable the `aws_ec2` Ansible inventory plugin in your Ansible configuration file, as shown in Listing 7-2.

***Listing 7-2.*** The ansible.cfg File

```
[inventory]
enable_plugins = amazon.aws.aws_ec2
```

It is important to verify that the following environment variables are defined containing the AWS_ACCESS_KEY_ID and AWS_SECRET_ACCESS_KEY:

```
export AWS_ACCESS_KEY_ID='AK123'
export AWS_SECRET_ACCESS_KEY='abc123'
```

You can interact with the Ansible Dynamic Inventory plugin using the ansible-inventory or ansible-playbook command line:

```
$ ansible-inventory -i inventory.aws_ec2.yml --graph
```

This ansible-inventory command generates a graph-style output with all the resources in the cloud provider.

- Tag: ansible-examples
- graph view

```
@all:
  |--@aws_ec2:
  |   |--ip-10-126-56-132.ec2.internal
  |   |--ip-10-125-56-129.ec2.internal
```

You can execute the code using the ansible-playbook command combined with the Ansible Dynamic Inventory for the ansible-examples tag:

```
$ ansible-playbook -i inventory.aws_ec2.yml ping.yml
```

Amazon Elastic Kubernetes Service (Amazon EKS) offers many options to run a Kubernetes cluster based on the amount of control that you want to have and the Kubernetes experience of your teams:

- **AWS fully managed nodes**: AWS Fargate is fully managed by Amazon Web Service if you want only to focus on the data plane and quickly spin up the pods, services, and so on.

- **Managed nodes**: You can manually add under Amazon Elastic Compute Cloud (Amazon EC2) instances in Amazon VPC if you need some special customization nodes.

- **Self-managed nodes**: For maximum customization, you can also add customer-managed nodes using Amazon Elastic Compute Cloud (Amazon EC2) instances in Amazon VPC.

Amazon provides a shared responsibility model, providing tools and infrastructure for creating the infrastructure. Choosing the fully managed service (AWS Fargate), AWS takes direct accountability for any failure of the Kubernetes data plane. In another type of service, the responsibility might be wary only if there is a failure on the underlying cloud infrastructure instances. You can focus on developing an application, data, and support.

AWS Fargate is powered by microVM (Firecracker) technology, a secure and fast microVM for serverless computing. Amazon EKS-optimized Linux AMI is the default AMI for Amazon EKS workloads. The AWS Build Specifications are available on GitHub for creating custom Linux AMI. For example, you could use Bottlerocket, a popular open-source lightweight Linux-based OS designed to run containers.

AWS Identity and Access Management (Amazon IAM) manages Authentication Authorization Accounting (AAA) permissions. RBAC roles allow mapping using ConfigMap to map roles within Kubernetes and IAM, specifying the `mapRoles` attribute.

You can map the IAM role to a Kubernetes RBAC for authentication.

For example, you can create an `aws-auth` ConfigMap currently configured to map the `EksNodeRole` IAM role to the `system:bootstrappers` and `system:nodes` groups. The `EksNodeRole` IAM role is applied to the control plane that serves the Kubernetes cluster. The username in RBAC for one of the nodes would be similar to `system:node:ip-node1.example.com`. If a node does not have the `EksNodeRole` IAM role attached to it, it does not have the correct permissions in RBAC to be included as a cluster node.

Amazon EKS requires an Amazon VPC network in order to operate. The Kubernetes cluster node hosts (in an auto-scaling group) are deployed in the private subnet. Traffic is granularly enabled to the public subnet via a NAT gateway that interconnects the private subnet with the public subnet. The public subnet inside the AWS cloud is connected to the Internet via the Internet gateway. Some use cases require a Bastion host (in an auto-scaling group) configured in the public subnet. You can control inbound (ingress) and outbound (egress) traffic to and from nodes in a security group and/or network security group.

Amazon also created an Amazon EKS API that you can use to interact with the control plane of your Kubernetes cluster. Table 7-3 shows a comparison between the Kubernetes API and the Amazon EKS API.

***Table 7-3.*** *Kubernetes API vs Amazon EKS API*

| Kubernetes API | • kubectl command-line utility<br>• Kubernetes objects: Pods, deployment, namespace<br>• Labelling |
|---|---|
| Amazon EKS API | • eksctl command-line utility<br>• Cluster management<br>• Managed node groups<br>• Fargate<br>• Tagging |

eksctl is an additional command-line tool created by Amazon to interact with Amazon EKS API. It requires Amazon command-line tools (AWS CLI), kubectl command-line tools, and IAM permission for Kubernetes (eksClusterRole). Check out the AWS Prescriptive Guidance for more details about AWS security best practices.

The following eksctl command deploys a small Amazon EKS cluster of two nodes in the eu-west-1 region as a control plane:

```
$ eksctl create cluster --name test-cluster --nodegroup-name test-nodes
--node-type t3.small --nodes 2 --nodes-min 1 --nodes-max 5 --managed
--version 1.21 --region eu-west-1 --zones eu-west-1a,eu-west-1b --role-arn
arn:aws:iam:1234567890:role/eksClusterRole
```

Each parameter of the eksctl command uses the following:

- name: The name of the Kubernetes cluster, test-cluster, in this example

- nodegroup-name: The Amazon EKS node group name, test-cluster, in this example

- node-type: The size of the EC2 instances for the nodes

- nodes: The number of nodes, 2 in this example

- nodes-min: The minimum number of nodes in the Amazon EC2 auto-scaling configuration node group, 1 in this example

- nodes-max: The minimum number of nodes in the Amazon EC2 auto-scaling configuration node group, 5 in this example

- `managed`: Create an Amazon EKS managed node group; it is an AWS managed node group in this example

- `version`: The version of Kubernetes of your Amazon EKS cluster, `1.21` in this example

- `region`: The AWS region of the deployment of Amazon EKS cluster and node group, `eu-west-1` in this example

- `zones`: (optional): Limit the AWS availability zones of the deployment of Amazon EKS cluster and node group, `eu-west-1a` and `eu-west-1b` in this example

- `role-arn`: (optional) The Amazon IAM role ARN identifier using the `eksClusterRole` or `eksNodeRole`

You can verify that the successful cluster was generated using the `kubectl` command:

```
$ kubectl get nodes
```

For each Kubernetes node, you obtain the release version:

```
NAME                                         STATUS   ROLES    AGE
  VERSION
ip-172-16-11-31.eu-west-1.compute.internal   Ready    <none>   2m
  v1.24.1-eks-fb459a0
ip-172-16-53-234.eu-west-1.compute.internal  Ready    <none>   2m
  v1.24.1-eks-fb459a0
ip-172-16-82-159.eu-west-1.compute.internal  Ready    <none>   2m
  v1.24.1-eks-fb459a0
```

As expected, there are three instances: (`ip-172-16-11-31.eu-west-1.compute.internal`, `ip-172-16-53-234.eu-west-1.compute.internal`, and `ip-172-16-82-159.eu-west-1.compute.internal`) in a Ready status from two minutes on the version 1.24, specifically Kubernetes version `v1.24.1-eks-fb459a0`.

When you request a large number of resources and nodes in Amazon, your cluster might fail to build because the current Amazon availability zone (AZ) doesn't have sufficient resources to serve your request. You will receive a `ROLLBACK_FAILED` error message. You can perform a more detailed root cause investigation from the CloudFormation Console under the Events tab.

> **Note**   Amazon Web Services Cloud9 (AWS Cloud 9) is a full online IDE that makes it easy to create AWS cloud resources to create, execute, and troubleshoot code using only your favorite browser and CloudFormation stacks.

Another interesting service is Amazon Elastic Container Registry (Amazon ECR), which provides a fully managed registry for Docker containers and Open Container Initiative (OCI) artifacts. Major advantages are 99,99 percent SLA, high availability and scalability, encryption at rest (requires an AWS Key Management Service [KMS] key), vulnerability scanners, and IAM integration. You can publish publicly or privately visible images and manage permissions using the IAM repository policy. Do not confuse Amazon Elastic Container Registry (ECR) with Amazon Elastic Container Service (ECS). Amazon Elastic Container Service is usually more affordable than the Amazon Elastic Kubernetes Service (EKS). Moreover, it can run images using the three launch type models:

- AWS Fargate

- Amazon EC2

- Amazon ECS on AWS Outposts

With the AWS Fargate launch type model, you pay for the resources that your containerized application utilizes. The amount of vCPU and memory is provided in sizes—from the tiniest of a minimum of 0.25 vCPU and memory of a minimum of 512 MB to a maximum of 2 GB to the biggest of 16 vCPU with memory from 32 GB and a maximum of 120 GB. This is in 8 GB increments.

Using the standard UNIX toolchain, you can create and publish files to the private SCM repository (`git`), generate a Docker image (`docker build`), and push (`docker push`) to the Container Registry, in this case, Amazon ECR.

AWS CodeCommit is a managed source control repository compatible with Git. It enables secure coding team collaboration and integrates all the popular features of its competitors (GitHub, GitLab, and so on).

Amazon provides the service CodePipeline to release software via Continuous Integration via an intuitive workflow-style step-by-step user interface. Through this service, you can create a CI/CD pipeline, a set of automated processes and tools that allow your organization's developers and operations teams to work cohesively to build and deploy code to a production environment.

You can define a pipeline in AWS CodePipeline that stores code in the AWS CodeCommit, triggering an image build that populates the AWS Elastic Container Registry. For example, the popular delivery pipeline in AWS uses AWS CodePipeline, Wave, and Flux.

AWS CloudWatch is the Amazon way to use meaningful metrics data in your cluster. AWS CloudWatch Container Insights is specialized for container data collection. It collects metrics and logs, aggregates at the cluster, node, pod, task, and service level, and visualizes metrics in a dashboard (CPU, memory, disk, network, container data). The EKS Control Plane can be configured to send logs to CloudWatch and the Data Plane Fluentd service. The Fluentbit is more lightweight than the Fluentd service, so most of the time it is preferred. Note that you need to enable the AIM policy `CloudWatchAgentServerPolicy` in order to be able to push the log from your EKS cluster to the CloudWatch.

Each API metric is collected in the dashboard inside a log group. This is a way to acquire data inside your cluster. Moreover, you can enable AWS X-Ray for tracing the service from the backend to the frontend in order to debug and analyze any latency in your system. The traditional debug process is difficult to troubleshoot and involves a combination of different components.

AWS X-Ray analyzes the traffic requests and organizes them into segments and subsegments to pinpoint bottlenecks and perform the service graph. It then drills down on the response code of your API, database, and so on, to understand what exactly is happening. Usually, you keep track of utilization, latency, duration acquiring raw metrics, performance metrics, and error metrics and combine them during every investigation and resolution.

It might be useful to consult the Amazon Well-Architected Framework in order to review the set of architectural best practices for delivering operational excellence for better ROI. This will allow you to secure your data and networks, deliver reliability, and recover after an incidents.

# Google Cloud Platform (GCP)

The most successful Google services, such as Google Maps, Google Photos, YouTube, and Gmail, run on containers. Some statistics estimate a real estate of 4 billion containers in their infrastructure.

Google Cloud spans 35 regions with 106 availability zones and is available for users of more than 200 countries and territories, as shown in Figure 7-2. You can try Google Cloud Platform using the $300 trial, which is enough to start a laboratory and try the basic tools.

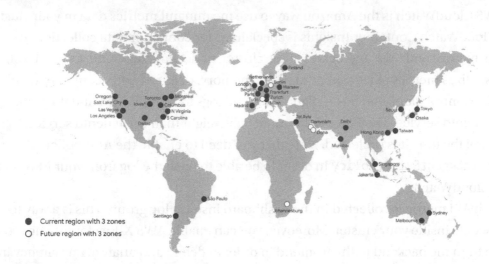

*Figure 7-2.* *The Google Cloud Platform (GCP) global infrastructure map*

As shown in Table 7-4, Google offers the Infrastructure as a Service (IaaS) called Google Compute Engine (GCE), which allows you as a customer to access powerful virtual machines. GCP Cloud Storage might be handy for organizing the entire database, raw video streams, and even a matrix for machine learning models. GCP Networking is grouped into one easy-to-use dashboard. The Google Cloud Identity and Access Management (IAM) manages access control by defining who has what access to which cloud resources.

Google Containers Registry (GCR) is the container registry in the GCP. You can interact with it by specifying `gcr.io` in your Kubernetes manifest files as a source of containers.

*Table 7-4.* *Google Cloud Platform IaaS, PaaS, SaaS Services*

| IaaS | PaaS | SaaS |
|---|---|---|
| Google Compute Engine (GCE) | Google Kubernetes Engine (GKE) | Google Cloud Run |

You can interact with GCP via the Google Cloud Shell directly or via the Google Cloud Console. The Shell appears at the bottom of your Console window when you choose the Console button on the dashboard. When creating your account, the first step is to enable the API of the services that you want to use—in this case, the Google Container API. This API enables the GCP service. In the dashboard, simply search for API & Services and search for the relevant API to enable.

Google Kubernetes Engine (GKE) is the Google-managed offer of Kubernetes for managing your deployments and scaling your containerized applications using the Google infrastructure. It integrates the latest release of Kubernetes plus all the specific patches for the Google infrastructure. The service is fully compatible with the Kubernetes API, four-way autoscaling, official release channels, multi-cluster support, and scales up to 15,000 nodes. The major advantage of using Google Kubernetes Engine (GKE) is that it closely follows the latest changes in the Kubernetes open-source project.

Google Kubernetes clusters are formed by a virtual machine running on the Google Compute Engine. At the moment of writing this book, there are two differences between AKS and GKE services. GKE supports only a few operating systems, and the SLA is different in the zonal clusters. The first weakness is that there are only two available operating systems for the server nodes: Container-Optimized OS and Ubuntu. Container-Optimized OS is an operating system image for the Google Compute Engine virtual machines optimized for running Docker containers. It is maintained by Google and based on the open-source Chromium OS project.

Note the Service-Level Agreement (SLA). Amazon Elastic Kubernetes Service (EKS) offers an SLA of 99.95 percent, whereas GKE offers 99.95 percent only for its regional clusters. The GKE for its zonal clusters has a 99.5 percent SLA. GKE has a lot of flexibility based on your workload and budget requirements. The smallest is the single control plane in a single zone "zonal cluster," but you can increase to multi-zonal and regional options.

One of the benefits of running in GCP is that it is fully integrated with Cloud Controller Manager to manage accesses on the cluster. As a managed service, it outsources the data plane that is managed by Google,. You can then focus on deploying your application or service. A cluster is the foundation of the GKE service. A cluster consists of at least one control pane and multiple nodes. The cluster uses some connected GCP services such as VPC networking, persistent disk, load balances, and cloud operations. Each node is managed by the control plane and runs your Pods (aka user pods). A typical workload completely in Google Cloud could use services like Cloud

Code as IDE, Code Repository ad SCM, and Cloud Build to create container images to store in Google Container Registry before being deployed in GKE. You can interact with your cluster using Cloud Console UI, the gcloud command-line interface, or Google APIs. One of the main benefits of GKE is the native integration between cloud monitoring and cloud logging Google services. These services are performed via cloud operations for GKE, are enabled by default, and provide a monitor dashboard specifically tailored for Kubernetes. You can also collect application logs for easy troubleshooting and further analysis.

Another option for running your cloud-native application is using the Google Cloud Run service. It is the Google serverless offer used by companies like MailChimp, Airbus, and MediaMarktSaturn. It supports the most popular computer languages (GO, Python, Java, Node.js, .NET, and Ruby) on a fully managed platform to create containerized and scalable applications.

You can retrieve the Google Cloud Compute Engine list of resources using the gcp_compute Ansible inventory plugin included in the google.cloud collection.

You can install the google.cloud Ansible collection using the ansible-galaxy command included in all Ansible installations:

```
$ ansible-galaxy collection install google.cloud
```

The following command verifies a successful installation of the google.cloud collection:

```
$ ansible-galaxy collection list google.cloud
```

The google.cloud collection requires the requests and google-auth Python libraries installed in your Ansible Controller:

```
$ pip3 install requests google-auth
```

The configuration file in Listing 7-3 returns the list of resources in an Ansible Dynamic Inventory format.

***Listing 7-3.*** The ansible.cfg File

```
[inventory]
enable_plugins = google.cloud.gcp_compute
```

Meanwhile, Listing 7-4's inventory.gcp.yml lists the resources in the ansible-examples project.

***Listing 7-4.*** The inventory.gcp.yml File

```
plugin: gcp_compute
projects:
  - ansible-examples
auth_kind: serviceaccount
service_account_file: /home/ansible/credentials.json
```

The `credentials.json` file is the service account credential file that contains the access token downloaded via the Google Cloud Console.

Google, like with the other competitors, has plenty of services to simplify your workload in cloud computing.

# Microsoft Azure Cloud Services

Microsoft Azure provides similar building blocks as Amazon Web Services and Google Cloud Platform, plus some specific services that might be useful for IT professionals. Azure spans more than 60 regions with more than 90 availability zones and is available to users of more than 200 countries and territories. Azure offers some free services the first year, and a selection of more than 55 services is always free. The free trial at the moment of writing this book includes 750 hours of B1s burstable virtual machines, 100 GB storage in one standard tier registry, and 10 webhooks in the Azure Container Registry.

Azure Compute is their Infrastructure as a Service (IaaS). There are many options for Platform as a Service (PaaS) and serverless with the Azure Functions service. See Table 7-5.

***Table 7-5.*** *Google Cloud Platform IaaS, PaaS, SaaS Services*

| IaaS | PaaS | SaaS |
|------|------|------|
| Azure Compute | Azure Kubernetes Service (AKS) | Azure Containers |

Azure Compute deploys Windows and Linux virtual machines (VMs) using the powerful Microsoft Hyper-V hypervisor technology. Azure Hybrid Benefit is the licensing model that enables you to use software assurance-enabled Windows Server and SQL Server licenses and Red Hat and SUSE Linux subscriptions on virtual machines in Azure. Azure Spot Virtual Machines is an option to use heavily discounted, unused computing capacity to run your workloads. Azure uses Azure Virtual Network (VNet) to connect virtual machines to public and private segments. Routing and access control lists can also be configured dynamically for enhanced security control. When you're embarking on your journey to the cloud, you might find Azure Migrate useful. It helps migrate Linux and Windows, including Virtual Desktop Infrastructure (VDI) resources. It enables a comprehensive security and compliance overview of your hybrid infrastructure. Azure Compute Virtual Machines also supports the latest Ampere Altra ARM–based processors (a complete multi-core server processors system on chip solution built for cloud-native workloads) since 2022.

The first specific Azure service is a resource group. Resources groups are essential to every architecture on Azure. They are logical buckets where you include all the resources needed by your application or project, and you can manage them as a group. Each resource exists in only one resource group, can be moved to another one, and can be from different regions. You can apply a common access control policy to all the resource groups.

Azure Resource Manager (ARM) is the deploying manager on Azure when it comes to creating, updating, and deleting resources. You can interact with Portal, PowerShell, Azure CLI, REST APIs, and client SDKs using the Azure Resource Manager API. The best practice is to deploy, monitor, and manage your resources through the Azure Resource Manager as a group rather than manually start one after another, individually. The major advantages are as follows:

- **Consistency**: Each deployment triggers the same workflow on each deployment

- **Dependency**: Ensures that all the necessary resources are in place at the right time

- **Access control**: Applies a common policy

- **Tagging**: Easily identifies and applies a label

- **Billing**: Simplifies audit and understanding

Virtual machines in an Azure cloud provider are called *Azure compute* and are widely used all over the platform.

Azure calls a group of identical, load-balanced virtual machines a *scale set*. The baseline is a single image that is deployed by the scale set. If one virtual machine in the scale set stops or fails, the others continue working and take over the load. The scale set enables automatic matching of the workload and adding or removing virtual machines to try to match the needs. The service is free, but you pay for the virtual machines. It can manage thousands of resources. Azure Service Bus is a message bus interface that you can use as a source event with Event Driven Ansible (see Chapter 8).

As the previous cloud providers, you can retrieve the list of resources using an Ansible Inventory plugin. First of all, you need the `azure.azcollection` Ansible collection in your Ansible Controller. The installation can be performed using the `ansible-galaxy` command included in all Ansible installations:

```
$ ansible-galaxy collection install azure.azcollection
```

You can obtain the full list of the installed Ansible collections using the same command with the `list` option:

```
$ ansible-galaxy collection list azure.azcollection
```

The `azure.azcollection` collection requires the Python plugins listed in the `requirements-azure.txt` file, which you can retrieve from the GitHub repository of the project[3] installed:

```
$ pip3 install -r requirements-azure.txt
```

The `azure_rm` Ansible inventory plugin of the `azure.azcollection` collection retrieves the resources included in the `ansible-examples` Azure Resource Manager, as demonstrated in Listing 7-5.

***Listing 7-5.*** The inventory.azure.yml File

```
plugin: azure_rm
include_vm_resource_groups:
  - ansible-examples
auth_source: auto
```

You need to enable the dynamic inventory in your Ansible project with the `ansible.cfg` Ansible configuration file, as shown in Listing 7-6.

---

[3] https://github.com/ansible-collections/azure

***Listing 7-6.*** The ansible.cfg File

```
[inventory]
enable_plugins = azure.azcollection.azure_rm inventory
```

As with other Ansible Dynamic Inventory plugins, you can interact with it using the `ansible-inventory` or `ansible-playbook` command line:

```
$ ansible-inventory -i inventory.azure.yml --list
```

The output of the `ansible-inventory` command is a JSON file with all the resources of the cloud provider:

- Namespace: `ansible-examples`

- `list` view

You can execute the code using the `ansible-playbook` command combined with the Ansible Dynamic Inventory for the `ansible-examples` resource group:

```
$ ansible-playbook -i inventory.azure.yml ping.yml
```

On the PaaS offering, the easiest way to deploy containers is via the Web App for Containers. Web App is a managed platform of Azure. It can host your existing container images. The container supports web applications written in popular computer programming languages (Python, Node.js, .NET, Java, PHP, and Ruby). There are also API apps that host and simplify the data backend services.

Azure Container Instances (ACI) is the primary service of Azure for managing and deploying your applications in a container. The service takes care of managing your workload on containers without the complexity of virtual machines. On batch workload, for example, you can spin up the container on demand, process the data, and turn off the containerized application. Using this workflow, you reduce costs and resources. ACI supports Azure Portal, CLI, and PowerShell.

When the workload becomes bigger, you can use the Azure Kubernetes Service (AKS) to orchestrate it. The setup is quick as the service already includes the standard Azure services, identity and access management, elastic provisioning, integration with Microsoft coding tools, and global reach using Azure Stack.

Azure Container Registry (ACR) is the Google-managed Container Registry that manages container image files and artifacts.

The major advance of using Azure Kubernetes Service (AKS) is its rich integration with other Azure services, for example, Azure Active Directory (Azure AD).

Azure Kubernetes Service (AKS) is an Azure-managed Kubernetes service with hardened security and fast delivery. Microsoft handles the control plane, so you can focus on deploying your applications. AKS also supports NVIDIA GPU-enabled node pools.

You can interact with the AKS cluster using Azure CLI, Azure PowerShell, Azure Portal, and template-driven deployment (Terraform, Azure Resource Manager templates, and Bicep).

# Other Vendors

With many vendors offering Kubernetes as part of their offer of cloud services, you need a way to compare the main features among them. The Certified Kubernetes Conformance Program, by CNCF, enables multiple Kubernetes cluster interoperability. At the moment, 90 certified Kubernetes offerings passed the Certified Kubernetes Software Conformance by CNCF (Sonobuoy). Software conformance certifies that every vendor's version of Kubernetes supports at least the community APIs of the open-source edition.

The benefits of the Certified Kubernetes Conformance Program are as follows:

- **Consistency**: Works with any installation of Kubernetes

- **Timely updates**: Updates at least once per year to the latest version

- **Confirmability**: All end users can run the certification conformance application (Sonobuoy)

According to IDC, Forrester, and Gartner international analysis, the current Kubernetes in the cloud computing marketplace is divided between Akamai, Alibaba, Amazon Web Services, DigitalOcean, Google, Huawei, IBM, Microsoft, Oracle, OVHcloud, Tencent, Vultr, Zadara, and Linode.

- Rancher, acquired by SUSE in July 2020, is an enterprise-grade and user-friendly Kubernetes management platform with more than 37,000 active users. SUSE is the company behind the SUSE Enterprise Linux operating system.

- Alibaba Cloud Container Service for Kubernetes (ACK) was one of the first certified platforms and integrates virtualization, security, storage, and networking capabilities.

- DigitalOcean Kubernetes (DOKS) from DigitalOcean Cloud is a managed control plane like in PaaS services such as Amazon Elastic Kubernetes Service (EKS). It includes the DigitalOcean CSI plugin and the Container Storage Interface (CSI) Driver for DigitalOcean Block Storage.

- IBM Cloud Kubernetes was one of the first fully-managed Kubernetes in the cloud, since May 2017 (formerly known as IBM Cloud Container Service). It runs on the IBM Cloud.

- Linode Kubernetes Engine (LKE) is a service known for its simple pricing model and ease of use based on the Linode infrastructure.

- Oracle Container Engine for Kubernetes (OKE) offers the same service in the Oracle Cloud Infrastructure (OCI).

With such a multitude of offerings, it can be difficult to make the right decision. Competition, in this case, is a good driver for the final user because companies are competing with each other to offer better services, at a better price, a better SLA, and a better infrastructure. Before making your decision, consider the alternatives. The Certified Kubernetes Conformance Program guarantees that you can always move your application between providers, thus avoiding vendor lock-in mechanisms.

# Key Takeaways

Ansible, Kubernetes, and cloud providers are an incredible combination of powerful tools, technologies, and cost-efficient ways to deploy applications or services at a world scale. Organizations all over the world are considering hybrid clouds and learning how to deploy container images faster and scale as needed. You learned how to easily maintain a remote data center in a cloud environment with Ansible and the right tools You already know to manage your local laboratory or on-premise data center. Ansible Dynamic Inventory is the critical tool for homogenizing, scaling, and maintaining your fleet of machines when the scale is simply too much. In the next chapter, you learn about Ansible for Enterprise.

# CHAPTER 8

# Ansible for Enterprise

One of the main benefits of Ansible is that it standardizes infrastructure automation among different technologies and programming styles (Perl, bash, Puppet, Chef, and so on). It is the Swiss Army Knife tool of modern operations engineers and can easily be used in Infrastructure as Code (IaC), Configuration as a Code (CaC), Policy as a Code, Code pipelines, orchestration (K8s), and event-driven automation.

Ansible runs literally everywhere. It enables organizations to speed up processes and become more efficient and productive. It is the rise of platform engineering tools: user-driven, self-service infrastructure and deployments that extend the principle of continuous integration and delivery, furthering infrastructure and operations (I&O) agility, faster, more efficient, safe, and compliant with international standards.

When you are part of an enterprise organization, you use Ansible in a slightly different way. Many organizations use Ansible because the amount of resources to manage is simply too big to handle manually. You can also use tools that make collaboration within your team more effective and dynamic. You can manage resources and relationships at a planetary scale nowadays. Also, organizations embrace the change of internal processes for fast-pacing decision-making. One of the main advantages of Ansible automation is that it produces code that you can store in a common source control repository and can be shared between your teams. The Red Hat Ansible Automation Platform grew up around the idea of creating a web service API and web user interface that teams can use every day. Some colleagues advantage of the uncomplicated web interface to trigger the automation, whereas all the operations can be performed via the RESTful API.

## The Ansible Automation Platform

The Ansible Automation Platform (AAP) is the commercial offering from Red Hat, the company leading the Ansible project. The Ansible Automation Platform subscription includes the latest software and official support, documentation, and additional

261

© Luca Berton 2023
L. Berton, *Ansible for Kubernetes by Example*, https://doi.org/10.1007/978-1-4842-9285-3_8

resources from Red Hat. The AAP is a platform of Ansible-based IT automation products, including Ansible Controller (formerly Ansible Tower), Ansible Core (formerly Ansible Engine), Automation Hub, and other enterprise features, including:

- Ansible Certified Collections

- Single sign-on

- Role-based access control

- Multi-cloud support

- Red Hat support and subscription

It allows organizations to automate IT operations, deploy and scale applications, and manage Infrastructure as Code (IaC) across multiple environments, such as on-premises, cloud, and hybrid.

Ansible Automation Platform includes Ansible Automation Controller (formerly Ansible Tower). This web-based management console provides a graphical user interface, role-based access control, and other features to make it easier to manage and scale Ansible automation across an organization.

It includes a RESTful API and enterprise Ansible collection to interact with it. It also includes Ansible Core (formerly Ansible Engine), which is the core of the platform. The release of the Ansible language provides the ability to automate provisioning, configuration management, application deployment, and many other IT needs. It includes enterprise-grade support in the subscription services. The platform includes more products that interact with the Ansible Automation Controller. The most important is the Ansible Automation Hub. In the same way that the Ansible Galaxy registry downloads community content, the corporate world relies on the Ansible Automation Hub to provide Ansible resources and content that they download from it. The Ansible Automation Hub manages resources from Red Hat product teams, ISV partners, and community and private contributors.

The partner list in Ansible Automation Hub is getting lengthier day by day and includes, at the moment, the following: Amazon, Arista, Aruba Networks, Check Point, Cisco, Citrix, CyberArk, Dell EMC, Dynatrace, F5 Networks, Fortinet, HPE, IBM, Juniper Networks, Kubernetes, Microsoft, NetApp, NVIDIA, 1Password, SAP, ServiceNow, Splunk, TrendMicro, and VMWare.

The Ansible Automation Platform provides centralized management, visibility, and scalability to the IT organization and improved collaboration among teams and departments.

The Ansible Automation Platform has a bi-yearly software release cycle, usually in May and November. The release 2.x+ fully embraces the Container software design paradigm with the full support of Kubernetes as an execution environment and operating system.

The latest release at the time of writing this book is version 2.3. Its main features are as follows:

- Automation Execution Environments

- Automation Mesh

- Automation Services Catalog

Currently, the Red Hat Ansible Automation Platform is supported on Red Hat Enterprise Linux versions 8 and 9 and Red Hat OpenShift. The Ansible Automation Platform Operator provides cloud-native, easy-to-install deployment of Ansible Automation Platform instances in your OpenShift environment. The Ansible Automation Platform Operator deploys and manage instances of the Automation controller and Private Automation hub in your OpenShift cluster. At the moment of writing this book, the Ansible Automation Platform Operator for installing Ansible Automation Platform 2.3 is available on OpenShift Container Platform 4.9+. It deploys Ansible Automation Platform instances with a Kubernetes native operator. The two types of instances are Ansible Controller and Private Automation Hub.

The easiest way to install the Ansible Automation Platform Operator is via the OperatorHub in the web console. Just search for the Ansible Automation Platform provided by Red Hat. The latest release is 2.3.0+0.1674778407, as shown in Figure 8-1. The Operator takes care of all the necessary dependencies, such as PostgreSQL 13.

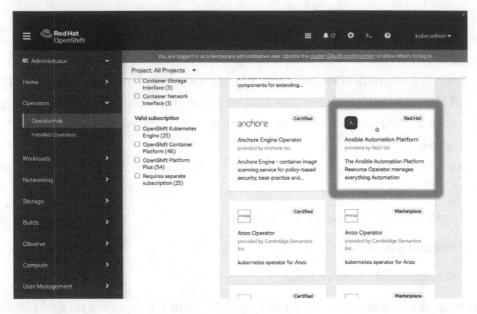

***Figure 8-1.*** *The Ansible Automation Platform Operator*

You can specify some installation parameters, as shown in Figure 8-2.

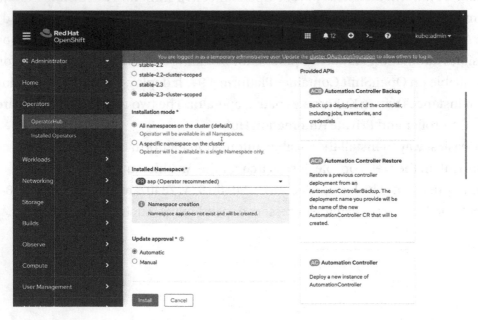

***Figure 8-2.*** *AAP operator installation parameters*

Here is a full list of Ansible Automation Platform Operator parameters:

- Update Channel: The exact version to install

- Installation mode: Install the operator cluster-wise or only in a specific namespace

- Installed namespace: Customize the default "aap" namespace

- Update approval: Manual or automatic

Once it's successfully installed, you receive a confirmation like the one shown in Figure 8-3.

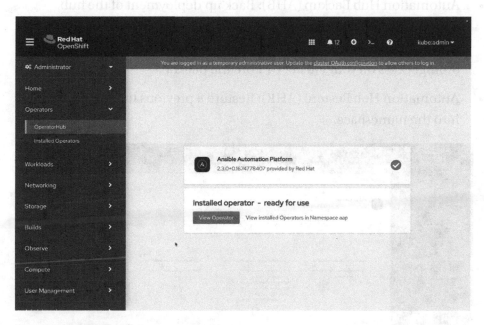

***Figure 8-3.*** *AAP operator was installed*

You can see the Operator Dashboard in Figure 8-4, which enables you to:

- Automation Controller (AC): Deploy a new instance of AutomationController.

- Automation Controller Backup (ACB): Back up deployment of the controller, including jobs, inventories, and credentials.

- Automation Controller Restore (ACR): Restore a previous controller deployment from an AutomationControllerBackup. The deployment name you provide will be the name of the new AutomationController CR that will be created.

- Automation Controller job template (JT): Define a new job template in the controller.

- Automation Controller job (AJ): Launch a new job via Controller.

- Automation Hub (AH): Deploy a new instance of Automation Hub.

- Automation Hub Backup (AHB): Back up deployment of the hub, including all hosted Ansible content, secrets, and the database. By default, a persistent volume claim will be created using the default StorageClass on your cluster to store the backup.

- Automation Hub Restore (AHR): Restore a previous hub deployment into the namespace.

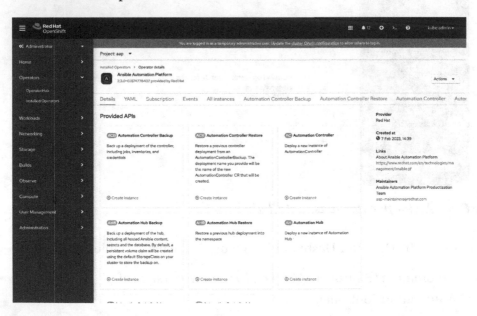

***Figure 8-4.*** *The AAP Operator Dashboard*

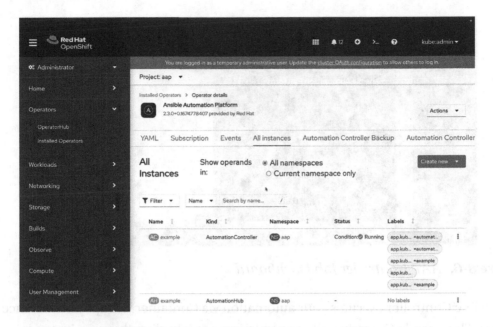

**Figure 8-5.** *AAP Operator running instances*

When all your instances are fully running, you can access the Ansible Automation Platform Dashboard (see Figure 8-6), and your automation journey begins. Inside the interactive web dashboard, you can create users applying RBAC access criteria, fetch Ansible projects from the most common SCM, and run your automation using the Job Templates. Every execution of an Ansible Playbook is called a *job execution*. A job execution can incorporate Credentials and Vaults and can be executed against Inventories or Hosts. One of the biggest benefits is that the dashboard centralizes your experience. You can store credentials, Ansible vaults, keys, and security tokens between the IT department team, customizing accesses using RBAC and integrating AAP with the most common enterprise-grade authentication systems.

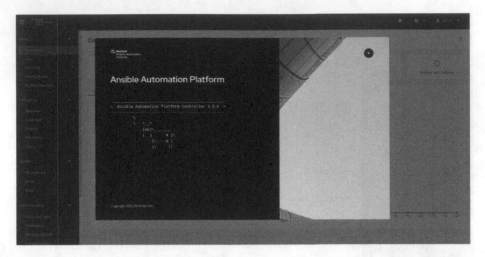

***Figure 8-6.*** *AAP Controller Job Dashboard*

Ansible Controller executes your automation via Container Groups and Instance Groups. The Ansible Controller allows you to execute jobs directly on an instance member, in a virtual environment, in a Kubernetes namespace, or a in a project in an OpenShift cluster.

When implementing your Infrastructure as Code (IaC), creating an IaC Ansible pipeline can be handy. It is a Git-centric continuous deployment pipeline using Ansible. DevOps teams create the Ansible resources and store them in a Git repository. Those commits are picked up by a CI/CD tool, typically Jenkins, or trigger an Ansible Controller WebHook to launch associated jobs (playbooks) or workflow.

All the book's code can be used in the Ansible Automation Platform for easy interaction between your IT department team.

# Event-Driven Ansible

Modern businesses use many different IT systems and services, with the consequence of increased complexity in managing integration and mode API interfaces. This often results in a "spaghetti infrastructure." Accessing a centralized event streaming service that acts as a message bus with event-driven architecture can achieve easier integration between different systems and services. The result is a more flexible system that can adapt to changes in the business environment.

An exciting evolution of automation is Event-Driven Ansible (EDA). It's highly scalable with a flexible automation capability. At the moment of writing this book, the EDA was released in October 2022 as a technological preview by Red Hat. Event-Driven Ansible contains a decision framework that is built using Drools. In a nutshell, it implements the ability to react to a system event and trigger automation. In this way, you can work smarter by applying Event-Drive Ansible and Ansible Rulebooks.

Think about the ability to apply "If-This-Than-That" logic or to minimize the Mean-Time-To-Resolution (MTTR) for outages in your systems. This is the latest evolution of smart automation, an understanding of how to execute automated scripts to mitigate and quickly remediate any event in your IT infrastructure. The key component is the Event-Driven Ansible Server, which runs in the system as a service and listens for events. The Ansible Rulebook (see Figure 8-7), similar to the Ansible Playbook, explains to the EDA Server what the playbook executes, specifying the relevant parameters.

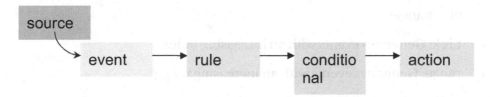

***Figure 8-7.*** *Workflow of an EDA rulebook*

The building blocks of Event-Driven Ansible automation are as follows:

- Event: Any changes from the source

- Rule: Evaluated for every event

- Conditional: The event expression that triggers the action

- Action: What to execute (playbook, modules, tasks)

In the rulebook, you can define the sources of events: hooks, alert managers, URLs, and files to listen to. For each of them, you can define and perform some action according to the rule that you write. Each rule defines the condition that triggers the action. Each rule has some conditionals. Conditionals evaluate some event status logically and define when to trigger an action. For example, it could be an event from the alert manager or when a specific HTTP status code is obtained, a newly created file, or a message from the webhook. When a condition is reached, one or more actions can be triggered. The most common action is `run_playbook`. Each source of event determines the type of event in the rulebook. A very interesting source of events is Apakce Kafa as a "message bus" or webhook.

At the moment of writing this book, the following source plugins are available:

- `alertmanager`: Receives webhook events from alertmanager

- `Azure_Service_Bus`: Receives Azure Service Bus events

- `kafka`: Receives Apache Kafka topic messages

- `url_check`: Polls URLs and sends events based on their statuses

- `watchdog`: Sends events when a file status changes

- `webhook`: Receives events from a webhook

- `file`: Loads facts from YAML files and reloads them when a file changes

- `tick`: Generates events with an increasing index

- `range`: Generates events with an increasing range

The installation of Ansible Event-Driven requires two components:

- The Ansible `ansible.eda` collection

- The Python `ansible-rulebook` command-line utility

  You can manually install these using the `ansible-galaxy` command or using a `requirements.yml` file:

  ```
  $ ansible-galaxy collection install ansible.eda
  $ pip3 install ansible-rulebook
  ```

The utility requires the Java 11+ runtime environment (Oracle, OpenJDK, GraalVM, and so on) and the `JAVA_HOME` environment variable, set accordingly. You can verify a successful installation using the `--version` parameter of the `ansible-rulebook` command to verify the current version of the software:

```
$ ansible-rulebook --version
```

The rulebook in Listing 8-1 exposes a webhook on port 8000 that is listening for messages. Each time you receive a non-empty message (a condition), it triggers the execution of the `playbook.yml` playbook, shown in Listing 8-2.

***Listing 8-1.*** The eda.yml File

```
---
- name: Listen for webhook events
  hosts: all
  sources:
    - ansible.eda.webhook:
        host: 0.0.0.0
        port: 8000
  rules:
    - name: webhook
      condition: event.payload.message != ""
      action:
        run_playbook:
          name: playbook.yml
```

***Listing 8-2.*** The playbook.yml File

```
- name: eda demo
  hosts: localhost
  tasks:
    - name: print a message
      ansible.builtin.debug:
        msg: "Event Driven Ansible"
```

***Listing 8-3.*** The inventory File

```
localhost ansible_connection=local
```

You can execute your rulebook using the following command:

```
$ ansible-rulebook --rulebook eda.yml -i inventory --verbose
```

You can add the optional parameter --verbose when you want more debug information.

You can also create a container image with the Ansible rulebook and deploy it in a pod to implement a scalable Event-Driven Ansible on Kubernetes.

The latest release of Ansible Automation Platform 2.3 integrated Event-Driven Ansible as a Developer Preview release.

# IT Trends

More and more applications are moving from monolith devices to microservices software design patterns. This is one of the reasons for the increased use of containers and the adoption of the Kubernetes container orchestration tool. An orchestrator helps you deploy high-availability applications with no downtime. They scale up or down when the traffic demands more resources, making applications more flexible. Latency is becoming the key metric to evaluate the quality of your applications. Kubernetes also has the ability to self-heal infrastructure to run your application when an event happens, such as a failure in the underlying server, storage, or network. The lowest metrics for Recovery Point Objective (RPO) and Recovery Time Objective (RTO) are available for a disaster recovery or data protection plan.

IT infrastructure is becoming the heart of organizations. International analyst agencies predict that the complexity and type of threats to rise yearly. The container and Kubernetes Security Market is in expansion. We often hear on the news about ransomware or supply chain attacks. The most impactful event on this side was the SolarWinds hacking in June, 2022. The hackers breached the Onion network in September 2019, malicious code had been injected into Orion for seven months. FireEye, the detection and response Cyber Security Experts and Solution Provider, was the first firm to publicly report the attack, called the SolarWinds hack "UNC2452." The attack was performed via a "Sunburst" backdoor, which connects to an external command-and-control server. The Orion software was turned into a weapon, thus gaining access to several global IT infrastructures.

According to the reports, the malware affected 18,000 SolarWinds customers and impacted many public and private companies. Famous organizations such as FireEye, Microsoft, Intel, Cisco, and Deloitte were impacted by this attack, as were government departments such as the U.S. Homeland Security, State, Commerce, and Treasury. It also significantly damaged SolarWinds' reputation, probably taking them years to heal and recover.

This event raised public opinion and consensus that companies needed to pay more attention to privacy issues. Corporations are obliged by law to report data breaches, and in the upcoming years, we are going to see a rise in data breach compensation claims. Starting in 2018, with the implementation of the European General Data Protection Regulation (GDPR), many data protection frameworks were created to protect data as an asset. For example, there is the EU–US Privacy Shield, California's Consumer Privacy Act (CCPA), Brazil's General Personal Data Protection Law/Lei Geral de Proteção de Dados (LGPD), and South Africa's Protection of Personal Information Act (PoPIA).

# Ansible Trusted Code

To minimize the risk of supply chain attacks, it's important to use only trusted code in your organization. In November 2022, Red Hat released the following:

- Ansible Trusted Ansible Collections

- Signed Ansible Projects

Ansible Trusted Ansible Collections is a feature available in the Ansible Automation Platform, Automation Hub, that enables the download of only digitally certified content signed via a GPG key. GNU Pretty Good Privacy, or GPG, is a popular program that authenticates contents with digital signatures of stored files.

In the same way that Ansible Certified Contents are digitally signed, you can use the same technology for in-house content. The `ansible-sign` command-line utility is designed precisely for project signing and verification. You can install the utility via the popular operating system package manager or the Python `pip` installer.

As general habits, we store our project in an SCM repository, usually Git. The list of files for signature is specified in the `MANIFEST.in` file, where we can specify which files to include or exclude. This is a famous format used in many open-source projects nowadays. You can `include` or `exclude` single files or `recursive-include` or `recursive-exclude` directories or only match some criteria with `global-include` and `global-exclude`.

Listing 8-4 is an example of a `MANIFEST.in` file for this project that excludes the `.git` directory, includes the `inventory` file, and includes all the files with the `yml` extension under the `playbooks` directory.

***Listing 8-4.*** The MANIFEST.in File

```
recursive-exclude .git *
include inventory
recursive-include playbooks *.yml
```

The full command to sign this project is as follows:

```
$ ansible-sign project gpg-sign PROJECT_ROOT
```

In the same way, you can verify the project using this command:

```
$ ansible-sign project gpg-verify PROJECT_ROOT
```

A signed project has an additional .ansible-sign directory with two files inside. The first is the sha256sum.txt file, which contains the SHA256 hash of each file. This is already an industry standard. The second file is sha256sum.txt.sig, which contains the GPG signature of the previous file. With the contents signature and verification, you obtain a success when the signature verification is valid. Two files exist, the checksum is valid and the signature is valid.

Here are the possible scenarios when something is not correct:

- The checksum is invalid when files are tampered with or are invalid

- The signature is invalid when the signature is tampered with or invalid

- There is a signature mismatch when the signature is wrong, expired, or inaccessible

The benefits of the feature outweigh the extra overhead in the effort. I'm happy with the outcome. Now you know how to use the ansible-sign utility for your projects. Taking a closer look at the utility by design, it already supports the expansion with more options and more hashing technologies in the future. Sigstore is a new standard for signing, verifying, and protecting software that might be embraced in the future.

Ansible enterprise customers can use the Signed Ansible Projects features every day as part of the Ansible Automation Platform 2.3 (November 2022) or the open-source AWX 21.7.0 with AWX Operator v0.30.0 (October 2022). The Signed Ansible Projects feature is implemented in AWX and Ansible Automation Controller. You can enable the feature of creating a credential using the GPG Public Key type and selecting it in your projects. Content verification will automatically occur upon future project sync. Every time your project syncs, the signature will be evaluated, and if it doesn't match, the execution will be forbidden. Under the hood, it uses the ansible-sign utility to validate the project.

# What's Next?

Ansible and Kubernetes are two open-source products that benefit from a vibrant community of people worldwide. Somehow, the holistic view is more powerful than each part of it. Kubernetes has more than 18,000 GitHub contributors, whereas Ansible has 5,100 contributors.

New trends emerge every day in this fast-paced IT world. Artificial intelligence-powered automation is already on the rise, and automated machines are expected to take over a growing portion of professions in the coming years. Sometimes machines can execute a task better, faster, and cheaper than humans. Other times, machines create big mistakes. Applying artificial intelligence to infrastructure could be a great boost in efficiency for the Infrastructure and Operations (I&O) of projects.

Since the OpenAI ChatGPT release announcement on November 30, 2022, the ChatGPT tool has seen great hype on the Internet. People around the globe tested in the most variant situations. The application of the GPT-3 (Generative Pre-trained Transformer) large language model is impressive with a massive amount of data. Applying this type of technology to your daily workflow could be interesting. At the moment of writing this book, you can interact with the tool in a chatbox user interface. The tool can generate some Ansible code that you need to revisit before running it.

Announced at *AnsibleFest* 2022, Project Wisdom will be released later in 2023 as the result of a close collaboration between the Ansible Engineering Team and IBM Research. The goal was to create an Ansible AI (Ansible Lightspeed with IBM Watson Code Assistant) integrated into the VSCode editor to create code based on the Ansible task text.

This type of technology scenario creates opportunities for IT professionals to step up, upskill themselves, and be part of the machine evolution. The unique ability to connect data, be creative, and imagine the future is a game changer for humans. "We are the master of our fate: We are the captain of our souls," as William Ernest Henley said in *Invictus*.

Intuition is the unarticulated, almost imperceptible gist that you get in a situation. That feeling that sometimes it's quite right, or that sometimes it is about to happen, that we can't explain, but know to be true. It seems like magic, but it is humans' unique ability that differentiates us from machines. Gut instinct is a valuable tool that we can use for the present to identify what to improve in our life without really thinking about it. It's the human essence.

# Thank You

Kubernetes is a very powerful but also complex technology for container orchestration. It solves the problem of managing many containers to deploy microservices of cloud-native applications and services. You learned how to automate and simplify many day-to-day operations using Ansible automation technology. These applications and services are used by people around the world—they interact every day with websites, bank accounts, and e-commerce, they reserve a table at a restaurant, order a delivery/pickup, a taxi, or a flight, and many other examples. The microservice application design has become very pervasive in just a few years at a world scale.

Briefly, Ansible and Kubernetes are evolving open-source products. Check out the official websites for the latest news and updates.

I'm so grateful to live in the information age, where ideas become businesses overnight, and as individuals, we have equal opportunities for success.

Using Ansible automation with Kubernetes for container orchestration with cloud providers opens up unlimited computing resources. The use of artificial intelligence and deep learning models is growing faster and faster. Altogether, this world enables a new class of cloud-native applications of tomorrow that is going to change our lives.

The future is uncharted territory, and the sky is the limit. I look forward to hearing your success automation story.

"Simplicity is the ultimate sophistication." —Leonardo da Vinci

Please be nice. Life is sweeter that way.

# Index

## A

AppArmor profiles, 193
AAP Operator, 263
AAP Operator parameters, 265
Alpine Linux distribution, 15
Amazon availability zone (AZ), 249
Amazon command-line tools (AWS
    CLI), 248
Amazon EKS API, 247, 248
Amazon Elastic Container Registry
    (Amazon ECR), 11, 250
Amazon Elastic Container Service
    (Amazon ECS), 11, 250
Amazon Elastic Kubernetes Service
    (Amazon EKS), 11, 246, 250, 260
Amazon Machine Image (AMI),
    11, 84, 247
Amazon Web Services (AWS), 3, 11, 56, 87,
    99, 109, 153, 201, 244
Ansible, 7, 169
    benefits, 27
    builder process, 57, 58
    code language, 37
    collection, 54, 55
    configuration file, 245
    configuration management, 29
    control node, 34
    DevOps, 27
    Execution Environment, 55, 56, 59
    Galaxy, 53, 54
    INI format, 39
    installation, 34

    inventory, 33, 37
    localhost, 38
    open-source *vs.* commercial
        options, 29
    Playbook, 40–42
        conditional statements, 45
        facts, 48
        filters, 44
        handler, 46
        loop, 46, 47
        magic variables, 48, 49
        plugins, 50, 51
        templates, 49, 50
        variables, 43
        Vault, 49
    Playbook/Inventory, 31
    plugins, 28
    provisioning, 28
    Role, 51, 52
    runner process, 60
    Ubuntu Linux systems, 35
    UNIX target node, 31, 32
    Windows target node, 32
    YAML format, 39, 40
Ansible Automation Controller, 262
Ansible Automation Hub, 262
Ansible Automation Platform (AAP), 126,
    261, 263
ansible-builder command, 59
ansible-builder command-line tool, 60
ansible-builder tool, 59
ansible.cfg file, 198

Ansible Community package, 35

Ansible configuraion
  error, 111
  installation, 111, 112
  kubectl, 113
  kubernetes.core collection, 109,
    111, 112
  kubernetes.core.k8s module, 111
  OpenShift cluster, 113
  PyYAML jsonpatch
    kubernetes, 111
  requirements.yml file, 112
  resources, 109, 110
  setup.py install method, 111

Ansible Controller, 82, 126–128, 130, 134,
  136, 160, 197, 205, 244

Ansible Dynamic Inventory, 194, 195,
  197, 232

Ansible Execution Environment, 123
  ansible builder, 123, 125
  Ansible Playbook, 125
  Ansible Runner, 123, 125
  bindep.txt file, 124
  context/Containerfile file, 125
  execution-environment.yml file,
    123, 124
  localhost connection, 125
  my_kube, 123
  pip package manager, 123
  Red Hat, 125
  requirements.txt file, 124
  requirements.yml file, 124

ansible-galaxy command, 270

ansible-inventory command,
  38, 246, 258

Ansible modules, 198

Ansible Playbook, 30, 31, 37, 40–43, 49, 52,
  185, 197, 198

ansible-playbook command, 69, 82,
  231, 246

ansible-rulebook command, 270

ansible-runner tool, 61

ansible-sign command, 273, 274

Ansible troubleshooting
  kubeconfig file, 118, 119
  401 unauthorized
    fatal error message, 114
    Kubernetes, 114–116
    Kubernetes authentication, 114
    OpenShift, 116, 117
    tokens, 113
  x509 error, 118

Ansible Trusted Ansible Collections, 273

AnsibleTurboModule class, 112

Apache webserver container, 78

AppArmor
  Linux security tool, 192
  *vs.* SELinux, 192

Application deployment, 29

Application.java, 173, 174

Applications
  containerized, 87
  Kubernetes networking
    ClusterIP service, 144
    ExternalName service, 147
    ingress object, 146, 147
    LoadBalancer service, 145
    nodeport property, 145
    NodePortservice service, 144
    pod status, 143
    YAML files, 148
  Kubernetes Service
    Ansible Playbook, 142
    inventory file, 143
    kubectl command, 142
    nginx-example service, 142

OpenShift cluster, 142
pod statuses, 141
service.yaml document, 141
stakeholders, 141
resilience, 148
scaling, 149
Ansible, 150
Ansible Playbook, 150–152
auto-scaling, 153, 154
changed status, 152
get parameter, 149
inventory file, 151
k8s.gcr.io registry, 154
kubectl command, 149
nginx deployment, 149
pod count, 152
READY column, 149, 150
scale parameter, 149
updation
ansible-playbook command, 157
automation, 156, 157
Kubernetes, 156
latest tag, 155
logs, 156
nginx deployment, 155
pod instances, 155
rollback option, 155
rolling updation, 154, 155
scaling, 155
Array variables, 43
Artificial intelligence (AI), 163, 239,
275, 276
Attribute-based access control
(ABAC), 235
Authentication, Authorization, and
Accounting (AAA), 235, 247
Automation Controller (AC), 29, 30, 262,
263, 265, 266, 274

Automation Controller Backup (ACB), 265
Automation Controller job (AJ), 266
Automation Controller Restore
(ACR), 266
Automation Hub (AH), 29, 262, 263,
266, 273
Automation Hub Backup (AHB), 266
Automation Hub Restore (AHR), 266
AWS fully managed nodes, 246
AWS Identity and Access Management
(Amazon IAM), 247
AWS Key Management Service (AWS
KMS), 243
AWS X-Ray, 251
Azure Active Directory (Azure AD), 259
Azure compute, 255, 256
Azure Container Instances (ACI), 258
Azure Container Registry (ACR), 255, 258
Azure Kubernetes Service (AKS), 258, 259
Azure Resource Manager (ARM), 257
advantages, 256
azure_rm Ansible inventory plugin, 257

**B**

Base Container Images (BCI), 16
Bitnami, 204–207
Borg, 88
Business-critical services, 148

**C**

Calico, 237
California's Consumer Privacy Act
(CCPA), 273
Certified Kubernetes Conformance
Program, 259, 260
Charts, 202, 204, 207, 211

Cloud computing, 61, 88, 148, 237, 239,
    240, 242, 255, 259
Cloud Key Management Service (Cloud
    KMS), 243
Cloud-native applications, 87, 171, 199,
    201, 202, 240, 254, 276
Cloud Native Computing Foundation
    (CNCF), 82, 87
    Kubernetes, 9
    Kubernetes distribution
        Amazon EKS, 11
        OCP, 9, 10
        public cloud, 11
Cloud-native environments, 87, 95
Cloud providers, 87, 96, 99, 109, 239
    architecture, 241, 242
Cloud storage services, 90
CloudWatch, 251
Cluster Autoscaler (CA), 153, 154
CMD instruction, 13, 19
CodePipeline, 250, 251
Common Vulnerabilities and Exposures
    database (CVE), 18
Conditionals, 269
Configuration as a Code (CaC), 261
Configuration class, 171
Configuration files, 5, 27, 39, 49, 82, 92,
    113, 183, 186, 197, 245, 254, 257
Configuration management (CM), 7,
    27–29, 99, 262
Containerfile, 5, 12, 123, 176, 235
Container Registry, 5, 6, 13, 22, 77, 178, 179
Containers, 4
    analysis tools, 17
    benefits, 6
    business applications, 6
    definition, 11
    deployment, 4

    lifecycle, 5
Container Storage Interface (CSI), 90, 260
Content verification, 274
Continuous Delivery (CD), 94
Continuous Integration and Continuous
    Delivery (CI/CD), 7
Continuous Integration (CI), 93, 94
Cordon, 229, 230
credentials.json file, 255
Customer-managed key (CMK), 243

D

DaemonSets, 91, 232, 233
Debian Security Advisories (DSA), 18
Deep learning (DL), 163, 276
Deployment, 232, 233
    container, 4
    traditional, 2
    virtualized, 3
Developers, 93–95
Devmode, 75
Digital Envelope, 243
Disaster Recovery (DR), 148, 272
Distribution Specification, 5
Docker, 63, 88
    Debian Linux, 65, 67
    Fedora/Red Hat Linux, 67, 68
    platforms, 64
    Windows, 70, 71
DockerCon, 88, 89
Dockerfile, 5, 12, 13, 18–19, 59
Drain, 229, 230

E

echo command, 12
eksctl command, 248

Elastic Block Storage (EBS), 90, 244

Elastic Compute Cloud (EC2), 244, 246

Elastic Container Registry (ECR), 250, 251

Elastic Kubernetes Service (EKS), 11, 244, 246, 250, 253, 260

Enterprise customers, 274

Enterprise Linux distribution, 16, 17, 64

Envelope Encryption technique, 243

Event-Driven Ansible (EDA), 268–271

Extra variable, 43, 126, 219


**F**

Fault tolerant (FT), 148

Fedora-like Linux operating system, 76

Fedora Linux, 14, 82

Fetch logs, resources, 220, 221

Flatpak, 63, 71–74, 85

Fluentbit, 251

FROM instruction, 13

Full command, 41, 52, 85, 112, 125, 127, 274


**G**

gather_facts variable, 48

General Data Protection Regulation (GDPR), 272

General Personal Data Protection Law, 273

Generative Pre-trained Transformer (GPT-3), 275

GitOps continuous deployment, 93–94

Google, 87–89

Google Cloud Platform (GCP), 3, 11, 87, 99, 109, 251, 252

Google Compute Engine (GCE), 3, 252, 253

Google Container Engine (GKE), 11

Google Containers Registry (GCR), 252

Google Kubernetes Engine (GKE), 89, 253

Gradle build tool, 172, 175, 176

Graphics Processing Units (GPU), 163

Guestbook application, 180–184


**H**

Hardware, 2, 88

Hardware security module (HSM), 243

HashiCorp, 82, 243

Hello App, 12

    Alpine Linux, 15

    application, 19–21

    browser, 20

    building, 22

    deploy in Kubernetes, 24

    deploy in Operator, 25

    Docker, 22, 23

    Dockerfile, 18

        ADD instruction, 19

        CMD instruction, 19

        EXPOSE instruction, 19

        FROM instruction, 18

        LABEL instruction, 19

        pip command, 19

        RUN instruction, 19

    Enterprise Linux distribution, 17

    Fedora Linux, 14

    Linux base images, 13

    RHEL, 15, 16

    source files, 18

    SUSE, 17

    Ubuntu Linux, 14, 15

Hello application, 19–22, 176, 177

Hello container, 177

HelloController class, 174

HelloController.java file, 173

Hello-deployment.yaml Manifest, 179
Hello-service.yaml Manifest, 180
Helm, 10, 109
Helm Chart, 207, 211, 219
Helm package manager, 111
    advantages, 202
    charts, 202
    commands, 202, 203
    directory, 202
    glib Python library, 203
    helm command-line tool, 202
    helm utility, 203
    kubernetes.core Ansible collection, 203
    Microsoft, 202
    modules, 203
    tasks, 203
    uses, 202
Helm packages
    installation, 207, 209
    removal process, 209, 210
    reporting, 210–212
Helm plugins
    commands, 212
    installation, 212–214
    removal process, 214, 215
    reporting, 215, 216
Helm repositories
    addition, 204, 206
    Bitnami, 204
    helm repo command, 204
    removal process, 206
Heroku platform, 170
Hetzner-ocp4, 103
High availability (HA), 6, 99, 104, 148, 155,
    184, 241, 242, 250, 272
Horizontal Pod Autoscaler (HPA), 153
Hybrid-cloud, 4
Hypervisor software, 96

I
Idempotency, 38
Identity and Access Management (IAM),
    247, 252, 258
Image Specification, 5
Infrastructure and operations (I&O),
    261, 275
Infrastructure as a Service (IaaS), 242, 244,
    252, 255
Infrastructure as Code (IaC), 1, 25, 27, 61,
    261, 262, 268
Integrated development environment
    (IDE), 95
Internet of Things (IoT), 74, 107
IT infrastructure, 1, 25, 28, 243, 246,
    269, 272

J
Java microservice
    configure, 171, 172
    Demo Java web application, 172
Jenkins Pipeline, 94
Job, 233
Job execution, 267
Job template (JT), 266, 267
JSON Patch operation, 222, 223
JSON Web Token (JWT), 236

K
keyed_groups option, 245
Key Management Service (KMS), 243, 250
Kubeadm, 9, 102, 104, 106–108
kubectl, 92
kubectl command, 249
Kubernetes
    manage services, 225, 227

Kubernetes' annotation, 193
kubernetes.core.kustomize, 185
Kubernetes data plane, 171
Kubernetes (K8), 8
   advantage, 89
   Ansible, 201
   benefits, 89
   Container Image, 133
   control plane *vs.* data plane, 91, 92
   definition, 87
   feature, 89
   Google, 87, 88
   K3s, 107
   objects, 90, 91
   self-healing capabilities, 87
   timeline, 87
   upgrades, 107, 108
   uses, 87
   YAML files, 166, 167
Kubernetes Operations (kOps), 109
Kubespray, 96, 99–100
Kustomization directory, 185, 191
Kustomization file, 184, 185
kustomization.yaml file, 111, 186
kustomization.yml file, 185
Kustomize tool, 184, 185

**L**

LABEL instruction, 13, 19
Laboratory
   creation, 95
   hetzner-ocp4, 103
   Kubespray, 99, 100
   OpenShift Local, 100, 102, 103
   Raspberry Pi, 97, 98
   virtual machines, 96, 97
Lei Geral de Proteção de Dados (LGPD), 273

Linux Containers (LXC), 2, 11
localhost inventory, 209, 211, 213, 214,
   216, 221, 223, 225, 231, 233

**M**

Machine learning (ML), 163, 239, 252
Magic variables, 48, 49, 61, 66
main() method, 175
Managed nodes, 246
Manual work, 7
Maven or Gradle build tool, 176
Mean-Time-To-Resolution
   (MTTR), 269
Mesos, 88, 89
Message bus, 257, 258, 270
method parameter, 72
Microservices, 4, 6, 7, 87, 171, 172,
   272, 276
Microservices software design
   patterns, 272
microVM, 247
Minikube, 96, 104
   kubectl command, 105
   memory/CPUs settings, 105
   memory parameter, 104
   minikube command-line tool, 104
   minikube dashboard command,
   105, 106
   node, 105
   output, 105
   packages, 104
   resources, 105
   Ubuntu 22.04 LTS, 104
   virtual machine, 104
Modern operating systems, 7, 8, 34, 96,
   104, 202
Modern processor chips, 2

Monitoring tool deployment, 216
   Ansible Collections, 218, 219
   Helm Chart, 219
   kube-prometheus project, 217
Multi-cloud, 4, 9, 262
mysql.yaml file, 186, 187

**N**

Namespaces
   creation, 126, 128, 129
   reporting, 129–131
   reporting deployments
     ansible-galaxy, 135
     Ansible Playbook, 133, 134
     applying deployment, 132
     changed statuses, 134
     deployment_list.yml file, 135, 136
     deployment.yaml file, 131
     inventory file, 134, 136
     jmespath library, 135
     json_query filter plugin, 135
     kubectl namespace, 132
     Kubernetes deployment, 131
     message, 132
     metadata, 135
     nginx deployment, 132
     output, 132
     pods, 132
     query lookup plugin, 134
Network storage protocols, 90
nginx container, 77
Nginx web server, 92, 155, 207

**O**

Open Container Initiative
   (OCI), 5, 11, 15, 250

OpenID Connect (OIDC), 236
OpenID identity provider, 236
OpenShift, 10, 89, 101, 113
OpenShift Container Platform (OCP), 9,
   10, 101, 103, 104, 263
Operator SDK, 25, 191
Oracle Container Cloud Service
   (OCCS), 11
Orchestration technologies, 89
Orchestration tools, 7, 272
Organizations, 1, 2, 4, 30, 89, 202
Over-the-air (OTA), 74

**P, Q**

Packer, 82, 84, 85
PersistentVolume, 186
PersistentVolumeClaims, 186
PHP Guestbook application, 180, 181
ping.yml file, 197
pip utility, 35, 111
Platform-as-a-service (PaaS), 4, 89, 95,
   242, 244, 255
Playbook, 38
PodDisruptionBudget (PDB), 148, 229
Podman, 5, 63
Podman Container Engine, 80
Pods, 12, 253
   Ansible Playbook, 137
   configuration, volumes, 163–165
   copying files/directories, 224, 225
   definition, 136
   inventory file, 138
   kubectl, 138
   Kubernetes file, 137, 138
   OpenShift cluster, 138
   output, 138
   resources

CPU, 158, 160
GPU, 163
memory, 161, 162
metrics, 158
namespace, 163
resource utilization, 150
service scenario, 148
Pod security, 191, 192
Pod Security Admission (PSA), 191–192
PodSecurityPolicy, 191
Pod security standard policy, 192
Pokémon Go, 89
Prometheus, 216
Prometheus Operator, 217
Promise Theory, 88
Provisioning, 28
Python
daemon, 112
dependencies, 111, 113
library, 111, 121–124
package manager, 111
virtual Environment, 120–122

**R**

Raspberry Pi, 8, 97–98
Recovery Point Objective (RPO), 272
Recovery Time Objective (RTO), 272
Red Hat Ansible Automation Platform,
29, 261, 263
Red Hat Enterprise Linux (RHEL), 9, 15,
16, 35, 64, 68, 123, 244, 263
Red Hat OpenShift, 263
Red Hat OpenShift Local, 10
Red Hat OpenShift Service on AWS
(ROSA), 9
Red Hat Security Bulletins (RHSB), 18
Redis leader deployment, 181

Redis Service YAML file, 182
Registered variables, 43, 44
ReplicaSet, 91, 150, 233
Replication Controller, 150, 229, 233
Role-based access control (RBAC),
29, 191, 235
Runtime Specification, 5

**S**

Scratch, 89, 96, 97, 235
Seccomp, 193, 194
seccomp profile audit.json file, 194
Secrets, 139, 141
Secure Token Service (STS), 236
Security, 233
AAA, 235
Calico, 237
cloud infrastructure, 234
cluster security, 234
code, 234
container images, 235
containers, 234, 235
directives, 235
OpenID identity provider, 236
Security pod resources, 192, 193
Self-managed nodes, 246
Service-Level Agreement (SLA), 253
Simple Storage Service (S3), 244
Single-board computer (SBCs), 97
Single sign-on (SSO), 236, 262
Single source of truth (SSOT), 94
Snap, 74, 75, 77
Snapcraft, 74
snapd daemon, 74, 77
Software as a Service (SaaS), 170, 242, 243
Software development lifecycle (SDLC)
methodology, 169, 170

Source control management system
(SCM), 94
Spring Boot, 172, 175
state parameter, 72
Stateful applications, 163, 186, 191
Storage devices, 90
SUSE Linux Enterprise Server (SLES), 244
Syscalls, 193, 194
System Integration Test (SIT), 6, 201

**T**

Taint nodes, 227, 228
Technology, 193
Total Cost of Ownership (TCO), 239, 242
Traditional deployment, 2
Traditional infrastructure, 1
Twelve-factor application, 170, 171

**U**

Standard ubi UBI images, 16
Multi-service ubi-init UBI images, 16
Micro ubi-micro UBI image, 16
Minimal ubi-minimal UBI images, 16
Ubuntu Linux distribution, 14, 15
Ubuntu Security Notices (USN), 18

Uncordon, 108, 229–231
Universal Base Image (UBI), 15, 16
UNIX toolchain, 250
Uptime, 2
User-defined variables, 43

**V**

Vagrant, 82, 83
Vagrantfile, 83, 84
Vendors, 4, 11, 242, 243, 259–260
Vertical Pod Autoscaler (VPA), 153, 154
Vibrant community, 9, 87, 89, 107, 275
Virtual Desktop Infrastructure (VDI), 256
Virtualized deployment, 3
Virtual machines (VMs), 2–4, 83, 84,
96–97, 255
Virtual Network (VNet), 256
Virtual Private Clouds (VPC), 244, 253
VMWare Tanzu Application
Platform, 95

**W, X, Y, Z**

Web-generated ZIP file archive, 173
Webhook, 255, 268–270
wordpress.yaml file, 189

Printed in the United States
by Baker & Taylor Publisher Services